# Seeking Signs of Sanity

D0874950

A bit of flotsam left when the tide of war went through her village, the little girl was the only person found alive in Cerisy-la-Salle, Normandy.

Two American soldiers tried to assure her that someone would soon be there to take care of her. This was probably a futile gesture, for they needed to move on, but at least they tried. They tried, and to this author, their compassion for a small child was a sign of sanity on a world committed to the irrationalities of conflict.

Drawing by Meredith Laurence, a student at Seekonk High School, Seekonk, Massachusetts. 2004

*(Suggested by a U.S. Army Signal Corps photo taken shortly after D-Day, 1944.)*

# Seeking Signs of Sanity

◆

## A Veteran's Account of His Role in World War II

Russell E. Spooner

iUniverse, Inc.
New York  Lincoln  Shanghai

# Seeking Signs of Sanity
## A Veteran's Account of His Role in World War II

All Rights Reserved © 2005 by Russell E. Spooner

iUniverse books may be ordered through booksellers or by contacting:

iUniverse
2021 Pine Lake Road, Suite 100
Lincoln, NE 68512
www.iuniverse.com
1-800-Authors (1-800-288-4677)

ISBN-13: 978-0-595-35615-7 (pbk)
ISBN-13: 978-0-595-80096-4 (ebk)
ISBN-10: 0-595-35615-X (pbk)
ISBN-10: 0-595-80096-3 (ebk)

Printed in the United States of America

# Contents

# *Acknowledgments*

It is not possible to complete a project such as this without the help of others. It's also not possible to list here all of those who participated in any way, so I'm constrained to limit mention to those who have done the most.

My wife, Bessie, has suffered through years of partial neglect while this book was in progress, yet she continually encouraged me to complete it. For that, I thank her.

My daughter, Lorelei, is probably one of the best proofreaders in the area today. She came to this from the eight years we worked together in our printing business. My thanks to her for catching all the typos and misspelled words that are apt to plague every writer who tries to go it alone through this wilderness of words.

Finally, and not at all the least, is Gilbert D. Woodside, Jr., D. Ed., who headed the veterans' writing program at Seekonk High School in Seekonk, Massachusetts. It was his encouragement that kept this account moving, and his suggestions that made it a better book.

These three, and others, deserve my gratitude and appreciation.

Russ

All the people in this account were real. For some, I've used fictitious names, because the descendants of those who served may have heard different versions of the events described herein. I have no wish to destroy even the least of their treasured concepts of what their ancestors did, or did not, do. I'm certain that my personal view of events is somewhat different from that of others, especially from the "official" versions allowed to the media by the military censors. I make no apology for this.

I have also used some imagination to supply a conclusion to actions that had none. In the rapid-fire events of an active war, "closure" was a rarity. Where supplied, the only intent was to make the reading easier. The reader is invited to draw his/her own conclusions.

Seeking Signs of Sanity

# *Prologue*

They are not long, the weeping and the laughter,
    Love and desire and hate;
I think they have no portion in us after
    We pass the gate.

They are not long, the days of wine and roses;
    Out of a misty dream
Our path emerges for a while, then closes
    Within a dream.

        *—(Ernest Dowson, 1867–1900)*

We knew little of the wine, and nothing of the roses. Those of us who remain now approach that second dream—the eternal sleep, perhaps, within which we may, or may not, find what was lost in the time that was taken from us.

Those who wished to rule the world used us to achieve their ends. This is not to condemn them, nor to deny the necessity of what they did. Someone needed to oppose those who had similar ambitions, but founded on more sinister motives and goals. Yet, the war that changed society, with a finality beyond any possibility of reversal, possessed much that could have been different.

All wars are an admission of failure. In the beginning, this is the failure of statesmen and diplomats. As war consumes ever larger portions of a nation's youth, its wealth, and its moral values, the failure inevitably belongs to the citizens themselves. The moment in which they might react, and halt the annihilation of

1

too many lives and too much honor, is likely brief. Yet, given a degree of courage equal to that demanded of their armed forces, people can change the course of events. This is never accomplished in the rabid howling of student packs, or the slanted reasoning of fanatical reformers. It is with the quiet assurances of those who know how to find a new direction without burning the bridges of the past.

Each of us is the sum total of our earliest, and latest, memories of the experiences life has thrust upon us. Much of that has been beyond our control. We can't change it. We can't run away from it. We can only accept it, for until we find that second dream, we must live with ourselves.

We must also live with the recognition that those who fight for freedom are not allowed to be free while they are so engaged. Ask any soldier serving in combat what he would like to be, and what he'd like to do. It's unlikely any of the replies will be the role of a soldier doing battle with other young men. All civilians owe their freedoms to those who have, for a period of time, surrendered theirs.

Wars have rarely, if ever, been a single, continuous event. They are collections of incidents, great and small, often with little more than a tenuous connection to each other. Generals, with the foresight of an education in the history of wars, can see a whole, where the average citizen, or citizen soldier, sees only that part of it that immediately concerns him.

I cannot write this account from the viewpoint of a general. I was not one. It must be presented, therefore, as the incidents in which I was involved, or those in which others, known to me, were involved. Their stories, if firsthand, are a part of this. All of it is a part of us. It characterizes us, even today. It's something we need you, if you're of the younger generations, to understand.

*Russell E. Spooner*

# 1

# *Solomon's Promise*

What bothered us more than anything else was that no one would tell us what sort of organization we were, or what we'd be expected to do. We lived each day in an information vacuum, and this was neither pleasant nor reassuring.

We were called a "company," but this made almost no sense. Four officers and thirty-one enlisted men were a number far below our understanding of what comprised a company. An infantry company had something like two hundred and forty men. Some special units, such as the parachute infantry, were smaller, but they were trained to do a specific job. Our group was a hodgepodge of young men and boys with varied backgrounds, experience, and levels of training. We seemed to be without purpose or proper organization. We were unprepared for nearly any assignment we could imagine. Only the cooks seemed to know what would be expected of them, and for reasons unknown to us, there were a lot of cooks.

Most of us had recently arrived in England from the States. We had never met each other, but that was nothing unusual in a newly formed unit. Our First Sergeant, Jim Grollin, was regular army, and had come from Iceland. Our Supply Sergeant, Frank Parsons, had also arrived from Iceland, and seemed to know what was expected of him, but there were no supplies to manage. Henry Furman was our company clerk, and obviously knew his job. I was the company armorer, a small arms specialist with excellent training at Aberdeen Proving Ground in Maryland, and the armory at Fort Meade, also in Maryland, but we had no weapons of any kind to maintain or repair.

We waited. Each day we waited some more, and tried to fill the hours with whatever we could find to keep occupied. We talked about the war, but it was a distant thing for us. All the action in this half of the world had been in Africa, the Mediterranean, or on the Russian front. The Soviets agitated continuously for a "second front" in Europe to relieve the pressure on their armies in the east. We saw no indication that this would happen soon, only suggestions that it was surely going to happen. When it did, how were we going to fit into the picture? Our officers may have known, but apparently it was army policy to keep enlisted men uninformed whenever possible.

We (our thirty-one enlisted men) lived together in a Nissen hut (similar to our "Quonset" huts in the States). There were two hundred identical units in this camp, all of them hastily erected steel shells on concrete slabs. For every two rows of huts, there was a dirt apology for a street, useable by our trucks. Trenches six feet deep occupied the alternating spaces between rows.

These were our bomb shelters. When the air raid sirens wailed, we abandoned the huts and jumped into the nearest trench. Shoes, trousers, and a jacket were always kept where we could put hands on them in the dark. Most air raids happened then. Newspaper articles we read all reported that the Luftwaffe (German Air Force) had been "swept from the skies of Europe," but someone neglected to inform the Germans about this. With remarkable persistence, their Luftwaffe turned up again and again where it was least expected and certainly not wanted.

Large letters and numbers, painted near the doors, identified each hut. We lived in row D, number 5. This was our only way to find "home" in a camp that lacked any amenities such as a recreation hall or game area. The builders had also put a low value on esthetics. Not a shrub or blade of grass challenged the dismal monotony of the place. When informed that we would move soon to an undisclosed destination, we treated the news with eager anticipation. It didn't matter where we'd be going. Any place was better than this. "Soon" became two hours. We hurriedly packed and climbed aboard our trucks.

First to Scotland, and a night ferry crossing of the Irish Sea, we arrived in Northern Ireland. A camp, far more pleasant than the one we'd just left, was ready for us. British troops had recently occupied it, and had made an effort to keep it tidy and as comfortable as we had any right to expect.

The place was on a country road, a side street leading up a small hill from the main road along the shore of Belfast Lough (pronounced "lock"). There was a view of the Lough past a thatched-roof country cottage at the foot of the hill. It was a beautiful scene, even in this cold late-winter season. We were halfway between the small city of Bangor and the fishing village of Donaghadee, each about three miles distant. Our immediate area was called "Portavo Point."

When there was no snow on the ground, Ireland lived up to its reputation for greenery. The "forty shades of green" in the old song were indisputably present here, or soon would be with the new spring growth.

We were given a name. We were a "replacement company." This was no more illuminating than any of the other sparse bits of knowledge gleaned from a reluctant chain of command. We had no idea what a "replacement company" was or did. Who did we replace, and where, and why? What, exactly, were we?

As soon as we'd settled in, we learned that our primary duty in this location was to house, feed, and supply training facilities for new arrivals from the States. Apparently, their preparation for overseas duty had been incomplete when they'd boarded a ship, or ships, to come to Europe. An infantry squad from a nearby camp came every day to do the hands-on work of showing these new recruits the proper handling of weapons, preparations for both defensive and offensive positions, and details of life in the field.

My armory was a former truck repair garage. Rifles and rifle racks arrived, and I arranged everything in a way that would make it simple and fast to issue the two hundred Springfield rifles to trainees, and return the rifles to their racks at the end of the day. I liked the Springfield. I'd qualified with it on the range at Aberdeen. It was World War I vintage, the 1903 model, developed in a hurry to catch up to the rest of the world in a race to have the best infantry weapon. It had been just that, for many years.

As a nation embroiled in a new war, we had now gone a step beyond the rest of the world with our M1, the Garand, probably the finest mass-produced semi-automatic shoulder weapon ever made, and certainly the most reliable. The Germans still used their 1898 Mausers, the British their 1917 Enfields. The M1 out-classed all of them. We did not have any M1s in this Irish camp, a disappointment. We did have a .30 caliber light machinegun, in my care when not used for training, and two mortars, a 60-millimeter and an 81-millimeter. Both were classed as "artillery" rather than small arms, so I had no experience with them. They stayed in a corner of the armory except when in use by the infantrymen.

The machinegun was an old friend of mine. I'd rebuilt and test-fired hundreds of them at Fort Meade. Its one serious fault was that it still used the old canvas belts. In constant use, these became frayed and altogether too likely to cause a jam in the mechanism of the gun. We had no cure for that, except to discard a belt that was worn, and hope we could find a replacement within a reasonable time.

There was no way to avoid the conclusion that this conflict was a continuation of the last World War. So much of our equipment dated from that earlier time, with just a few outstanding examples of newer and improved items. The M1 rifle was the prime example. Our helmets were of a new design, and superior to those old "tin pots" used in 1918. Ours came in two parts, a steel shell and a fiberglass liner with adjustable straps inside. Yet, our uniforms were essentially the same. We wore canvas leggings from shoes to just below the knees, with a strap that went under the shoes and a lacing up one side, using metal hooks in the canvas. These replaced the yards-long piece of material, like an Ace bandage, that we had wrapped around our legs first thing each morning, and removed the last thing each night.

Slowly at first, but with increasing confidence, we accepted our individual roles in this strange company. The first sergeant, supply sergeant, company clerk, the cooks and I all found our situation not too far removed from the sort of things we'd been trained to do. The others, with varied backgrounds, were rapidly promoted to sergeants and became responsible for groups of new arrivals. They saw to the housing for these recruits, moved them from one training session to another, kept them in formations for marches of any distance within the camp, and generally nursed them through this phase of their military experience.

Only one member of our company was not included in this "shakedown" of duty assignments and organization. This was Solomon Vance, a "striker" for our four officers. Sol did those things that were deemed beneath the dignity of an officer to do for himself. He cleaned their quarters, made their beds, pressed their uniforms, and polished their shoes. Each day he obtained the coal ration for the Nissen hut in which they lived. He removed the ashes and readied the stove for its evening fire. They wanted him to make the fire an hour before they finished their duties for the day, so the rooms would be warm when they returned to them. Sol never quite got around to doing that. Each of the officers paid him fifteen dollars a month for his services, a fee that effectively doubled Sol's military pay. He was a private, and would remain a private while the others advanced to their designated ranks in the T of O (Table of Organization).

A first-generation American of Polish/Jewish ancestry, Sol was a little shorter than most of us, with a dark complexion, dark eyes, and a nose that would betray his ethnicity in any gathering. "Vance" was a contraction of something like "Vancelovonich," a name rarely referred to by either Sol or others.

Sol hated his job and he hated officers. When we first arrived at Portavo Point, all the enlisted men shared a single Nissen hut. It was in a small depression, a hollow in the landscape of the camp. A cart path led up the hill, with the officers' hut at the top. Sol was always the first to rise each morning, and indulged in a routine that he seemed to feel was necessary for his mental stability. He opened a door at the end of the hut. While he ignored the pleas of the rest of us to save what heat was left in the place, he shouted, at the top of his lungs, at the officers' hut above.

"You friggin' officers!" he screamed. "You're all too stupid to be good for anything. Those bars on your shoulders don't mean shit, because you haven't got enough sense to know your ass from a hole in the ground. You can't even light a match. I put papers in the stoves. I put kindling on the papers, I put your coal bucket next to that, and you can't light a match to make your place warm. You can't do anything. You're good for nothing. Because you're so stupid, you'll probably live through this crazy war. You're not worth the price of a German bullet to put you out of the way."

Sol could go on like this for a half hour, and often did, without repeating himself. The officers undoubtedly heard him, but never made an issue of it. Where could they find another striker?

After his morning diatribe, Sol's attitude toward officers was one of careful disregard. He was a master at playing dumb. New men were arriving regularly now, and with them came new lieutenants. They were quartered in a separate Nissen hut from our own officers, so were not Sol's responsibility. Perhaps this was why he felt it was an imposition when one attempted to give him an order.

Sol's work was normally done by noon, except for picking up the coal ration and preparing the stoves in our company officers' hut. He spent the rest of the day wandering around the camp, observing the training exercises but never participating in any. From each hand hung a large bucket to be used for the coal. In nearly any confrontation with a new lieutenant, the officer was likely to come off second best. It was interesting and educational to watch.

This lieutenant had just arrived the day before, and knew nothing whatever about Solomon Vance. Shortly after lunch, he stopped Sol and asked, "Where are you going with those buckets, soldier?"

Sol stared at him for a time calculated to infuriate, but not quite long enough to create a basis for charges of insubordination. "Going to get coal for the officers' hut," he finally replied.

"But the coal bin doesn't open until four o'clock," the lieutenant insisted. "Shouldn't you be doing something else until then?"

"I want to be first in line when they unlock the gate," said Sol.

"Sir!"

"Huh?"

"Sir. I'm an officer. You should address me as 'Sir'."

"Will that get my coal any sooner? Sir?"

"No. It has nothing to do with your coal. It's a matter of military courtesy, which seems to be a problem for you."

"My only problem," Sol stated, "is getting the coal and getting out of the wind and bad air here."

"What bad air?" the lieutenant innocently asked.

"The bad air that's always around an officer. Sir."

"You should also salute an officer, but I suppose you know that," the lieutenant persisted.

"Can't do that. Got these huge coal buckets in my hands. How could I salute anyone? Sir?"

"You could put them down."

"Then who would get the officers' coal?"

The new lieutenant surrendered at this point and walked away. Sol knew exactly what he was doing.

On a chilly evening, with several of us gathered around the coal stove, he'd tell us about it.

"They all think I'm crazy, you know. Maybe I am. Maybe we all are, here in Europe when we ought to be back home doing something useful. So if anyone ever asks you, just tell them sure, Sol's as loony as they come—a real wacko. That's exactly what I want them to think."

No one offered to comment.

"But I'll tell you something." He'd point in an easterly direction. "Real soon, you're all going over there, to France. You're going to France, where a lot of you will probably get yourselves killed. I can promise you one thing for sure—Sol Vance will not be going with you when that happens. Sol will be in New York, living easy on the money his wife is sending him now. You wait and see!"

Sol was married, but not exceedingly happy about it. Once a month, he wrote a letter to his wife. "Send me fifty dollars" was the total message. A week later, he'd receive a money order for fifty dollars from her. They exchanged no other communication.

Sol had another source of income, beyond his army pay, beyond his striker pay, and beyond the fifty dollars every month from his wife. Some in our company had difficulty stretching their money from one payday to the next. Sol had an answer for that problem. He let it be known that he could relieve small deficiencies in funds with a loan. In a black pocket notebook, he carefully recorded the amount advanced to each borrower.

On the next payday, Sol waited outside the HQ (headquarters) hut, book in hand, and collected the amount he'd loaned, plus ten percent. It made no difference whether the loan had been for three days or thirty. Interest was always ten percent. Sol's book-keeping system was remarkably simple. He sent his gains to his personal bank account in New York, to which we assumed he also sent his striker's pay and the fifty dollars from his wife. Within the rules of life as Sol defined them, he was scrupulously honest. He provided a service to those who needed it, at a fee they were willing to pay. Many fortunes have been made following the dictates of this rule.

Whether his conviction that we would soon go to France was founded on the overheard conversation of the officers, or was simply a logical deduction, it made sense. This war could not be won in Ireland. That was the reality we needed to face. The easy camp life we enjoyed was going to end, and a day would come when we'd need to say our farewells to this land so favored by nature and so tortured by human antagonisms, most founded on religious differences.

In the beginning, it was here, at Portavo Point in Northern Ireland, that we became a company with a purpose. It was not our eventual purpose, but that appeared to be clothed in secrecy during our stay in Ireland. Here, we learned to work together, to function as a unit, to deal with other soldiers who were, for the most part, transients.

We learned to give orders to a couple of hundred of Europe's royalty. In the process, we found out that they were not so terribly different from ordinary people, like us. There were good and bad among them, those who made the most of their situation, and those who did not.

Portavo Point, halfway between the small city of Bangor and the little fishing village of Donaghadee, was a pleasant place. The Point was where Belfast Lough opened out into the North Channel of the Irish Sea. The sea was always there, a presence changing with the wind, the sun, and the storms. It was here that Kay and I first met.

# 2

# *Anzacs and Fishheads*

There was less concern about a definition for our company as we assumed the various duties involved in keeping the camp at Portavo Point running smoothly.

By the end of the second week, we were allowed a twelve-hour pass every other Saturday, starting at noon. Most of the time, this meant going to Bangor on the bus for a beer or two in the local pub (public house), and spending some time in a slot machine emporium close by. There, we could empty our pockets of an enormous weight in those huge copper pennies used by the British. Or, if daring enough, we could get rid of a few thrupenny bits (three-penny bits, worth about a nickel) or even a few six-pence, equivalent to a dime. As the value of the coin increased, the number of machines to accept it grew smaller. This was a nickel-and-dime operation, but most of us didn't care. Feeding our loose change to the slots passed the time of day. Now and then, one of the machines produced a return, and the games went on for a few more minutes. Anyone who dreamed of winning enough to leave richer than when he'd arrived had created a fool's paradise for himself. It wouldn't happen.

On a pleasant day, just walking along the sea wall and watching the fishing boats come and go was relaxing. An arm of Belfast Lough extended almost to the center of Bangor.

It was at the pub that I first met the Anzacs. These were Australians and New Zealanders. They were large, hearty men with big voices and ready smiles. They wore those cowboy-style hats, with one side of the brim turned up, and this gave them a devil-may-care look. Most, I learned, had grown up on a station. A "station" was a sheep or cattle ranch, and could be many thousands of acres.

Anzacs were handy with horses and with guns, and were generally considered the finest soldiers on either side in this war. It was a reputation well earned in Greece and Crete, and on some of the Pacific islands.

One of the ten gathered in the pub spoke to me. "Could I buy you a beer, Yank?" he asked. I hesitated at first. It was a week until payday, and I had very little money—not enough to return the favor for all of them here.

"Come on, Yank," the Anzac prodded. "What'll it be? A Guiness?"

"No," I replied. "If you insist, I'll have a Younger's Pale Ale." I'd tried this before, and liked it, although I'd just turned nineteen and was far from being an experienced drinker. A second glass would probably leave me passed out on the floor.

"Ah! Good choice." The Anzac ordered, the barkeep poured from a bottle into a glass and set both in front of me.

"How long have you been in Ulster?" I asked.

"Arrived a fortnight ago," said the Anzac. "You?"

"About the same. We formed up in England, then came here."

He nodded. "Good to have you Yanks in this thing with us now. It'll make the difference, you know. We might have held them off for another year or so, but doubt we'd have been able to pay the price much longer. Having you here really matters."

"Where were you earlier?" I asked.

"Crete." He hesitated. "That is, Crete was where we were a complete battalion, a year and a half ago. A bloody disaster. Thousands of German parachutists and airborne. First real battle where the Huns used them. We should have beaten them off, but didn't, as you know if you paid attention to the news. A lot of them will never leave Crete, though. Of course, neither will ours." He waved his hand at the others. "We're all that's left of that battalion."

"Oh," I said. "I'm sorry. Where have you been since then?"

"Egypt, Palestine, parts of the Balkans—all minor police actions. We'll never be committed to anything large again. They want us back home, and we may just go there next. The Japs already have part of Borneo, and are threatening Australia. There's no more than a handful of troops there to defend it."

"Well, I wish you luck," I said. "It seems to me you've paid your share in this whole business, and deserve to go home now. Many thanks for the beer, and I apologize for my inability to reciprocate. I've nothing but a couple of sixpence in my pocket."

"No apology needed. You'll soon be paying your share in the whole bloody mess on the shores of France. That's got to happen, you know." He lifted his glass. "Cheerio, Yank."

I left, wondering how Americans at home would deal with the sort of losses the Anzacs had suffered—wondering how we ourselves, here in Europe, would handle it. This was a gloomy thought, tied to gloomy prospects. There had been stories around that Britain had sacrificed the Anzacs to buy time, when England itself was almost undefended, with something like one gun for each five miles of coastline. There may have been a grain of truth in this, but it had been a mixed force that had fought in Crete. They were British, Indian, Anzacs, and others, with ten thousand untrained and weaponless Greeks. They had all lost heavily, the Anzacs most because they had fought as the rearguard when many of the others had been evacuated. It was, as my Anzac friend had said, a bloody disaster, with the Germans victorious after just eleven days of fighting. Would it be like that for us on some as-yet-unnamed French beach, when our time came? Many would die. That was a certainty. Not only that, but since men had fought wars, it seemed to be always the best who died first. I returned to camp before dark, in a thoughtful mood.

The next day was Sunday, a time of light duties, but I was in the armory, doing a few housekeeping chores. Jim Grollin, our top kick (first sergeant) came in. He was a lean, wiry man, slightly shorter than average, with a dark beard that needed to get close to a razor twice each day.

"I'd like to borrow one of the Springfields," he said.

"Sure, Sarge. '03 or '03A1? I've some of each."

He looked at me with a quizzical expression. "You know the difference?"

"Sarge, I'm an armorer. Of course I know the difference. How did you plan to use it?"

He grinned a little. "Manual of arms. Actually, I want to practice the Queen Anne Salute. It's been a while, and I'm probably so out of practice, I'll flub the whole thing. I still want to try, though."

"I don't know that one, but if it's any kind of manual of arms, I'd guess you want the '03, without the pistol grip. Is that right?"

His grin became a smile. "Corporal, you're okay. Have you ever seen the Queen Anne?"

"I've never heard of it before now," I replied.

"Then come outside and watch if you want. I'm regular army, as you probably know—nine years in, now. When I was a fresh-faced kid going through basic, the instructors were fanatics about manual of arms drills. One of the most difficult, and yet the most beautiful, was the Queen Anne. I'd guess it started as a British thing. Sergeant Parsons is outside, checking over the lay of the ground. We need a nice level spot about thirty yards long. Beside this garage will do, I think. Let's go."

"Armory," I said. "It's now an armory, Sarge, if you don't mind."

"Right. Armory it is. Let's go."

We went out. Staff sergeant Frank Parsons, our supply sergeant, stood near the end of the building. He, too, was a man smaller than average, with what has sometimes been called a "fetal" shape to his head. He had a high forehead, a narrow chin, and almost no beard. I'd already worked with him a brief time, helping to convert a Brit meat storage hut into the supply room. Unlike the Brits, who kept a week's supply of meat packed in ice, our meat came to the camp every day in a refrigerated truck. Parsons was also regular army, but with six years instead of the top kick's nine. They seemed to know each other.

He pointed along the building's side. "Right here, Jim. It's level enough, and I couldn't find any small stones you might turn your ankle on, or gouge your knee. How are you going to get the marching beat?"

"Randall is in the HQ hut with the PA system. He's got a Souza march ready to play." He looked at me. "Would you go over there and tell him to start the music in exactly five minutes?"

"Sure." I ran the short distance to HQ, went in, and gave the information to Danny Randall, our assistant company clerk.

He nodded and sat beside the PA controls. A record was on the turntable.

When I returned, Sergeant Parsons explained a little about what was going to happen. "Jim will shoulder the rifle and march to the other end of this place along the building. He'll turn and come back, keeping in step to the beat of the music. He'll turn again here, and after a few steps, do the Queen Anne. This will probably be the last time you, or any others, will have a chance to see it done."

"Can you do it?" I asked Sergeant Parsons.

"Just barely, and nowhere near as well as Jim."

The top kick came back, rifle on his right shoulder, marching in time to the music. He turned, still in time, and began the final leg of the march. Sergeant Parsons called out the order, clearly and sharply, "Queen Anne salute!"

Jim Grollin twirled the rifle from his shoulder, dropped to one knee as the rifle butt touched the ground, stepped forward as he brought the rifle back to his shoulder, and marched on, without once losing the beat. It was truly awesome, and I could imagine an entire company, with a band playing nearby, doing the same thing, rank after rank, all in unison and all in perfect time. If the manner with which a rifle was handled could ever be a thing of beauty, this was it. It could not be done with an M1, with a carbine, or with a host of other weapons. Only the Springfield, the Enfield, or perhaps the German Mauser could be used for the Queen Anne Salute. I felt privileged to have seen it this one time.

In spite of its beauty, there was also a serious question in my mind about the utility value of the Queen Anne, or any other manual of arms drill. Here we were, embroiled in a serious shooting war, in which we could expect casualties, even many deaths, and our army seemed to give an unreasonable priority to fancy show maneuvers rather than more hours or days on the firing range, perfecting our skills with weapons. How much, I wondered, of all that we were doing here was little more than play-acting and showmanship? When the crunch came, and it was no longer a drill but exchanges of live fire and explosives, of what practical value was all that saluting, marching back and forth, and standing at attention? I really wanted to know.

Sergeant Grollin handed the rifle to me. "Mind putting this back in the rack for me?" he asked.

"Not at all," I replied. The music stopped, apparently the end of the recording. I looked at Grollin. "Got a question for you, Sarge," I said.

"Then spill it. What would you like to know?" he replied.

"That thing you just did was fantastic. I really enjoyed watching it, and I admired your ability in doing what must have been a difficult thing to learn. But it seems to me it's nothing much more than a peacetime maneuver, done to keep you on you toes and impress visiting politicians. What good will it be where we're going—to France?"

He smiled. "Right now, it probably looked like something a troop of Boy Scouts, or even Girl Scouts, might like. And sure, done right, it did, and still can, impress visiting dignitaries. But like all such things, there's an underlying purpose that is always present. It's to train every soldier to instantly obey each command given by a superior, and to do that without giving it a thought. Imagine a full regiment passing a reviewing stand, marching in order twelve columns wide.

"As each rank passes the stand, and the order for the Queen Anne Salute is given, they absolutely must be in perfect alignment, in perfect step with the music and each other. If one man fails to twirl his rifle and touch the butt to the ground at the same time as every other man in that rank, you'd have a catastrophe. Then, if he fails to rise from the kneeling position and bring the piece back to his shoulder with the others, rifle barrels could hit the back of the man ahead. A miss-step could have the man behind running up your backside. The entire regiment would dissolve as a coherent unit. The theory that we'll soon be testing is that men in combat must react in exactly the same way as those who march in a parade and do a difficult maneuver, such as the Queen Anne. There's no place for any independent action. It could destroy the effectiveness of the entire regiment, or battalion, or company."

"In other words," I said, "we're supposed to do certain things—take certain actions—on command without ever thinking about them."

"That's the idea," said the Sarge. "Learn to obey an order instantly without stopping to think about it. Turn it into a debating session or examine the pros and cons of its correctness, and you plus a lot of others could be dead."

"But..."

"No buts. That's the whole point. Instant obedience without thinking about it will save your life and that of others. You just hope that your officers and noncoms know what they're doing, because you'll need to trust them in that. There's no other way an army can function in wartime. The things taught and learned in peacetime, much of it through endless repetition, eliminate the need to ask questions. Satisfied?"

I nodded and looked at Sergeant Parsons. "Did you two know each other before?"

Grollin answered. "Some. We were in different companies, but in Iceland at the same time. Shipped there together, on a troop transport from New York."

"When was that?" I asked.

He and Parsons both gave me a strange look. "I'm not sure you're supposed to know this," he said, "but guess we're never going to be in any situation where it would matter much. It was a few days before Pearl Harbor—before we were officially at war. We were on our way to kill some Germans and shut down a sub repair and refueling base on Iceland. Their U-boats were raising hell with our convoys to Britain, and it had to be stopped. Last winter, the one of '42 and '43, they sank half of all the ships that tried to cross."

"What about the crews of those ships?"

"There were no survivors. In the Atlantic south of Iceland in the winter, you can't live more than twenty-two minutes. If any subs tried to pick up the guys in the water, it was too late by the time they surfaced and reached them."

"And you did this before we declared war?" I asked.

"We were on our way there when war was declared. It made no difference, really. Declared or not, we were at war, and our orders would have been carried out regardless." He turned to Parsons. "Have you ever run into any other fishheads since we got to England, Frank?"

"Fishheads?" I asked.

"That's what we called anyone who served in Iceland," the top kick said. "After nearly two years of eating fish practically every day, it seemed appropriate."

"Damned appropriate," Parsons added. "And no, I've met none of the others. Most went to other places, I guess. Just you and I wound up in this sort of outfit, Jim."

"How did the local government treat your attack on the German sub base?" I asked.

They both laughed, but with a note of bitterness rather than joy.

"They protested," said Parsons. "They protested loud and long. They liked the Krauts and hated us, and would almost have rejoiced if no American ship ever reached England again."

"Why? Did the Germans treat them so differently, or so much better?"

"Not so you'd notice," said the top kick. "It was mostly international politics and trade agreements, I think. The Icelanders weren't great admirers of German Nazism, but still thought there were benefits in good trade relations with Germany, and probably none with England or with us. There's always an economic angle in every war."

There are also a lot of unknowns, I thought. I'd shipped overseas believing it would be us, Britain, Western Europe and the Russians against Germany and Italy. That, it seemed, had been a false assumption. Nothing was as clear-cut as that. We were not universally admired or treated as friends. The Germans were not universally hated. You picked your friends, and your enemies, as you went along, almost on a day-to-day basis, and frequently disregarding nationalities.

# 3

# Counts, Dukes, and the King of France

Among the groups that arrived at our camp from the States was one composed entirely of European royalty. These were people who had escaped from their respective countries ahead of the invading German army, sometimes by a matter of just hours. Many had abandoned their family estates and sold valuables to secure space on a flight or ship to the United States.

They'd fully expected to find sanctuary, perhaps political asylum, in America. That didn't happen, at least not in the manner they'd wanted. The U.S. Army had its own plans for them. Each of these foreigners possessed intimate knowledge of the language, culture, and geography of that part of Europe from which he'd come. They all spoke English, some of them fluently. The army thought they would be invaluable when we eventually established our own presence on the continent and replaced the Germans.

Before they arrived in our camp at Portavo Point, our company, except the cooks, had been divided among the Nissen huts, so that at least one of us was living and sleeping with each group of new arrivals. Our cot (pallet) was next to the door, and we were responsible for awakening the inhabitants of the hut when we were awakened by the "charge of quarters" on duty at the time. Next to me was Charles deBourbon, who, if his nation should ever elect to return to a monarchy, was possibly first in line to become the King of France.

He was a quiet man, reserved and polite. He never protested about any duty assigned to him, something a few of the others did constantly. He was thin, with a carefully trimmed moustache. He seemed tall, but that may have been only the impression he created. DeBourbon was a "presence" in any group of which he was a member. In just a few words, he could establish himself as the temporary leader of all who associated with him, yet he never attempted to assume authority that belonged to those who operated this camp, or the infantry units that arrived on most days to handle the training programs.

Whatever else he might be, or might one day become, deBourbon was likable, and I respected him. So, apparently, did nearly all of the other members of Europe's royalty present. There were a couple of dukes, a few counts, and numbers who possessed lesser ranks in the aristocracy of Europe. Harry, an Austrian count, went out of his way to be friendly with me. I was sure this was because he saw me as a very young and inexperienced American soldier, who could benefit from the advice offered by an older person. Harry went to Bangor with me one time, when we each had a pass. There, he did his best to "fix me up" with a pretty young Irish girl in one of the small stores. She was not interested, but I had to give him an "A" for his effort. He went off on his own after that, possibly looking for female companionship more suited to his age and experience. Harry was probably thirty years old.

Like deBourbon, Harry never seemed to have a problem with any assignment given him. He was Austrian, which meant he should have been closely allied, psychologically, with the Germans. They used the same language, and shared much in their history and heritage. None of this seemed to affect Harry. He spoke excellent English, and possessed an awareness of the current world situation that forced him to realize he must serve in some sort of military capacity, so perhaps he believed the American army was as good as, or better than, any other.

Others were not quite as accepting of their condition. They were a mixed lot, these dukes and counts and marquis, or whatever designation was used for their particular place in the hierarchy of a system that now belonged to antiquity. DeBourbon was the only one among them who immediately created an image of "nobility." He had, in his speech, actions, and attitude, that intangible superiority to normal men that could be neither defined nor denied. He was a king, and not far removed from the time when that title had possessed a literal meaning.

Among the others, some worked hard, some were lazy. Some were highly intelligent, and some were stupid. It was likely that the majority resented their hasty induction into the U.S. Army, and their return to the Europe from which they believed they had escaped. A few were vociferous in their condemnation of this, and their loss of status by being made into common soldiers. They were Europe's nobility, and if this was now a fantasy as far as any real meaning was concerned, they wanted to live out that fantasy, and not be subjected to the indignities of taking orders from inferior men.

In the list of conditions they might resent, one was certainly the accommodations in this Irish camp. Nissen huts were bad enough. They were always either too cold or too hot. To add insult to injury, the "bed" on which we all slept was a pallet of wood about thirty inches wide, placed on supports that held it six inches above the concrete floor. The "mattress" was a huge cloth sack, which each of us filled with straw from a pile dumped on the ground. The full sack was called a "palliasse." It was usually lumpy and never comfortable, but at least dry.

One of my duties, before I went to the armory and opened it for the day, was to take my group to the parade ground, where a roll call was held and announcements concerning the program for the day were made. That was the end of my official association with the royal trainees for that particular day, a fact that did not depress me in the least.

There were frequent problems with some of them. A couple remarked, loudly enough for all to hear, that I did not "count cadence" properly as they marched to the morning briefing. They referred to me in the third person when they discussed my failings, as if I were incapable of understanding all their well-meant criticisms. Maybe their military background was more extensive than mine. That wouldn't have been surprising. Maybe European methods were different, also likely. Maybe (and this I suspected), they just liked to complain. I ignored all such comments, although I would readily admit that I wasn't much of a soldier. I could never do the Queen Anne salute, but I doubted any of these could, either.

More aggravating were those who could not wake up in the morning. I supposed these were "night" people who simply shunned the daylight hours, perhaps through a hereditary disposition toward vampirism, or sensitive eyes, or an inability to accept whatever they could not directly control. I had a whistle, like a policeman's whistle. Those still under covers five minutes before it was time to march heard my whistle, loudly and clearly, at a distance no greater than a foot or two from their ears. They grumbled and sometimes screamed, but they arose and hurriedly dressed to greet the day.

To be completely fair, there were a few who were incapable of meeting the requirement to be up and dressed before breakfast. Call him Heinrich. A Hungarian kid, he was a member of a minor noble house. He'd apparently had a personal servant to dress him each morning. He was totally incapable of doing it for himself. He could not find a single article of clothing, and while the others donned their uniforms, he spent his time dumping all his possessions from his barracks bags onto his pallet, then shoving them all back in the bags. Each such procedure might result in the discovery of a sock or undershirt, but he was then lost as to how he should wear them. It always took the combined efforts of two or three of his bunkmates, now fully dressed, to find a complete uniform and get it on the young aristocrat in time for roll call. Even this was difficult, for beyond his complete lack of physical ability, he was grossly overweight—he must have been over three hundred pounds. Like most of the group, this fine young representative of Europe's upper class was now a member of the Military Intelligence branch of the U.S. Army. Military Intelligence? Could a greater oxymoron exist?

We wondered how it had been possible for our government to draft citizens of other nations for military service. Was this legal? It hardly seemed so. Yet, once war had been declared, all acknowledgements of such things as diplomatic immunity went by the board. The army demanded and the army received. What it received in this case was Heinrich, who, once dressed, waddled along puffing and blowing at the end of a line of Europe's finest, destined to make his contribution to the field of intelligence, military style.

In addition to deBourbon and Harry the Austrian, there were others who were competent enough. I just never found any in the detail assigned to clean our Springfield rifles one day. I supplied them with cleaning rods, cloth patches to use in the barrels, rags, cans of sperm oil (the world standard of the time for protecting and lubricating all firearms), and linseed oil for the wooden stocks.

Anger was an emotion to which I rarely succumbed, but these morons, sitting in a circle on the ground and chattering away in languages I did not understand, soon had me screeching well-enunciated obscenities.

When every European was a quarter mile away, I used some gasoline to "swamp out" the rifle barrels and remove every trace of linseed oil from the metal parts. If these precious Springfields of mine were fired with linseed oil in the working parts, it would turn to a gummy substance that could ruin any firearm. Linseed was for the wooden stocks, and only for that. It could bring them back to a wonderful soft sheen, and if used regularly, helped preserve the walnut finish for decades. It took much of the remaining stock of sperm oil to then properly swab the barrels and lubricate the bolts of all the rifles.

The First Sergeant duly noted my formal request to never again allow those mentally deficient play soldiers near my armory, my rifles, or my machinegun.

It wasn't long after that when all of the Europeans moved out, transferred to some other camp, where they were probably educated in the finer points of military intelligence, such as how to dress themselves in the morning. We wondered if we'd ever see any of them again. It would be no great loss if we didn't, except I'd grown fond of deBourbon and Harry, and would always recall my association with them as a source of pleasure and pride.

# 4

# *An Anchor in the Gathering Storm*

A mile away, on the other side of the road to Bangor, was an ATS camp. This meant "Army Territorial Service," and it was the British equivalent of our WAC (Women's Army Corps).

Danny Randall, our assistant company clerk, asked me one Saturday morning if I'd like to double date with him. "Sure," I replied, "with which girls?"

"A couple of very nice ATS girls at the camp down the road," he said. "Nothing really special. We'll just go to Bangor with them, stop at the pub, maybe take in a movie, then get a taxi back to their camp, and ours. The buses don't run after dark. I've already dated one of them. The one who'll be your date is Irish. That is, she's a volunteer from Eire in the Brit army. It might surprise you how many of them there are. I think people in the south are generally pretty poor. The Army is one of the few ways to get away from a place where opportunities are scarce for anything better than some kind of serving girl."

"That's interesting," I said. "I thought the border between Eire and Ulster was closed to Allied military. Does that mean they can never go home again until the war's over?"

"Not sure about that," said Danny. "I think they're allowed to cross if they lived in Eire, but must be dressed in civilian clothes. We can ask the girls. That is, if you're going with me."

I did, and it changed things a lot. With our passes in hand, we rode the first afternoon bus to Bangor, and stopped at the ATS camp. The driver waited while we called for the girls from the front guard post. They were expecting us, because Danny had phoned them from our own headquarters, something I hadn't known was possible. They soon appeared, we all boarded the bus, and something new began to happen.

A teenager thousands of miles from home, family, and friends can become depressingly lonely, even in the midst of many others in similar situations. I was one of those teenagers, and well aware that the loneliness, in a strange land and circumstances far from anything ever experienced before, could color my perceptions. It might even distort my judgment, but how much judgment does a nineteen-year-old really have? More, I thought, and sincerely believed at the time, than most people would give us credit for. Military training had pushed us along the road to maturity, maybe not always in the direction we might have chosen, but with "grow up or get out" as a most effective goad. Those of us who were not afflicted by either psychological or physical impairments grew up.

Her name was Kay, for Kathleen, and she was as pretty as any girl I'd ever hoped to meet. Blond hair, green eyes that laughed at the slightest provocation, in a round, pleasant face that grandchildren would certainly love. She was full-figured, something even the severe lines of the uniform couldn't hide. Kay was born the same year I was, a few months earlier. Our view of the world was similar, even if our nationalities and backgrounds were not.

The weather, though cool, was nice. We walked around much of Bangor after the beer, fish and chips we enjoyed at the pub. A visit to the movie theater followed, and this was a novel experience. The seating was the same as in any small town American movie house, with one notable exception. On the back of every seat was an ashtray, for the convenience of those who sat behind that seat and wished to smoke during the film. We did, as did many others. Before long the air was dense with tobacco smoke, the beam of light from the projector a bright slash through the swirling cloud, doing its best to illuminate the screen and make the movie visible.

No one seemed to mind, or complained. For the most part, these were American cigarettes making all the smoke, and the locals had rapidly become accustomed to the superior quality of our tobacco. English cigarettes were decidedly inferior, nearly tasteless. The availability of the American product was the basis for many friendships with the locals.

The movie was a war film about the firefighters of London. They were, for the most part, men who had been rejected by the military for minor disabilities or age. The movie made heroes of them, as they risked their lives (and sometimes lost them) putting out the nightly fires resulting from thousands of incendiary bombs dropped by German planes. There were no winners in these midnight battles against the incessant flames that devoured the city. There was just the commitment by a pitifully small number of men to fight on and do, over and over, what little they could to save some part of what was left.

This was, I supposed, a microcosm of the war and much of the world at large during this time. In the end, there would be many dead and injured, but no real winners. On all sides, we would simply do what we could to ensure something we may call a victory, but which was far more likely to be simply a change. This was not a defeatist attitude. As long as we were able to do something even slightly better than our opposition, we'd never admit defeat. That "slightly better" was all that might determine the course and shape of things to come. It was all that remained to the British people after four years of warfare. They hung on and held out, while their leaders talked a far better fight than most of the people were capable of sustaining.

We were here to change that, and the Brits knew it, just as had the Anzacs in the pub. America had the numbers, the industrial capacity, and the resources to tip the scales in favor of the Allies and against Germany. The only question was how much of all that would we commit to the war? How much would we be willing to pay for a world without a German or Japanese aggressor?

Danny rarely wanted to discuss these issues, nor did his date, Mary. For that matter, few in our company ever talked about such things. They did whatever they were told to do, and let it go at that. Conversation inevitably focused on girls, drink, and how to spend the next twelve-hour pass.

Kay was different, and seemed interested in any subject I broached. I did not know her well enough at the time to judge if this were just a façade to help our relationship grow into something deeper, or if she really did have an interest in world affairs. I'd need to see her again, several times, for an answer to that.

We found a taxi for the ride back that night. As with all privately owned and operated vehicles, the owner/driver could not buy gasoline. In its place, the taxi carried a huge airtight cloth bag, as large as the vehicle itself, on the roof. The bag contained a flammable gas (probably methane, because they could manufacture it from wood or coal), which was piped to the engine and burned for power. This worked well, except it took all the skill and strength of the driver to keep the vehicle on the correct side of the road when the wind was blowing. Sharp corners gave the passengers a real thrill.

I held Kay closely. With four of us in the back seat and the taxi threatening to take to the air at any time, it was the only way to go. When we arrived at the ATS camp gate, we kissed and quickly agreed that we'd see each other again.

We did that, every day when we could get passes at the same time. We often visited the little park in Bangor, where we fed the ducks in the pond there with stale bread bought for a few pennies in a nearby store. There was a bench on which we could sit if the day were sunny and warm enough. Kay liked to walk, and one day we hiked the four miles from her camp to Donaghadee, a quaint little fishing village at the end of Belfast Lough, and back. We saw another movie or two, explored the streets of Bangor, and often just stood at the seawall to watch the water and boats.

In addition to her interest in world events, she displayed a knowledge of literature and a love of poetry that matched or exceeded my own. Her father, I learned, was a district manager for the Irish railroad, which placed the family in a somewhat better financial position than the majority of Irish. Kay's parents were not desperately poor.

She had a sister and a brother, both of whom were members of the British army, just as Kay was. Of the two, she was more concerned about her brother, because all-Irish units would certainly be a part of the British fighting forces when we all moved to France.

Kay had no definite plans for after the war. Neither did I, except a vague idea of returning to printing, or going to work as a gunsmith in civilian life. Of the two, I believed that printing offered the best prospects for the future.

We grew closer with every hour we shared, until we both realized we were in love. Hampered by the inability to make anything that resembled plans for a permanent relationship, we consoled each other with vague promises about "when the war is over." Beside the road to Donaghadee, we stopped at the sea wall for a time and watched the waves break on the rocky shore.

"Will you consider moving to America with me?" I asked her.

"Yes," she replied, "but what's in America that we don't have in Eire?"

"Opportunity," I said. "I've been unable to see much here. Even in Ulster, people spend far too much of their time, energy, and wealth in hating each other and committing acts of violence against their neighbors. There do not seem to be any goals beyond perpetuating the status quo, which is, to me, a pretty sad state of affairs and not something I'd care to be a part of."

Kay was silent for a few minutes. "Yes," she said finally. "That's all true, and I'm afraid it will never change in our lifetimes, but it's better in the south, in Eire. There, we have few of the more violent confrontations common in Ulster."

"But no more opportunities for a good life," I added.

She shook her head. "I'm afraid not, if you're referring to the ability to earn much money. Most Americans seem to measure any sort of success in monetary terms. I can understand that, to a point, but cannot heartily agree with it. A couple who love each other deeply, as I believe we could when our circumstances are better, can have just as fulfilling a life in a two-room cabin as others might in a great manor house. Our minds and spirits do not necessarily need great gobs of money to find life's deeper meanings. In fact, I believe wealth may at times be a hindrance rather than a help."

I pulled her to me and kissed her. "I love the way you think. We're totally unable to make any decisions about this right now, but it's something we'll need to seriously discuss at a later time, a time when war and all its trappings does not dominate our lives. Maybe you'd be willing to try America for a few years first, then decide if its what you want. Maybe?"

She smiled. "Yes. Maybe. And maybe by then we'll have children and be unable to choose anything else."

I had to tell her what I knew was highly probable in the very near future. "We'll be leaving soon, I think."

Her eyes widened. "For where?"

"England, I suppose. The buildup seems to be speeding up, which means a landing somewhere in France must be in the wind, although no official word has yet been released, and probably won't be until it becomes an established fact, with some of us on the continent and others on the way."

"In other words," she said, "we'll know about it when it's a fait accompli."

"Yes. That's about the size of it. I'm not even sure how much warning I'll have when we leave the camp here. The army is not fond of allowing enlisted men much notice before a move."

"When you do know, and if it's only a matter of hours before you leave, telephone me. I'll demand a pass and come over to your camp. They'll not likely let me inside, but you could meet me just outside your gate, and we could spend at least a few last minutes together."

I nodded, and we walked hand-in-hand the rest of the way to her ATS camp. The sun was going down, the day nearing its end. We held each other closely for several minutes, after which she went through the gate, and I trudged back to Portavo Point under a darkening sky, carrying somber thoughts.

It was just a few days later that we were notified to pack our things and be ready to move in two hours. I was not allowed to use the phone, but Danny Randall could, and made the call for me. Less than a half hour later, a messenger from the sentry informed me that someone was asking for me at the gate.

We sat on the ground at the side of the road, close enough to the gate so I could be easily notified if I should be needed. In the field across the road, spring flowers bloomed. Insects hummed in those closer to us. Pleasant warmth gave notice of better days to come in the greenest land known to men.

We each smoked a cigarette and tried to find words that might have some meaning to them. Kay had twin rivulets of tears flowing down her cheeks. My eyes were threatening to overflow with a similar release of moisture. I kept telling myself that I could not cry. Soldiers don't cry. Young men don't cry. The world could be falling apart, but we were not allowed to express our feelings in anything as weak and insignificant as tears.

We'd had about twenty minutes, when a messenger appeared to inform me that I was needed in the armory. A crew had arrived to load everything there, and I should supervise most of it.

We stood, hugged and kissed a final time without a care about who might be watching. Kay left. I went through the gate to face my immediate future.

# 5

## *Irish Green to Major Mud*

We left by truck that same day and went to Bangor, where we boarded the train for Belfast. Here, we stayed the night at a "casual" facility (temporary accommodations for traveling soldiers). After an early breakfast, trucks took us to the ferry, this time for a daylight crossing. A British Spitfire flew overhead, circling and returning frequently, our escort through waters that not long ago had been infested with German U-boats. I stood in the bow, felt the gentle touch of the breeze we made in passing, and with feet spread well apart, rode the small swells of the sea. If I closed my eyes, I could easily imagine that this was my father's boat, and we were sailing down Mount Hope and Narragansett Bays, on the way "outside" to do some fishing. The ferry was much larger, but blind fantasy made real again the sensations of a pleasanter time.

The shoreline of Scotland was barely discernible, far ahead, and I realized that whatever Kay and I had experienced—whatever we had meant to each other—was equally distant, now on hold and something we might, or might not, be able to renew at a later time. It was out of our hands, and far beyond our powers to even think that we could control the smallest part of our lives. Others would do that, usually without the slightest concern about what we wanted or how we felt. It was the way the world operated in these times, and we had about as much chance of changing this as one of those wheeling gulls ahead of us had of flying to the moon. The only consolation was that we were far from being alone. Even German soldiers, I imagined, were no different from us in their personal desires.

So be it, I thought. If all that we wished were not possible now, then we'd do our part to shorten the time until it became possible. We'd obey our orders, whatever they were. We'd give the extra effort when that was needed. Kay and I would write to each other, often and at length, because what we could say in a letter—even a heavily censored letter—might just be all that really mattered in our personal lives at this time. Many of the others, I knew, felt the same way. It was impossible to overstate the importance of mail to young men facing a host of unknowns, many of which were potentially fatal. Letters could be the signs of sanity we'd need on a world gone over the edge with irrational hatred and the wholesale extinction of human lives once precious to someone. Kay and I would write to each other, and this was all that we could reasonably do.

The ferry arrived at a dock, where trucks waited for us. Trucks were everywhere, evidence of the greatest mobile army ever gathered on earth. It seemed obvious that these vehicles, with their ability to move men and supplies quickly, would be a deciding factor in the contest ahead.

Most of the drivers were black, and we saw now that they handled their vehicles with a professionalism of the highest order. We were a segregated army, living under the impression, passed down through the ranks from highest to lowest, that black men were "unfit for combat." Where that idea originated was uncertain. They had proven themselves in the Civil War, in the Indian Wars of the West, and in countless other ways since. Yet, at some point before World War I, a high-ranking general or politician had decided they lacked courage, patriotism, or ability with weapons, or perhaps were just not quite bright enough. No one seemed to know, so the topic was rarely mentioned.

When we returned to England, our first camp was a temporary affair, partly Nissen huts and dirt "streets," partly pyramidal "squad tents" erected over wood floors raised a step above the ground. Each of the tents held bunks for eight men. The season had advanced well into spring, and we were comfortable enough sleeping under canvas rather than steel.

Our cooks went to work in the kitchen, and I set up a tiny armory in a room behind our HQ, in the same Nissen hut.

I worked there only briefly. Orders arrived to send me to a small arms school for two weeks, to study European firearms, primarily British and German. It was an interesting time, divided between classroom work and experience firing various weapons in a huge open field, with a hill for a backstop. I'd not have believed, earlier, that England could contain such large open spaces. The actual firing was principally a refresher course in our own weaponry, such as the pistol, the M1 rifle, the Thompson submachine gun, and the BAR (Browning Automatic Rifle). Ammunition for the European arms was apparently scarce or non-existent.

Without actually firing them we did, however, become familiar with the German Mauser, the MG34 and MG42 (the early and later versions of the same light machinegun), the Luger pistol and its modern replacement, the P38 pistol, and, finally, the Schmeisser machine pistol, the well-known "burp gun." These weapons were well made, although none were any better than our own M1 rifle. The British Enfield was already familiar. American forces had used it during World War I, altered to take our .30-06 ammunition. It was not quite the equal of the Springfield, but apparently in 1917, American arms manufacturers had been unable to produce rifles quickly enough, so we had relied on the British to make up the shortage.

The French Lebel rifle was represented, but deserved little notice and no comment. A tiny machine pistol of Italian origin demonstrated a degree of ingenuity but little else. Designed to mount on the handlebar of a bicycle, and issued to troops who peddled out from their villages to meet the enemy, it could spit out a stream of small-caliber bullets, but typically dumped the bicycle soldier in the nearest ditch when it was fired. There was no way to steer the vehicle and aim the weapon at the same time.

The British Sten gun was novel. It was a throw-away weapon, cheaply made and issued to Commandos for quick hit-and-run raids. Fully automatic, it had little accuracy and a short range, but in close quarters, such as inside a building, it served well enough. When the ammunition was gone, or if there were any difficulty with the Sten, the Commando would simply throw it away and try to make his escape. Another would be issued to him before the next occasion when he might need it.

On my return to the company, I faced a real workload. We needed to be armed, in accordance with our T of O (Table of

Organization). This meant carbines for all but six men, each of whom would have a Springfield, three with grenade launchers. I ordered the weapons, and found that we needed five more carbines. I was the only one who would accept the Springfield. The others all thought it was too heavy, compared to the little carbine, and the ammunition, when we received it, would also weigh more. That was true enough, but the Springfield was far more accurate, with much greater range. I liked both of those features. Although we had no idea whatever about what we'd face in France, it wasn't at all difficult to imagine situations in which a Springfield could stop an enemy two to three hundred yards away, far beyond the effective range of the carbine.

We were not issued ammunition, except at the rifle range, where everyone was supposed to spend a little time becoming acquainted with his weapon. This was an activity much underutilized, and I feared that in a position where firepower was important, my company would perform poorly.

An armored battalion shared this camp with us. They, too, needed weapons, plus time on the range. As the only qualified armorer in the camp, it was up to me to arm them. Members of a tank crew could be issued either a pistol or a submachine gun. Nearly all of them wanted a pistol, but these were chronically in short supply. I never received more than a tenth of the number ordered. A new submachine gun, the M3, was substituted. This was not a popular choice with the tankers. The old Thompson (the "Chicago typewriter") was a well made weapon, but apparently too time-consuming and expensive to manufacture in quantity. The M3, with only two machined parts, the bolt and the barrel, was fast and cheap. All the other parts were stamped out of sheet metal.

It fired the same .45 caliber cartridge as the pistol and the Thompson. Everyone called it the "grease gun," because that's what it looked like. Target practice on the range proved that it was far from accurate, but that was not a critical necessity. If a tank were knocked out, the crew usually needed to bail out in a hurry. An M3, lifted above the hatch opening, could spray the surrounding countryside with a lot of bullets in a matter of seconds. This, it was reasoned, would discourage a nearby enemy from any attempt to interfere with those who needed to abandon their tank. Firepower, rather than aimed fire, was becoming the rule of the day.

We were issued a company weapon, a .50 caliber heavy-barreled machinegun on an anti-aircraft mount. It was a monstrous and cumbersome thing, without any means of aiming it beyond watching the tracers when (or if) it was fired. The mount was designed for a water-cooled MG, and came with one of those spider-web sights that clamped to the water jacket. There was no water jacket, and even if there had been one, we had the wrong kind of barrel for it. A water-cooled weapon, on this mount, was principally used in a defensive position, such as on shipboard, where the coolant permitted long bursts of gunfire. Our gun was the type used on, and against, armored vehicles. We possessed a mismatched set of gun and mount, but apparently would receive nothing else. The machinegun had sights, but there was no way a gunner could see them in this mount.

Because we had a machinegun, I was appointed the training instructor for it, and soon had a group of truck drivers who needed to know how to fire and maintain this weapon. I felt totally inadequate as a teacher, but tried. I soon learned that if I taught these men as I had been taught, focused on nomenclature (names of the parts) and the mechanics of the thing, I'd have them all yawning in minutes. They weren't going to be armorers. They were going to drive trucks, and if they knew how to use an MG, they'd have one in a ring mount cut into the roof of the cab on the passenger side. Ordnance was busily installing the mounts at this time, one in every fifth truck. This was considered sufficient to protect a truck convoy from attacking aircraft.

I forgot about names of parts and operating functions, just showed them how to feed the belt into the side of the gun, how to crank the operating handle twice to load, and how to use their body against the enclosing padded "hook" to swing and aim the piece. They learned that the spent cartridges would drop out the bottom of the gun, and would be hot, and the metal links that made up the belt would spit out the side and would only be warm. With that small bit of knowledge, the drivers went to their individual companies.

We soon moved again, and realized we were part of a living tide of military personnel flowing from north to south through the length of Britain. Something like a million and a half of us were all aiming at the ports on the south coast. A few of the camps were pleasant. Most were crude and gloomy, the ubiquitous Nissen huts on concrete slabs in the middle of a desolate nowhere. Yet the season progressed, and for those who looked, lilacs flowered on the hillsides and daffodils in the front of country cottages. Nature had awakened from her winter's sleep.

We lost Sol Vance at the next camp. Army psychologists had determined that Sol was mentally and physically unfit to serve where the possibility of hostile gunfire existed. Sol would be going home to New York, just as he'd promised us he would. We wished him well.

Three others soon left, but not headed for home. They'd be used to fill shortages in an infantry company. One was Reilly, who had developed a personal hatred for lieutenant Markinson, our "by the book" officer. Reilly's criticism was often vocal, and so were his threats of violence, at whatever future time an opportunity presented itself. He'd become so absorbed in his plans to wreak vengeance on the lieutenant, most of us could understand why he was sent elsewhere. Markinson could not function as he should, if he must constantly be looking over his shoulder for Reilly with a weapon in his hand.

Another to leave was the only person in the company younger than I was. Selfort was a good-looking kid, but not completely whole mentally. He was a petty thief, and I'd caught him with some of my personal items. We had no locks on the barracks bags, and Selfort managed to find excuses to visit the hut when no one else was around. My schedule, as armorer, did not always coincide with that of the others, and I walked in on him one day while he was going through my things. I challenged him, and offered to settle any differences we had with fists, outside the hut. He broke down, sobbing, and went through his own barracks bag until he'd found every item that had been mine, and returned all of them. I never reported this, but suspected the officers knew about it anyway, and got rid of Selfort when there was a chance to do it. There was no place for a thief in any company preparing to move into danger. I felt sorry for him, because he'd not survive long. If he were not shot by the enemy, one of his own company would likely do it.

One of our cooks was the last to go. No reason was made public, and we could only guess that he might have become involved in the black market. Cooks worked with a vast wealth of easily sold materials.

We arrived in Southampton on June 13, a week after D-Day. Once again, it was a camp of Nissen huts on concrete slabs, with mud. It rained much of the time. Getting from one place to another was a slow slog through oozing muck over halfway to our knees. There were no shower facilities, but we'd expected none. No one in Britain seemed to understand what a shower was. No home had one, and baths were commonly taken in a public bathhouse, every month or two or as needed. Only the American Air Force had showers.

Camp life at Southampton was dull and boring. The place was never designed with long-term occupancy in mind. There were no recreational facilities at all, no movies, not even a small library. Those who arrived here were expected to leave within days, maybe within hours.

Possibly to relieve the tedium, someone had the bright idea to send an inspection team to visit us. It consisted of a major and two captains, from headquarters, someone said, but did not say from what headquarters. Adolf Hitler's personal bodyguard, maybe? Someone called "Attention!" when they walked into our hut. The major was short and rotund, possibly from far too much time spent sitting at a desk. His uniform was spotless, or nearly so, except for the shoes, which were, of course, thickly coated with mud. He had folded up the pants legs to protect them. His insignia of rank were brightly polished, and his sandy-colored mustache was just long enough to bob up and down when he talked, as if to emphasize his well-chosen words of contempt and anger. He was red-faced and practically apoplectic when he entered our hut.

"What is this?" he screeched. "Don't you men have even an elementary knowledge of housekeeping? Every hut in this camp should be condemned. Look at this filthy floor! There's an inch of muck on it. This must be cleaned up and kept clean. Heads are going to roll about this, I promise you. There will be a court-martial."

He stopped in front of Sergeant Alonzo Truhall. Lon stood at rigid attention, staring straight ahead, with an unlit cigarette in his mouth. He'd apparently been about to use his Zippo when the inspection team arrived.

The major became even more incensed. "What do you think you're doing, Sergeant? Don't you know any better than to smoke during an inspection?"

"I'm not smoking, Sir," Lon said.

"What do you mean, you're not smoking? Do you think I'm blind? You've a cigarette in your mouth. Cigarettes are made to be smoked, aren't they?"

"Yes, Sir. But I'm not smoking."

"Do you deny that you've a cigarette in your mouth?"

"No, Sir," Lon replied. "But I'm not smoking."

"Are you calling me some kind of fool, Sergeant? Cigarettes are made to be smoked, and you have one in your mouth right now."

"Yes, Sir. I've got my shoes on, too, sir, but I ain't running."

The captains looked at each other, barely able to suppress their grins.

The major, with a mean glint in his eyes, turned to Frank Parsons, our supply sergeant. "Do you live in this pig sty, Sergeant?"

"I live in this hut, Sir," Frank replied.

"Then I hold you responsible. You appear to be the ranking NCO here. What is your position in this sorry excuse for a military unit?"

"Supply Sergeant, Sir."

This was almost too much for the major. He danced up and down, fists pumping as if he were pulling the ropes on a bell tolling the doom of the world. The whole display was ludicrous. He was ludicrous. He was also a major in the U. S. Army, with enough authority to make good on any threats.

"Supply Sergeant?" he screamed. "You're the Supply Sergeant? Then where are the cleaning supplies? Where are the brooms and mops every man in this cesspool should be using relentlessly to stay ahead of the filth?"

"They were requisitioned a week ago, sir, but as yet are unavailable."

"Unavailable? I'll not hear it. You understand, Sergeant? I'll not hear of it. You get those brooms and mops. The moment they appear, I'll have you court-martialed. Dereliction of duty, that's what it is. You'll spend the rest of your life in Leavenworth, learning something about keeping floors clean."

He stalked out, waving his arms and lecturing the captains about the benefits of a speedy court-martial. The captains followed, saying nothing. Each of the three left a pile of mud where he'd stood in the hut.

Our own Lieutenant Cicciloni came in a few minutes later. "That major and the captains give you a bad time?" he asked Sergeant Parsons.

"Sort of," Frank replied. "I'm to be court-martialed for not getting supplies that were unavailable."

"Forget about it," said the Lieutenant. "We'll be long gone before he can get the paperwork through channels." He glanced at the floor. "It is pretty bad here, though. Bring a couple of men with you to the HQ hut. We found some thin boards there, and used them to scrape up the stuff and toss it outside. You can do the same."

A half hour later, Frank and the others returned. We took turns scraping mud and throwing it out the door.

With each passing day, we wished more strongly for word from the beachhead. We knew we'd be going over soon, and needed details about what was happening there. What would we face, and what would our role be once in Normandy?

Information was doled out to us through The Stars and Stripes, the army weekly newspaper. It cost two cents American, and that was about how much news value it had. We bought it for Bill Mauldin's cartoons.

There was another way to acquire information that we considered essential. The army "grapevine" was probably just as accurate as any of the bits of news released by the censors to the media. A steady stream of seriously wounded now arrived in England, on their way to hospitals where the level of care was much above what could be given them in the field. They talked. They talked to nurses and orderlies, and what they said was passed along, until it entered the generally accepted knowledge that flowed through the "grapevine." Errors developed, unavoidable in any word-of-mouth transmission, but much of it was at least as accurate as anything the media presented. We accepted the stories passed to us in the grapevine as essentially true, and learned to discount the wilder tales at the same time that we developed a healthy respect for the rest.

We learned, for example, that our men on the beachhead were outnumbered nearly three to one, but that many of the opposing troops were not Germans. They were Russians, Poles, Czechs, Latvians and Lithuanians, and others. They fought for Germany, but not with noticeable enthusiasm. In some units Gestapo agents accompanied them, ready to kill any who tried to surrender to American or British forces.

Supplies were scarce on the beachhead, notably artillery ammunition. The big guns were limited to three shots per day, except when under immediate attack. Our tanks were of little help. Those sent over on D-Day, equipped with special flotation devices to get them ashore, did not. They all sank, with their crews. The tanks that made it later, from LSTs (landing ship, tank) that were driven up on the beach, were no match for the German armor. It seemed, for a while, that all news from the beachhead was bad news. Yet, Allied infantry had managed to secure almost twenty-eight square miles of Normandy. This whole amphibious operation now looked at the possibility of success.

Meanwhile, one delay followed another. We began to wonder if we'd spend the rest of our lives slopping around in Southampton mud, waiting for the return of the mad major; or, as a few preferred to call him, the "Mud Major."

# 6

## *The Beachhead*

We boarded an LST (Landing Ship, Tank) on July 4. This was a relatively large vessel, capable of delivering tanks right on shore by lowering a ramp in the bow. As a troop carrier, its use was occasional and limited. In the early part of the Normandy invasion, the LCIs (Landing Craft, Infantry) took most of the men ashore.

A "craft" was far smaller than a ship, but served essentially the same purpose. Instead of armor, it brought men close to the beach, where it dropped a bow ramp in shallow water. The men ran out and hoped they'd make it to land alive. Many did; many others did not.

We were the last group to board the ship. This meant there was no space for us. Standing orders seemed to require that any vessel used as a troop carrier be overloaded at least fifty percent. Lon Truhall and I looked at the packed mass of humanity and elbowed our way to an enclosed portion of the main deck. There, we found a trapdoor that opened to a ladder ("companionway" to the sailors) leading down into the hold. We went down.

There was a solid bulkhead to the rear, another toward the bow with a door in its center. On the wall above the door was a small electric light bulb, about ten watts, enclosed in a wire cage. Apparently, it was never turned off, and provided just enough illumination to see our way around, and to read the sign on the door. In large red letters were the words "DANGER— HIGH EXPLOSIVES."

"It's probably the ammo locker for the deck gun," said Lon. "You want to stay here? The sailors said there are still lots of mines offshore over there. If we hit one, and we're down here with all that HE, no one's likely to find more of us than a tooth or fingernail."

I nodded, and we removed our packs, leaned them against the bulkhead, and gratefully sat down. With our legs stretched out and our backs against the packs, we experienced the first real comfort of the day. There was a risk involved, but if we did hit a mine, there would probably be few survivors anyway. For us, the end would be mercifully quick.

After a few minutes of relaxation, we left the packs and went topside to see what was happening. Distant thunder came across the water form Normandy.

"Artillery," said Lon. "I heard a sailor say there'd be a Fourth of July salute to American independence. Even the British guns have joined."

Beach commanders, we soon learned, had arranged a TOT exercise to mark the holiday. TOT stood for "Time on Target." Every artillery piece on the beachhead fired at the precise second that would allow the projectiles to land and explode simultaneously. We heard the rolling bass drum beat of guns firing, soon followed by the grand crescendo of exploding shells. The Krauts in the target zones must have thought the world was coming to an end. That was the whole idea, plus giving a boost to Allied morale. On our ship in Southampton harbor, it was an assurance that we had ample artillery already ashore over there. All they needed was more ammunition. At high tide the following morning, we sailed for Normandy.

Sergeant Parsons told us he'd once more ordered brooms and mops, but if they arrived, it was too late. The mad major never returned and, as far as we knew, never instituted court-martial proceedings. We could only guess that calmer or wiser heads somewhere in the headquarters from which he'd come had quashed his plan to fill Leavenworth with all those who did not meet with his approval. There was also a suspicion that he'd been sent out on his inspection tour just to get him out of the way.

Lon and I went back down to our "nest" in the hold. We talked for a few minutes, mostly to keep the fear at bay. We could rationalize our presence next to all that high explosive. We had the most comfortable place on the ship, and the odds were fairly good that we'd not hit a mine. Yet, only by sharing thoughts with each other was it possible to mentally compensate for the knowledge that violent death was both possible and imminent. No matter what the odds, we were very much aware of what could happen on this voyage to the beachhead, while we still knew nothing at all about what our purpose would be when we arrived.

Lon was a sergeant now, as were all of our company who had responsibilities directly related to training schedules or the welfare of new men arriving in a steady stream from the States. Lon was a good man and a good soldier, even if he did sometimes keep an unlit cigarette in his mouth. He was in the army because he'd been offered a choice between this and doing time in a penitentiary.

It was not that Lon was a criminal, in any way familiar to the rest of us. Call it drunken anger or call it a response to unnecessary goading by an in-law. Maybe it was all justified, even if questionable on a legal basis.

He was from Tennessee, and had once been a coal miner. He had a "lantern jaw" which jutted out from his chin in a way that gave him a pugnacious look totally out of character with his usual easy-going nature. A mine cave-in had buried him under seven tons of slate, and demolished his jaw beyond the ability of doctors to properly reconstruct it. It had healed this way.

Out of a job while he recovered, he'd turned to moonshining for income. Like many in that area, he'd probably done a little in the past, although that was something he'd never admit.

All had gone well until, following a family disagreement, his brother-in-law had informed the revenue agents about the location of Lon's still. They had smashed everything, an action Lon had not appreciated. Fortified with some of his own product, Lon had shot his brother-in-law, but not fatally. After that, he was offered jail time or the army. It had not been a difficult choice, since he expected to be drafted soon anyway.

Lon still could not handle drink well. It aroused old angers and made him want to fight, anyone and everyone. After we'd known him for a while, we could ignore all this, because Lon couldn't fight. He'd dance around, feint, wave his fists and make wild claims about his boxing prowess, then invariably wind up with a bloody nose or black eye when his opponent became tired of it all. Sober, there was none better than Lon. Drunk, he was hopeless and useless.

In reply to his questions about me, I told him enough but not too much. I'd been philosophically opposed to this war from the beginning. It had been my opinion that most, if not all, of it was arranged for the benefit of our politicians and leaders of industry. This was obviously why Germany had gone to war. Hitler had promised his people financial security. War was the only way he could make good on that promise.

We weren't terribly different. President Roosevelt needed to bring us out of a world depression and give us "a chicken in every pot and a car in every garage." He, too, needed a war to do all that.

Lon, the rest of our company, and I, were about to play a more active and vital part in this war, whether we liked it or not, and whether we thought it was right, wrong, or were indifferent to it. Our choices had been expropriated, our opinions and philosophies made pointless. As taught in the training film we'd been required to watch months ago in the States, the time had come to "kill or be killed." There were no other choices, no other path we might follow. It was too late to register as a CO (conscientious objector). It was too late to transfer to the medics. That wouldn't have done much good, anyway. Medics were killed as often as any others. They just weren't required to kill someone else before they died.

We heard the noises of increased activity above us, then the rattle of the anchor chain. We'd arrived. We heaved into the straps of our packs and climbed the companionway.

On deck, we waited. When our company was called, we climbed into one of the small boats and dropped into the sea. We seemed to be about a mile from shore, and questioned the sailor who started the engine and commanded this boat.

"Have to be this far out," he said. "Tides here are some of the highest in the world, probably second only to the Bay of Fundy. Thirty feet is common. Closer in, and the LST would soon be on the bottom."

We looked around. This place was a graveyard for ships of all sizes and descriptions. There must have been two hundred, sunk or partly sunk and damaged, some with steel cables still rising from them, attached to barrage balloons. Where the water was deep, the cables ended at the surface. Somewhere below was a ship that would never sail again, and probably a lot of bodies, both sailors and soldiers.

We bumped against a sort of floating boardwalk, supported by empty fifty-gallon drums, and trudged ashore. Smashed landing craft were strewn about on the beach. So were numbers of trucks, burned and scorched and blown apart. One lay on its side, the cab completely blown off. It didn't take a lot of imagination to know what had happened to the driver. He was probably part of the landscape now, as were the bulldozer operators who had managed to get ashore. From the looks of the mangled remains, Kraut artillery had targeted bulldozers in preference to anything else.

Thousands of jerricans (five gallon gasoline cans) were scattered everywhere, some with bullet holes, some burned or torn apart, some apparently whole. All kinds of supplies lay in jumbled piles. Ammunition of every description covered the sand, with empty shell casings wherever someone had fired a weapon.

It was a surrealist's nightmare, spread out for us to see and wonder about. We moved in, over coarse shingle, to the base of a hundred-foot cliff of mostly white chalk. This area, someone said, was part of the same huge deposit that lay beneath the English Channel and continued on land as the cliffs of Dover. England and Normandy shared ancient ties long before the Norman Conquest. A narrow goat path, with many switchbacks, struggled up the cliff. We climbed this, all the time wondering how anyone could have done it while under fire from above. Casualties had been heavy here, contrary to what we'd been told about overall losses.

A large German gun emplacement, empty and silent now, was at the top. Shells from our naval guns had pockmarked its four feet of reinforced concrete, like the wall of an inverted bowl. We learned that although the big guns of the battleship offshore had provided remarkably accurate fire, it was not quite enough.

Each of these coastal defense emplacements had to be neutralized by the infantry. They would force an entrance at the rear door, and with rifles, grenades, and flame throwers, eliminate the German crews. This saved lives among those who landed later.

We hiked to a position occupied by another company like ours. They'd been bombed the previous night and had casualties. The survivors we saw, and to whom we talked, were badly shaken. In the next field, we each found a spot in the ditch beside the hedgerow, and settled in for the remainder of this day, our first in Normandy.

A couple of our guys explored the area, and found a dead German soldier at the other end of our field. A few others indulged their morbid curiosity and went over to look at him. Lieutenant Markinson came to me and told me not to do that. I was the youngest in the company, and suspected he'd taken a somewhat paternal interest in my welfare. This was both reassuring and unnecessary. I could take care of myself.

In the morning, we hiked again, about ten miles to what became our own hedgerow-enclosed home field. The small town nearby was Isigny. From the country road that ran by the field, we could see the Vire River delta and the coast, three or four miles away.

Our company truck, a one-and-a-half ton, was now ashore. It brought company supplies, such as pyramidal tents for HQ, supply, and the cooks. It also had our .50 caliber anti-aircraft machinegun, on its mount.

In a couple of days, our reserve supply of ammunition arrived. In all, this was seven tons of rifle, carbine, pistol and sub-machinegun cartridges, with thirteen of the ammo canisters that attached to the side of the .50 caliber. Each held 265 rounds, loaded with a sequence of two armor piercing, two incendiary, and one tracer. The tracers were, of course, critical to aiming the piece. The incendiaries were intended to set fire to the gasoline or oil in aircraft fuel tanks or engines. Armor piercing was self-explanatory. We also had a rocket launcher (a "bazooka") and three rockets, and rifle grenades for our Springfields, but of a World War I type, useless against any modern German armor. As the company armorer, all of this was my responsibility. Wherever we went, I was to dig a hole for this ammo, then another next to it for myself.

Here in this Normandy field, we began to learn the nature of our work, and a definition for our company. None of it was good. We had a name, meaningless thus far. We'd started as a "replacement" company, had that changed to "reinforcement" company, but at no time were we told whom we should replace or reinforce. We did learn that we'd be "attached to," but not a part of, an infantry division. It was not specified which division that might be, and this was a clue to the army's paranoia concerning numbers. No matter who we were or what we did, numbers must always be kept secret. If the enemy ever learned how weak our defenses usually were, disaster could quickly follow.

We also soon realized that we were one small piece in a system dating back to World War I and never changed. We were probably the most despised members of the armed forces, but our assignment had never been a matter of choice, and we did not, at this time, have any clue as to why we should be so disliked. In due time, all this would become clear. Our job was furnishing the "warm bodies" to the infantry companies as replacements for those who had died or been seriously wounded. We were in the supply business, handling the "cannon fodder" of war. The men we "processed" would go from us to the front line. We were important in the scheme of things here, because without us, no infantry unit could long be a coherent fighting force. Combat losses would soon reduce them to ineffectiveness. If we failed in any way to meet our obligations, we ourselves would join those going to the front, likely to die there. If we did well, others would die while we remained in a demeaning job meeting inhuman expectations from army or corps headquarters.

I was a little better off than most. With my highly specialized training, my specific assignment was to see that before he went to the line, every replacement had his proper weapon, that it operated correctly, that he had fired it, if and when that was possible, and that he had his combat load of ammunition. Beyond that, my duty included making field repairs to any and all weapons used by the replacements or us. If one man could not move up to the line because his rifle or carbine would not fire, this was my fault.

I'd been issued an armorer's tool kit, a forty pound reinforced box I carried with me everywhere. In it were the tools and gauges used to keep World War I weapons functioning. There was nothing else. With pieces of found scrap metal, using a file and a sharpening stone sent to me from home by my father, I shaped some of the tools I needed for our modern rifles and carbines.

Also issued to me was a booklet that described exactly what I could and could not do within the definition of "field repairs." The limitations were insane, and if I'd followed regulations, no weapon would ever have been repaired outside a base ordnance depot. I disregarded all the rules, and did what had to be done. In following this action, I realized that there could not be more than thirty or thirty-five armorers in all of Europe who had the advanced training I'd received. Those classes at Aberdeen were small, usually no more than ten men in each. The course had lasted thirteen weeks, followed by my assignment to the armory at Fort Meade, where valuable hands-on experience was gained, followed also by those two weeks at the small arms school in England. I could have gone to the ordnance company of any infantry division and known what to do. Instead, I'd been assigned to this minor, but necessary, part of the United States First Army.

Obviously, the regulations were not made for me. Once resigned to my position, I took the responsibility seriously. I worked even harder and more carefully, and before any soldier fired a weapon I'd repaired, I fired it myself, usually a full clip, or eight rounds, with the M1.

There was no way to come out a winner, though. Whether I properly repaired a replacement's M1 rifle, and sent him to the line on schedule, or I sent his rifle back to ordnance for repairs, while he missed his shipment, I'd be damned if I did and damned if I didn't.

Our first group of replacements arrived on our third day in Normandy. There were only a few—not more than fifty men. They'd spend the night with us, possibly another, while division HQ decided where they were most needed. Trucks would be sent to take them forward. Although no place on the beachhead was far from any other, we were becoming used to the idea that we were a mechanized force. Transportation was quicker and more efficient than hiking. These replacements were all young men, with one who looked as if he might have lied about his age when joining the army and was just seventeen. He was a nervous kid who kept mostly to himself and had little to say to anyone else.

They were all afraid, and we understood this. Anyone who was not afraid was a liar or an idiot. We'd been afraid, and found the only cure for it was to stay busy and not to think about the fact that young men were dying not far away. This was not an easy thing to do, but we needed to accept the reality of the situation, which was that we no longer owned our bodies or minds. They had been taken from us, to serve what was ostensibly a greater purpose. These replacements would soon face other young men they had never known, who would try to kill them simply because our two political systems were anathema to each other. The politicians owned us, and their major concerns were never far removed from self-interest. This would include the generals. They could not attain that rank without first becoming involved in politics, because all generals and admirals became what they were through congressional appointments.

In the next few days, some soldiers came in who had recovered from minor wounds and were returning to their companies. They'd already accepted the realities of their present life, and resigned themselves to the inevitable. They would continue to be wounded, healed, and returned to the front line until they became fatalities.

They talked about it sometimes. They knew there were just two ways out. One was in a body bag, the other with a million-dollar wound. This would be the loss of a hand, a foot, or an eye. They'd be sent home if that happened, given an honorable discharge and, probably, a partial disability pension. They'd be treated as heroes.

What many of these returning wounded came to realize was that the replacement system represented their best chance of getting home alive. Without replacements, the remnants of their company, or regiment or division, would be bled dry, a victim of attrition until the only survivors were those recovering in a hospital. Replacements kept their units up to strength and gave them all a chance to live. Therefore, when the workload was next to impossible, when we'd been going straight out for twenty to thirty hours, running on coffee and nicotine and too exhausted to see straight, it was the returning wounded who pitched in and got us through the next day. Squad leaders organized the new men and kept things in order. Riflemen, machinegunners, and mortarmen talked to the replacements and stopped panic attacks before they could start. Platoon sergeants helped us with food and supply. Without their help, the entire system would have fallen apart. Thirty-one men and four officers could not feed, clothe, tend to health problems, check weapons, issue ammunition, and handle the endless paperwork involved for a thousand or more replacements every few days. It was too much to expect, and it was the veteran infantrymen who saved us all.

This latest group already had their ammunition, and had fired their weapons, so my job was minimal. The night passed, and at mid-morning, we heard the report of a rifle. Someone yelled for a medic. The young kid among those first arrivals had shot himself in the foot. He was not going to the front this day. The chances were good that someone had told him this was a way out. Of course, he claimed it was an accident, while cleaning his rifle. Of course, no one believed that. With the M1, it was a near impossibility. The medic removed his shoe and sock, dressed the wound, and put him on a truck returning to the beach. He'd be sent to a hospital in England, healed, and then court-martialed. The charge would be "cowardice in the face of the enemy." The kid would spend a large part of the rest of his life breaking rocks at Leavenworth. He'd lose his citizenship, and have difficulty finding any sort of paying job if and when he was released from prison. He was out of the war, but at a price few of us were willing to pay.

We never bothered to learn his name, although it was on the orders that had come with the group. Maybe we just didn't want to know, because knowing who he was might in some way make us accessories to his crime. Our bucket of guilt was already overflowing, without bearing the responsibility for self-inflicted wounds.

We had a visit the next day from a select group of officers. They were three generals and an admiral. With them were what appeared to be four bodyguards. Maybe they thought we were going to attack them, because these were Soviet officers, Russians as far as we could tell. They also had an interpreter, and the three American officers who accompanied them had another. The Soviets were here on an official visit to what they called the "second front," something for which they'd been clamoring in past months.

Each of the four wore enough ribbons and medals to sink a fair-sized ship, or awaken a sleepy sentry with their jangling. Maybe this was the purpose, but the Soviets, from what we knew of them, seemed addicted to "fruit salad," the multiple rows of campaign ribbons on the uniforms of most officers, ours as well as theirs. Each ribbon stood for a medal, when it became available. The Soviet Union apparently kept their medal factories going around the clock, cranking out replacements for the fruit salad. Ours would wait until the war ended. Ammunition took precedence at the moment.

These representatives of our allies in the east wanted something. Our officers assigned to escort them about on the beachhead, and ordered to cooperate, offered to show them our tanks.

"Tanks?" one of them replied. "You have no tanks. You have toys—metal coffins for your young men to play with, but nothing we consider worthy of the name "tank.""

"How about the artillery?" one of our escorting officers asked. "Would you like to see that?"

With a look of disdain, one of theirs said, "Is same as with tanks. You have nothing worthy of the name. Soviet tanks and artillery are much superior."

"Our aircraft?" the American officer persisted. "We have a small fighter field near here."

"Ah!" said one of theirs. "You have excellent aircraft. But each needs a Soviet pilot to be effective. We can see them at home, those we have purchased from you."

Purchased? When did the Russkies ever purchase anything from us?

"Our infantry?" the American asked. "We could take you to the front line, show you how we hold against greater numbers."

"Greater numbers of Latvians, Czechs, and Poles, you mean. We know the kind of troops you fight here. Soviet infantry is much superior. They fight for Mother Russia."

None of our officers mentioned the fact that a division of their vaunted infantry was at this time fighting for Germany. Maybe they didn't know about that, but it was not our duty to tell them. Or maybe they did know, and would take offense if the subject were brought up.

"Then what can we show you that might be of interest?" one of ours asked.

"Logistics!" they all answered. "Where is this Red Ball we have heard about? How do you move your supplies so rapidly? How do you know what to send where? How do you keep your fighting divisions up to strength all the time? What sort of records do you keep to put together—to coordinate—everything? Can we adapt your systems to the greater distances involved in our geographical area? Nothing else is of any interest to us."

Our officer had struck a responsive chord at last, but what could anyone tell them? And how did they know about the Red Ball? We had no details, but were aware an organization already existed that would guide our supply system as soon as we broke out of this beachhead. Construction engineers and quartermasters were making thousands of signs right now. They were simple things, a round sign painted red and mounted on a post. These were going to solve supply problems? We hoped so, and the Soviets seemed sure of it.

Logistics as a whole was still something of a mystery to most of us. We were marginally aware that it was important, that the logistics of battle was a science that could make the difference between victory and defeat. We were also aware that we ourselves were a part of it—the poorest and most ignored part, perhaps—but the part that supplied manpower quickly and efficiently when it was needed. But how could we explain this?

One of our officers tried. He waved his hand at the hedgerows around the field. "They are here. The replacements come in here, are checked for proper equipment, and leave from here to go to their companies."

The Soviets looked around. One of the generals asked what, to him, must have been an obvious question. "They do not escape?"

No, general, we did not escape.

# 7

# *A Taste of Things to Come*

On the next day, we had a different kind of visitor. Jacques was a French kid, who said he was ten. He was about the size of a six-year-old American. We guessed he really was French, because that was the only language he spoke. Many of the present inhabitants of Normandy were not natives, but had been "imported" here by the Germans from other areas, such as Belgium and the Netherlands. The French of Normandy had been moved out, their homes and farms given to the new arrivals. This had been a move calculated to lessen the chance that an invading force would receive sympathy or assistance from the civilians. We guessed that Jacques came from the bombed-out remains of a nearby village, or maybe from a culvert under the road. A lot of French kids lived in those.

In the process of "softening up" Normandy for the invasion, many thousands of civilians had been killed, many homes destroyed, villages bombed into oblivion, and altogether too many kids left as orphans. Jacques was one, a survivor who may well have been the only one left in his village. He was smart, resourceful, an inveterate smoker of our cigarettes, and hungry when he first showed up. His clothes were shabby, and he wore dirty wooden shoes, as did most of the natives. He soon learned a few of our words, and with frequent interjections of "sacre bleu" (a phrase our lieutenant Markinson said was a mild sort of profanity) made his needs known.

The cooks saw that he had enough food, something that was strictly against regulations. He was given castoff uniform shirts and trousers, which he wore with the sleeves and pants legs rolled up, again something frowned upon by military authorities. Jacques chattered endlessly when he was with us, always greeted everyone with a huge smile, and left when he knew his visit had lasted long enough. He was no trouble, and we all liked him. We wondered if he might have a family member somewhere, but there was never any indication of that, or even any sign that he might have a friend his own age. He seemed to be totally alone on a world where little remained that was not damaged, and nothing of much that he had known. We worried about what might happen to him when we were gone.

To some of us, this kid was what the war was all about. We cared little about the political differences that were the underlying cause, but if we could win, Jacques and others like him might have a far better life than anything they'd so far experienced. There was really no other reason why we should be here, caught in the middle of other people's arguments. On this world where the bulk of humanity had now abandoned any excuse for its own existence, and a war in which rationality was often a tortured fugitive, we would willingly flaunt regulations to provide life and care for an innocent kid.

We developed a degree of skepticism for most of what we'd been told about the natives. They did not hate us. We did not hate them. We'd simply killed thousands of them, and they seemed to understand why we'd done that. If there were blame, they placed it squarely on the Germans for putting them here, in harm's way. Our skepticism about much that we'd been told graduated into cynicism regarding the political motives behind everything we were expected to do, and many of the orders we were expected to obey. Just as the leaders of Nazi Germany undoubtedly did, our own leaders seemed to bend the truth to suit their own purposes. We needed to learn how to recognize that when it was done. Not that it made any difference in our daily lives, but it could affect the way we responded to being here, or any place where we had no wish to be. Our presence in a foreign and frequently hostile land needed to be supported by a mental attitude that could endure any and all discomfort, both physical and psychological. As often as not, any attempt to sustain this attitude was marked by its deficiencies rather than any strong principles. We griped and complained a lot, and thoroughly endorsed the old saying, "never trust the army." In spite of this, we did what had to be done.

The dog showed up about the same time that Jacques did, although the kid let us know he and the dog were strangers to each other. It was a nondescript mutt who approached the cooks fearfully, his tail between his legs. He was ready to high-tail it out of there if anyone spoke crossly to him, but no one did. A few scraps of food, and he became much more trusting. Like Jacques, he showed up each day for a handout, after which he vanished. Military authorities disapproved of this, too, but we fed the mutt anyway. A temporary company mascot wasn't such a terrible thing to have.

One other animal came every day, now that the front line had stabilized a few hundred yards away. An old man brought it every morning, and tied it to a stake driven into the ground of our field, just far enough from the traveled area along the hedgerows to be out of everyone's way. It was a cow. It munched grass most of the day, and the farmer came in the afternoon to lead it home and, presumably, to milk it.

They walked slowly, for the cow had just three legs. Its right foreleg was entirely gone. It had obviously tripped a mine, most likely an S-mine. This area had been well seeded with them, and we'd been warned to use only the edges of any field, not to move out into the open. Our engineers had cleared the hedgerows and the ditches next to the hedgerows, but no more than ten feet into the fields. Many places still had signs left by the Germans that read "Achtung! Minen." It was wise to believe them.

It was also wise to treat the matter of mines with utmost caution. The S-mines, which we called "Bouncing Betties," came in several varieties. They were all nasty devices, feared more than any other weapon. The local type was a can, a little larger than a soup can. Inside was a smaller can, which held the explosive charge and the fuse. Between the two cans were 360 steel balls, or sometimes a hundred or more pieces of jagged, broken bits of steel and iron. The whole assembly was buried on a base containing a compressed spring, to a depth that left the top level with the ground. Trip wires ran out to small metal stakes ten feet or more from the mine. When a trip wire was touched, the spring in the base was released and the mine flung into the air, where it exploded. Steel balls or bits of metal sprayed out in all directions.

The range was nothing great, but the thing was specifically designed for one purpose. It exploded at just the right height to tear a man's genitals to bloody shreds. This was a psychological weapon of tremendous effectiveness. No soldier who had seen it do its work on another would willingly walk into that same field. At a different angle, it would destroy a leg, as with the cow. This would also put a soldier out of action, but with less impact on his mental well-being. We loathed and respected the Bouncing Betty.

I accepted the job of deactivating live hand grenades, when one was brought in to me. The German "potato masher" was simple. It had a wooden handle with a hole through the length of it. At the top was a metal ring, attached to a string that went down through the hole to the fuse in the grenade itself. The handle could be unscrewed and removed. The string and its attachment to the fuse came with it. Then the grenade was just a can filled with explosive. Dump the powder out, and the whole thing was harmless.

Our own fragmentation grenades (the "pineapple") were different. The fuse was an integral part of the handle assembly. The handle itself was spring-loaded to fly off when the pin had been pulled and the grenade released. This would normally happen in the air, after the grenade had been thrown. The time from this point to the explosion varied. It could be seven seconds, five, or three, or any other, but always fairly soon. No one wanted to throw a grenade and have it tossed back to him. That was strictly a Hollywood stunt.

Where the fuse and handle had been screwed into the body of the grenade, a sealant had been applied. This had to be broken, by holding the grenade in one hand and tapping the handle and fuse with a hammer. Then the handle, with pin and fuse, could be removed, the powder dumped out, and the grenade made relatively harmless. The fuse would still explode if the pin were pulled, but it would be like a large firecracker in its explosive force. This was not one of my pleasant duties, but a part of the job and necessary.

I'd never touch an S-Mine, and was not asked. They were left for the engineers, who were far more familiar with these devices, and had been properly trained in the job of deactivation. We'd run a cloth tape around the spot, fastened to a few stakes, and thereby mark it for those who would dispose of the problem. We did the same with UXBs (unexploded bombs) that we found. They were less dangerous, at least for us, because they had no trip wires.

UXBs were a problem, though, simply because there were so many of them. When we walked along any of the fields here that had been bombed (which was most of them), we couldn't help but notice that almost every third bomb had failed to explode. There would be the hole, like an oversized rabbit hole, boring down into the ground. Close by was the tail fin of the bomb. They always broke off as the bomb itself burrowed in. The presence of a tail fin was an almost positive sign that a UXB was close by. Why, we wondered, were there so many? Were the armament factories half filled with German agents, engaged in sabotage? It almost seemed that way. Or were American factory workers so incompetent, they never inspected the parts used?

Another, perhaps more realistic, suspicion was that greedy industrialists and self-serving politicians wanted it this way. Maybe they let a lot of sub-standard materiel pass, with the result that many bombs proved useless when used. Therefore more would be needed. More government cost-plus contracts would be awarded. A politician who swung the contracts in the right direction could surely expect recognition for his efforts. We all knew that many politicians became very rich on salaries that could not possibly justify such wealth.

When we considered the thousands of tons of worthless armament now buried in the soil of Normandy, trust in the support we needed on the home front faltered. Why should we die for a government that cared mostly for its own agenda of special privileges, or for manufacturers who refused to look beyond their immediate and obscene profits? Granted, not all of those people were "on the take," but too many were, and it seemed the more honest among them were powerless to correct the situation.

Military decisions made here in Europe could be equally upsetting or unnerving. We weren't professional soldiers. With the exception of a few regular army members, such as our First Sergeant and Supply Sergeant, we were "citizen soldiers," and even in that phrase, the word "soldiers" was stretching things a bit. We'd been drafted to do a specific job, and were here doing our best to finish it so we could go home. Beyond that, nothing really mattered much.

The professional soldiers, the higher grade officers and our leaders in all that we did, seemed to see things differently. Even if we were citizens, serving in an emergency and doing what we'd never think of doing otherwise, we should still act, and be treated as, soldiers. Temporary or regular army, it made no difference. At least, none was recognized, even when we learned about some of the hideous practices ordered or condoned by our commanders.

There was a field hospital on the beachhead now, and some of our lightly wounded had gone there, then returned to their companies through our unit. They talked about their experience, and the experiences of others, in the hospital. Some of it was difficult to believe, although we heard the same story from more than one source, so were forced to give it credence.

The victims of S-mines, mortars and artillery fire rarely had clean, antiseptic wounds. War was a dirty business, and so were the wounds suffered. Gangrene was common, in which the flesh in and around a wound blackened and died. Death of these tissues spread to others next to them. It was painful, with a characteristic odor that could make the unaccustomed gag and retch. Amputation had for years been the only sure method of stopping it. This was usually effective, but left the victim less than whole. It was the "million dollar wound" for many, but loss of a limb or eye could reduce life itself to a consuming despondency that questioned the value of all things.

Something new had joined the arsenal of medicine, though. It offered hope that the large piles of hands, feet, arms, and legs associated with military hospitals might be significantly smaller in the future. This was penicillin. It could stop gangrene. The problem was that there was never enough of it.

On orders from SHAEF (Supreme Headquarters, Allied Expeditionary Force) the wounded were not allowed to have penicillin. The reason was very clear, and completely rational within the context of military thinking during warfare.

Penicillin, it was quickly learned, was supremely effective against venereal diseases. If a soldier went AWOL (absent without leave) and made his way to a town or village where he could pick up a companion for the night, he was apt to learn later that he'd also picked up gonorrhea or syphilis. The Germans may have planned this in advance. The use of easily transmittable diseases as weapons was nothing new in warfare. If the infected soldier reported to an aid station, he'd be promptly treated with penicillin. In a matter of a day or two, he'd be back on the line, ready for duty. This could make a difference in the next battle.

In the case of a wounded soldier facing amputation, penicillin only created another serious casualty, alive but militarily useless. He may need intensive care for a prolonged period of time, at the end of which he'd still be of no value to his former company, regiment, or division. He would tie up medical personnel who might be needed elsewhere. He'd take bed space in a hospital in England. He would create transportation problems, and not one bit of all this would ever be of any benefit to the army. Therefore, it was far more practical to use the limited supply of penicillin on the unthinking clod who had picked up a dose, and get him back on the line where he'd pick up a weapon instead of VD. He'd then make a contribution during the next bit of action.

So reasoned our High Command, our Supreme Headquarters.

The wounded soldier with gangrene would live or die by the skills of the surgeon who amputated the affected limb or limbs. Morphine, always plentiful, was allowed for the pain. This, at least, was what we heard from several returning wounded. We could find no reason to doubt them. They'd been there. They had seen what we had not. It was a demonstration of the extent to which an army in the field would go to ensure maximum "efficiency" in the use of combat troops. When an individual was no longer useful on the front line, he was no longer of any real concern to military commanders, regardless of what they might say to the media.

Somewhere back in time, a situation was responsible for another "military necessity." Every soldier in Europe carried a gas mask. We hoped they would never be needed, but feared that they might.

The Germans had initiated the use of gas in World War I. It was a desperate and stupid move, because gas is carried to its destination mainly by the wind. Prevailing winds in continental Europe are from west to east. The Krauts could send gas by artillery shells, and they did, but it would soon blow right back at them. Of course, they would know in advance when a gas attack was scheduled, and have time to prepare. To the Allies, it was too often a surprise.

If this kind of warfare ever started in our time, we were prepared to return three times as much gas as we received, and keep it up as long as it would take to convince the Krauts it was a bad idea.

We had thousands of cylinders of several types of gas in a field not far away. The cylinders looked like those used by welders to hold acetylene gas. The contents were very different, of course. Some held mustard gas, much used in that older war. Some were phosgene, which acted in a similar manner. We had nerve gases that would leave a man twitching and thrashing on the ground as he died. We were ready. Yet, we were unprepared for the reality when it seemed to arrive.

We'd complained bitterly about the new masks recently issued. It was called the M3 Lightweight. The old masks had been held in a canvas bag that hung on our left side, by a strap going around the neck. To access the mask, we ripped open snap fasteners on a flap, pulled the mask free, and slipped its straps over our head. We temporarily put our helmet on the ground or held it between our knees. The canister remained in the bag, connected to the face piece by a tube.

This was too easy, apparently. The whole thing was redesigned. Instead of at the side, the new masks, in their canvas bag, were carried on the back, attached to the backpack, something rarely worn except when moving. The new bag was difficult to reach and hard to open. The mask was slow to put on, and the whole thing bounced against the back of our heads with nearly every step. As a final insult to common sense, it was heavier than the old unit. Apparently, this was why the army designated it as a "lightweight." Most troops threw theirs away the first time they walked any distance with it.

We didn't do that, nor did we allow replacements to do it. Therefore, we were more or less prepared when, on a calm summer evening, the cry of "GAS!" passed from sentry to sentry across the beachhead. There was little panic. We donned our masks after a brief struggle, checked our weapons, and waited.

One of the replacements was in serious trouble, though. We'd all been warned to never keep food in the mask/canister bag. Especially dangerous was storing fruit there. Moisture in an apple or orange would be absorbed by the crystals in the filter canister, rendering it useless. No air could get through to the mask.

In every group, there seemed to be one who ignored orders and the best advice from those who knew what could happen. We had one such, a young man of such superior knowledge (he thought) he had no need to listen to anything others told him. He was suffocating now, thrashing about on the ground, unable to breathe and dying, yet refused to remove his gas mask. Three men finally held him down while another pulled the mask from his face. He never thanked them, but sat glowering as he munched on an apple retrieved from the gas mask and canister bag.

This incident was a valuable lesson for all of us. It proved that the army and its instructors could be right about some things. It also proved that we had some level heads among our officers. No gas counter-attack was ordered. Instead, an investigation was immediately undertaken to learn the source of the gas. This proved to be our own supply of cylinders in that field not far away. One of them had leaked. The valve was tightened, and the gas alarm became history. It had been mustard gas, easily identified, and not enough had leaked to cause permanent harm.

Each passing day seemed to bring more duties. In one sense, this was a welcome departure from the kind of military routine with which we were familiar. Throughout training, it was nearly always "Hurry up, so you can wait." Here, it was hurry up without the waiting. Things happened, often in rapid succession. Replacements continued to arrive from the beach. Division continued to have casualties and need replacements. We had no time to think about any of it, and barely time to do all that was needed.

"Bedcheck Charlie" became a fixture overhead every evening. This was a small, light reconnaissance plane. We and the Germans both used such craft for artillery spotting. All U.S.

planes were grounded a half-hour before sundown each day. After that, the sky belonged to the AA (anti-aircraft) guns and Charlie. We could time our watches by his appearance, just ten minutes after our planes were down on the ground. He'd fly low over the heavy guns, such as the 90 millimeters. By the time the gunners could traverse their pieces to aim at him, he was gone. Then he'd climb for all he was worth over the lighter stuff, like our own machinegun. Everyone shot at Charlie, but no one ever hit him. He became familiar, a joke in the almost-night sky. We grew careless about staying under cover when he was overhead. We were even more careless about leaving telltale worn areas on the grass in our field, when we went to the mess area for our meals, or when we went to the straddle trench to relieve ourselves.

Yet, it was not our carelessness that resulted in our first encounter with the Luftwaffe (German Air Force). It was early, and our fighters should have been up there, but they weren't. Three ME109 fighter planes came swooping down over the beach, strafing everything in sight. Rather than let the German planes get away, our AA crews started firing, although it was still early enough to have our own planes aloft.

They shot down one plane over the beach. They hit another almost directly over us. It left a perfect smoke ring in the sky, which hung there for over an hour. The pilot bailed out, and his parachute opened.

Using a machinegun has a strange effect on some men. It gives a sense of god-like power. They're sending a hammering stream of death, in the form of hundreds of bullets, at another human being who had intended to do great harm to the gunner and his associates. It's payback time, for everything the targeted person did or might have done to our side. The machinegun recognizes no moral code, nor does it offer any obstacle to destructiveness barely within the control of the gunner.

That is, unless the gunner and his mate were our own company's gun crew. Sergeant Jinks and sergeant Weldon were assigned that duty. They had set up the MG in a large bomb crater at one end of our field, positioned sandbags around it, then stayed as far away from the thing as they could. They convinced themselves, if few others, that any use of the gun would surely bring retribution from the Krauts, in the form of a tank roaring up to their position and blowing them into very small pieces with its cannon.

It was lieutenant Markinson, our gunnery officer, who eventually rousted our reluctant warriors from the deepest and most secure foxhole on the beachhead.

"Get out there and fire that gun!" he shouted. "If you don't do it now, the rust in the barrel will be too thick to clean out. Shoot at anything. Shoot at flak bursts. There are enough of them up there to give you some practice. Now move!"

Move they did, and cleaned out the rust with a couple of bursts aimed at not much of anything. Later, I cleaned the barrel and oiled the gun until it was in prime condition. Jinks and Weldon were never dedicated to wanton destructiveness, and in this instance, it turned out that their efforts were not needed.

The pilot of that second ME109 fighter plane was probably a seventeen-year-old kid, out on his first combat assignment. While Jinks and Weldon fired at cloud formations on the horizon, we watched the tracers from four or five other guns alter their trajectory from the plummeting plane to the pilot dangling beneath his chute. He must have been practically cut in half when he landed.

Gunners farther inland targeted the third plane of the group, and disposed of it. No pilot jumped from that cockpit.

The next day, a supply truck brought us a very large, square carton, about four feet on a side. Sergeant Parsons asked me to open it. The contents of that carton were some sort of miracle, an answer to our most urgent need in our dirt foxholes in the litter-filled ditch beside the hedgerow. Our water ration was two quarts a day, for all purposes. Naturally, the mad major of Southampton, the "mud major," would assume that we'd use all of our available water with these wonderful string mops he'd apparently had shipped to us from a supply depot in England. He was determined, at least.

# 8

# *Variations on a (Military) Theme*

The attitude displayed by Jinks and Weldon was not typical. If every soldier had looked at his duties as they did, it was doubtful we'd have been able to conduct a proper war at all. Still, they were fun people to have around.

Jinks was an older man of twenty-seven or eight, and had been regular army before the war. He was a little shorter than average, and lightly built, ideal for the horse cavalry, in which he'd served. He was now serving out the sentence of a court-martial, doing penance for an infraction he never discussed, but which cost him all of his pay every month. We suspected it had something to do with alcohol and horses. Maybe he'd given, or sold, some army horses to the Indians. Jinks survived by a quick wit and inventive bargaining, and had earned his sergeant's stripes by his ability to manage groups of newly arrived replacements with a combination of humor and firmness. He could see in an instant what motivated most people he met, and adjust his treatment of them accordingly. This worked well with enlisted men, but not with officers, and the nonchalance with which he often treated the upper ranks earned him some enemies. Not everyone laughed at his antics.

Sammie Weldon was a first cook. Twenty-four years old, he'd been offered the job of mess sergeant when the company was first formed. He tried it in Ireland, and begged to be relieved. He didn't feel he was cut out for the endless detail work that went with such authority. Instead, he accepted responsibility for one of the shifts, and worked with them during their normal schedule of twenty-four hours on duty, then twenty-four hours off.

65

He had few responsibilities beyond the kitchen, and during his off-duty hours found ways to make life interesting, if not always perfectly legal. Sam was a good-looking and affable man, usually possessing a large portion of common sense, except when he paired up with Jinks.

Some might consider the two of them together as a prescription for disaster. We didn't, because they could be funny, and humor was a precious commodity, altogether too rare in any combat zone. We were also quite sure that when push came to shove, and lives were on the line, they could be depended upon to hold up their end of things.

They shared a foxhole, something more like a bear's den. It was dug into the ditch along the hedgerow and then covered with logs, a large piece of sheet metal, and a foot of earth. The entrance was down some earthen steps to a blanket hung as a door. Visitors passed through that to a second blanket, beside which was a small electrical switch. This turned on battery-powered lights inside. There, shelves cut into the earth walls held cigarettes, soap, candy, and usually a bottle of calvados, the local intoxicant. All who entered were offered a drink and a smoke by these gracious hosts.

If our gun crew were not fanatics about firing tracers and incendiaries and armor-piercing bullets into the air, the gunner in the next company made up for that. Horace Mortis (we called him "rigger") wore a well-waxed handlebar moustache, and deemed himself the epitome of all that was desirable in a man. He was as gung-ho as anyone could be, and manned his gun when even a rumor of enemy aircraft floated through the air. He fired at flak bursts. He fired at cloud formations. He fired at the sound of distant thunder. He followed enemy planes right down to the ground with tracers marking the stream of his accurately aimed machinegun fire.

Unfortunately, he wasn't always accurate enough. One day, the top of our colonel's large pyramidal tent, three fields away, was decorated with several .50 caliber bullet holes. The colonel, upset about the fact that rain could now drip through a previously perfect shelter, made inquiries. We kept quiet, knowing it could not have been our gun or crew that was responsible. We neither accused nor defended Horace. He'd have to stand on his own, and somehow he managed to convince the colonel that the source of the stray bullets could have been almost anywhere in Normandy. Lots and lots of anti-aircraft fire filled the sky any time the Luftwaffe dared to approach.

Horace ran out of ammunition in three days. That was 3,445 rounds of .50 caliber in thirteen canisters. He came over to visit me, after our gun crew had refused to discuss the matter with him. We had twelve canisters plus 245 rounds still left. Lieutenant Markinson was nominally in charge, because he was the gunnery officer. He was present, and I looked at him, questioning what might be proper.

"How much can we spare?" he asked me.

I shrugged. "At the rate Jinks and Weldon are using it, we could get by on a handful of cartridges for the next year or two."

"Use your own judgment," the lieutenant told me.

"Okay," I said to Horace, "bring me three empty canisters, and I'll give you three full ones. In the meantime, see if you can requisition more on your own."

"Good," said Horace. "I'll be back with a coupla guys to help, and I'll try to be more selective in my targets for a while. Did you see those three ME109s I shot down? Got every one of them. Two others showed up the next day, too far away for you to see from here, but I got them, too. That there Kraut Air Force ain't goin' to fool around this neck of the woods much more, I can tell you. See you later. Thanks for the three canisters."

He returned shortly with help and three empty canisters. They picked up the full ones and headed back.

Lieutenant Markinson watched. "Going to be just a bit easier loading and unloading now," he remarked.

I nodded. "Those full canisters are heavy suckers, that's for sure."

While the colonel worried about bullet holes in his tent, we had our own concerns about stuff falling from the sky. What went up must come down, and when our own 90-millimeter AA guns were firing, there was a lot of it. At the first flak burst above us, we adopted a well-practiced drill. We donned our helmets, stood, and looked at the ground. This made us the smallest possible target for the rain of jagged shrapnel that filled the air. It punched holes in the tent, it tore leaves and small branches from the trees, and it could easily have done bodily harm if we'd not taken these precautions. Jinks and Sam escaped by going underground to their den. Often, two or three or four others would decide it was a good time to visit them. If the AA firing were prolonged, calvados might be consumed. The next best thing was staying close to the trunk of a large tree, again standing, with helmet on, and staring at the ground to protect the eyes, because even a tiny bit of hot shrapnel could do irreparable damage there.

We needed humor, and jokes were a part of everyday life. Even some of our officers participated. Lieutenant Cicciloni came into the supply tent one day. "On all future requisitions," he said, "make five copies. Send one to headquarters, keep one, and send the other three to the officers' latrine. We're out of toilet paper again."

It was a fair joke, and like most, it had a serious underside to it. We were frequently out of toilet paper. Leaves of trees worked reasonably well, as did a handful of grass, but the absence of paper was not always realized until it was time to use it. Squatting over a straddle trench, ready to leave, was not the ideal circumstance in which to learn of such a shortage.

My personal solution served well for the rest of the war. When paper was available, I pulled off about ten feet, folded it, and put it inside my helmet liner, where it would always be dry. This was my emergency cache. Sometimes, I'd share a little with a friend in obvious distress. Some guys carried tree leaves in a pocket. Without those, or easily reached grass, or paper in the helmet liner, it was a pure and simple case of doing without. It was never difficult to detect who was in that category.

Almost any joke was worth a chuckle or two, but we noticed as time went on that the quality of humor declined. Dark humor became more common. This was probably a sign of disaffection with the progress of the war and our part in it. Whatever glory might once have been thought to exist was long gone. We realized that it probably had never been there in the first place, beyond the vivid imaginations of a few journalists thousands of miles away. More often than not, their stories were the product of their own fantasies, based on distorted reports from a distant relative or former acquaintance. The reality was that war was always gritty, always filthy, always depraved, and filled with enough inconsistencies to provide material for jokes that became more and more gross. Still, we laughed at them. What else could we do?

There was another kind of humor that might have worked well enough in other circumstances, but was totally unappreciated here. This was the "practical joke," that relied on the discomfort, embarrassment, or humiliation of others. It could be outright dangerous in the here and now, as was demonstrated one day by a pair of replacement lieutenants just up from the beach.

Richard and Robert were identical twins, something unusual in itself. The military always tried to separate close family members, afraid they would be caught in circumstances that might kill them both. That would make for "bad press," a concern of all the world's leaders. It was Hitler who had remarked that this war must be won with the best propaganda that could be devised, and might be lost by too much bad news.

These twins were young, tall, blond, and handsome. They gave the impression that they were accustomed to wealth and privilege. This may have been true, for it would have taken great political influence to persuade the military to allow them to remain together through training and eventual assignment. Political influence is usually bought with large sums of money. Richard and Robert apparently felt that the world owed them far more than anything the "common" people were entitled to receive. They made this evident in their behavior. No one else really mattered, and they had no compassion for those on whom their actions placed added burdens.

One night, I was assigned to "charge of quarters" duty. We all had a turn at this. It consisted of staying in the headquarters tent for half the night, to answer the field telephone, provide information for any who needed it and had the right to it, and to be generally useful. One enlisted man and one officer, not necessarily known to each other, served together. At 2:00 or 3:00 in the morning, another pair would take over for the rest of the night. Lieutenant Johnson, a replacement, served with me on this night.

After 2:00, I was to awaken those who would relieve us. My own relief was no problem. He knew he'd have this duty, and had slept lightly, ready to move when I mentioned his name. Lieutenant Johnson's relief was Richard, one of the twins. I woke him on time, but he told me he was Robert, not Richard. I should wake the other twin. He said the same thing, that he was Robert, not Richard. There was no way I could tell them apart, so returned to the HQ tent and informed Lieutenant Johnson.

He swore a little, but understood. "The bastards are doing it again," he said. "Forget it, Corporal. Neither of us will be able to make them own up to doing anything wrong. It's an old story with those two. They've ducked out of more duty assignments than a lot of us have ever had, and they always laugh about it."

My relief came, and I waited an extra half hour, hoping one of the twins would awaken with a troubled conscience. That didn't happen. I was told later that Johnson stayed the night, and at 6:00 gathered his gear to move out. He went to the line lacking even ten minutes of sleep for the night. The twins thought it was a great joke.

Late the next day a medic, returning from the beach, stopped and gave one of our guys an account of what had happened. He'd taken Robert to an LST headed for England. The twin was picked up from the ground just behind our line. He'd been sitting, his knees drawn up to his chin with his arms wrapped around them. He would not speak, just moaned and rocked back and forth. He was an obvious section eight case (section eight was the psychiatric ward in military hospitals) and needed treatment. The medic had asked about the reason, and learned from a fellow medic that it was simple enough. Richard, his twin, had been killed in his first few hours on the line. No longer would either of them be able to use the other as an instrument to confuse fellow soldiers. Their practical joke days were over.

As far as most of us were concerned, the twins' lack of consideration for others had tapped our faucet of sympathy dry. Making a joke of a front line duty assignment was their final act of willful negligence. The enemy had not seen the humor in it.

This enemy, we soon discovered, was not always what we'd expected. Those Russian generals had mentioned Poles, Czechs, Latvians, etc. in their belittlement of our infantry. We now knew how accurate that had been. But of all the nationalities arrayed against us here in Normandy, Russians themselves composed the greatest numbers.

Some of our guys would, when time permitted, explore the surrounding area. They found all manner of military hardware and lots of ammunition. They usually brought the latter to me.

Some of it was at first puzzling. The rifle and machinegun ammunition was not ours, not British, and certainly not German. Close examination disclosed Cyrillic characters on the base of the cartridges. They were Russian, made for Soviet weapons. Why, I wondered, were they here? Were the Germans so desperate they were using captured weapons and ammo from their eastern front? This hardly seemed likely, yet I held the evidence in my hand.

The answer, soon known, was a lot more direct than that. In our sector of the front, our troops faced an entire division of Russian infantry. Stories gathered from a few prisoners, and passed on to us through the grapevine, explained why this was so. The German army, when it first entered Russia, was greeted as liberators from the yoke of communism. The people fed them, quartered them, and made them welcome. Some Soviet units, including a few complete divisions, changed sides to help the Germans. With their weapons and supplies, they were sent to other areas, including Normandy, where the Germans were certain an attack would eventually come. So were battalions and companies of Czechs, Poles, Hungarians, and others. The German army was far from being all German. It was an international force, with many volunteers. This put a whole new twist on the way we looked at our involvement here. We, the Canadians, and the Brits were at war with a mixed group of continental Europeans. It made no difference in the way we followed orders or did our duty, but did make us wonder how and why we'd become involved in one more mixed-up European war. The issues involved were never as clear and sharp as we wished they could be.

A little later, we learned that Hitler had personally taken command of all German armed forces. This led to the kind of ill considered orders that alienated most troops from Eastern Europe.

If they had not already, German officers replaced all others in positions of command. Members of the Gestapo joined each unit, with orders to kill any who tried to surrender to the Allies. The result was more surrenders than ever.

We gained from such blunders, but it was a short-lived triumph, for our own leaders were quite capable of just as many poorly thought-out orders and reports. For example, the news media, such as it was, had assured us that the Luftwaffe was no longer a threat, and that it had all but vanished into history. That announcement was, at best, premature. We'd already had that experience with the three fighter planes strafing the beach, and were familiar with Bedcheck Charlie and his seemingly harmless excursions over our heads each evening.

One time, it was not Bedcheck Charlie who flew over. It was a flight of medium bombers, from the air force that didn't exist. They came in low, right over us, and dropped flares. These floated to earth under small parachutes and, for a short time, made the sky and ground brighter than daylight. We knew well enough what to do, which was to stand perfectly still and look down. Upturned human faces, without camouflage paint on them, can be easily spotted from a low-flying plane. Motion can be detected, too. So it was heads down and don't move. When the planes had passed, we ran for our foxholes, dove in, and loaded our weapons.

The bombers circled and, while the flares still burned, made their bomb run. We waited, holding our collective breaths, and listened as bombs exploded two fields away. Another company was the target. A convoy of trucks had come up from the beach, late in the day. The drivers had not taken the time to drive the vehicles under trees or use camouflage netting. We guessed Charlie had seen them, radioed the nearest bomber base, and this was the result.

The new arrivals were quartermaster truck drivers, with their trucks. If we were to break out of this beachhead, a necessity was a good, fast-moving supply system. These men and their trucks were a part of that, probably a part of the Red Ball Express, not yet operational but rumored to be close to that status. The men were all black, not uncommon in a quartermaster company.

They'd not had an easy day, or an easy channel crossing, and were tired, hungry, and out of sorts.

A sergeant met them and told them to immediately dig in along the hedgerow. They'd refused, said they could do nothing until they'd first eaten. They milled around at one end of the field while the sergeant checked with the cooks. They were there, moving around, complaining, and exposed, when the bombers came over.

They were hit hard. One bomb landed in the reserve ammo pit, dug by my counterpart in that other company. For the next two hours, small arms ammo exploded, .50 caliber tracers scored the night sky, with rockets and grenades adding a bass section to this orchestra from hell. The earth shook and men screamed.

The truck drivers were caught in the middle of it all. Around the perimeter of the field, everyone else was well dug in, and casualties were light. The drivers had no place to go.

The worst of it was that we could do nothing in the dark of the night to make things any easier. We were helpless while we listened to what was happening in that other field.

Someone yelled for a medic. They were already on the way, running down the road past us. We had a doctor, a trained medic, and two litter bearers. That was our total aid station personnel. They reached the field where casualties screamed, cried, and called on Jesus, God, or their mother at home to help them.

I stayed in my ditch and thought about that. We'd been here just long enough to lose any illusions we'd had about right, wrong, or justice in this war, or any war. The cries continued, and many were pitiful.

"Jesus, sweet Jesus! Save me. Save me, Lord. Please stop this, and I'll always ever after do only what's right."

"Medic? Medic, over here. Medic, I can't feel my arms any more. Medic!"

"Oh God, oh God, oh God."

"Mother? Mama, take care of me. Mama?"

It went on like that.

God? I thought. What God? Those guys didn't know yet that on the belt buckle of every German uniform were the words

"Gott mit uns." (God with us.) The Krauts believed that. The kids flying those bombers believed it. They believed they were fighting a war against American atheists and their allies. They were bringing the blessings of God to a people in need. We were doing the same, of course. God must have been doubly pleased, for each side was asking his blessings on every attempt to kill, dismember, and bloody the other.

A million miles and an eternity away, I'd listened in church to the admonitions of our minister. He'd slapped the lectern and pounded on the bible as he shouted, "Remember this, people. Remember it well. In the foxholes, there are no atheists." The same words were repeated in churches across the country. What a gang of pompous asses! They displayed the heights to which arrogance can reach. How could those people know, from three to six thousand miles in the rear, who was in the foxholes and what we thought? How could they, in their stupendous ignorance, make such a judgment call?

So who, I wondered, did have a direct line to God, and what kind of a God was He? Was it the same God who had watched with total impartiality as various religious or political groups aroused hatred in their followers and brought butchery and genocide to others? History was filled with obscene horrors, perpetrated by people who placed themselves above all others in the eyes of their God. Much of that had happened right here, in this corner of France. The soil of Normandy was rich with the blood of those who had fought and died here, and for what purpose? What had ever been gained but fear, terror, suffering, and death?

I grabbed a handful of dirt from the ditch bottom next to me. Was this what we fight for, this dust so rich with ancient blood? Or was it merely a receptacle for something that was once human? We do return to the dust at the end—the dust already burdened with its full share of shattered human dreams and lost moral values. It was a blend far too rich to be considered mere dirt. If there were a God, a deity impartial and just, this must be it. We might as well pray to common dirt as to something unknown, uncaring, and a trillion miles away. The explosions continued, and I wished for a bit more of this holy dirt between my ammo and me.

Eventually quiet came, and then the dawn. It was time to count the dead. There were thirty-five of them, not a massive number but enough to bring tears and sorrow to a couple of hundred family members and close friends. Our company truck driver told me one of the dead was my counterpart in that other company, their armorer.

As we all did who had this job, he'd dug his foxhole next to the ammo. He'd dug it deep, with straight walls and room at the bottom to stretch out and sleep. It had not been the explosions that had killed him, although that close to them, he'd almost certainly have been deafened. He'd died because, as with the shrapnel from the AA guns, what went up also came down. The .50 caliber ammo, like ours, was loaded 2-2-1, armor piercing, incendiary, and tracer. In about as freak an accident as could be imagined, one of the incendiary bullets had gone straight up, turned around, and come almost straight down. When the medic found him, his head was in a pool of blood and there was a .50 caliber hole burned completely through his neck.

Of the truck drivers who survived, most were injured, some seriously enough to be sent home. The war was over for them. When there was time to think about the incident and reflect on it, some conclusions could be drawn, and something learned.

Perhaps most important was that regardless of how meaningless they might seem, and no matter how disagreeable on a personal level, orders had to be followed without hesitation, especially in a combat zone. Slack off or dispute the point, and death could soon follow. First Sergeant Grollin had told me that back in Ireland, when he'd practiced the Queen Anne Salute. These black soldiers had not been well trained in instant obedience to a command, and this had killed them. Possibly no one expected them to be selected by the enemy as a target. That didn't matter. The possibility was there, and that should have been enough.

Their families at home would care little about the odds, and it wasn't unreasonable to expect some of them to look for someone, or something, to blame, in addition to the enemy. No one should fault them for that. The fact that they were black was not a consideration. There was no color line in death, and particularly in death that should have been avoided.

The medics had gone past exhaustion to a state of numbed shock. They were one doctor and one trained medic with over seventy casualties, all needing attention at once. They'd done what was humanly possible. They had saved some lives. They'd worked through the night without a triage nurse, and with the only light that of exploding ammunition. They surely felt frustrated, with a sense of partial failure, when it was over. They shouldn't have. No one could have done more. If there was a single lesson in it for all of us, it was that when this war was at last finished, each of us needed to be able to say the same—that no one could have done any more. Belief or disbelief in a deity made no difference. Faith or lack of it didn't matter. Nothing mattered except the will to do our best at all times and under all circumstances.

# 9

# *Buildup and Deceptions*

Maybe to help compensate for a very bad night, we were surprised the next morning by something every soldier serving away from his native land cherishes. We had our first "mail call" in some time. We gathered at one edge of the field and the mail clerk read off the names on the envelopes. There were a half dozen for me, including two from Kay, still in Ireland.

She'd had an opportunity to connect with her sister Maureen, also in Ulster and also serving in the ATS. Strangely, there was nothing in the letter to indicate whether it had been a happy meeting or otherwise. Kay did say that her company would soon move to England. As a military staging area, Ireland had apparently served its purpose and would now be allowed to revert to its former status as a land of intense beauty and seething religious hatreds.

Kay's other letter was more about us, and about the hopes we harbored for a life neither of us could fully imagine at this time. At least, we would be a few miles closer together geographically, although how much good that would do either of us was debatable. She closed the letter with a short love poem. Whether this was original or from a book, I had no way of knowing. It was sweetly sentimental, and I loved it, as I loved her.

It took a couple of days to settle back into our routine after the bombing. During that time, some of us found it impossible to avoid thinking about, and occasionally discussing, our attitude toward black soldiers. We were a segregated army, but contact with them was obviously going to be frequent. They'd drive the trucks that brought us our supplies. In many cases, they'd load and unload those supplies. They'd probably do innumerable menial jobs that were necessary to keep an army functioning in the field. There were even rumors that selected black troops might be formed into combat units. Why not? They were as involved in this war as any of us.

My personal feelings ran the gamut from approval of the status quo to an honest wish to be part of an integrated army. We all base our judgment calls on personal experience, and I'd seen both positive and negative sides to this issue. I had not, however, had as much contact with blacks as the majority of others in our company.

In my hometown there had been a single black family. The father was a small businessman, hard working, honest, and highly respected. He and his wife had two children in my age group, but we never had a chance to meet and know them, because they went to a private school. We could not argue with that decision, but neither could we form an opinion about the desirability of having black kids as friends.

In the small arms school at Aberdeen, classes were integrated, although barracks were not, and were generally a mile or more apart. I walked a mile to classes. The two black soldiers who studied with us walked at least two miles.

George was one of those black soldiers. He was bright, grasped the material quickly, and was both friendly and easy to talk with. He was treated like dirt by some of the base cadre, and I witnessed this.

As we neared the completion of our course of studies in small arms, two base personnel soldiers called us outside, one at a time. First was the student with the best grades. I was second. They asked if I'd like a permanent appointment at Aberdeen. This was no small thing, because such duty would mean there was little chance of being shipped overseas. Staying at Aberdeen was probably the best insurance against being shot or otherwise subjected to the harsher realities of the war. With other plans in mind, I turned down the offer, as had the soldier ahead of me. When I opened the door to return to the classroom, George was called out. The moment they saw that he was black, they told him to go inside, and went to the next name on their list. No offer was made to George. It was blatant discrimination, and not one of us in that class liked it. Yet, we could not entirely blame the cadre who had been sent here to find a knowledgeable addition for the base staff. This was army policy. They had simply obeyed the orders of the day. So we fumed and murmured about the unfairness of it all, but were powerless to change anything.

An incident no less disturbing happened on the troopship while on my way to Europe. This was the old French luxury liner, the Louis Pasteur, a former cruise ship that carried 800 passengers on pleasure trips from LeHavre to Rio. It now had 4,000 troops on board. The Pasteur was round-bottomed, built for calmer waters than our route across the North Atlantic. This was November. The sea was rough and deadly cold.

The Pasteur rolled from one side to another, 47 degrees each way according to the instrument we could watch in the main passenger salon. My section was on "C" deck, three levels above the waterline. When our side of the ship rolled down, water pressure on the hull was great enough to burst a porthole. Seawater poured in as if from a six-inch high-pressure fire hose. The compartment had inches of water on the deck by the time the ship's engineers could weld a plate over the broken porthole and stop it.

Almost all of the troops were seasick. I'd had enough salt-water experience on my father's small cabin boat to be relatively immune, and liked to go on deck to smoke a cigarette now and then, just to get away from the horrible stink of the ship. We were not allowed to go fully outside, but could stand in an open doorway (or hatchway) and watch the huge wall of gray water rise beside the ship as she rolled down, and then feel the ship's hull shudder and rise until we pointed at an equally gray sky. Every three minutes, there was a change in the course. This was a standard anti-submarine maneuver, intended to prevent those who might fire a torpedo at us from calculating a precise interception course for their weapon.

An armed guard stood at the opening at all times. His job was to prevent anyone from going any closer to the rail or the water. He was also there to stop anyone who might strike a match or use his cigarette lighter. A candle flame, it was said, could be seen a mile away, and any light that strong could become a target for a lurking sub. There would be no survivors. As sergeant Grollin had told me, twenty-two minutes was the longest any person could live in that sub-arctic water.

This meant there was an element of danger in standing at this spot and smoking a cigarette. SOP (standard operating procedure) was to light the cigarette inside, out the line-of-sight of anyone watching from the ocean, especially anyone watching through a periscope. To actually smoke the thing, it was held inside the hand, almost inside a clenched fist, so no faintest spark could be seen. When finished, the glowing ember was squashed between the thumb and index finger of one hand, wrapped within the other hand, and the butt put in a pocket.

I was doing all that when a black soldier appeared next to me. He must have done this before, because he seemed to know the routine.

"Going to England," he said.

"Sure looks like it," I replied.

"Yeah," he said. "Gonna fuck me some white girls there. Gonna fuck me all I can catch."

I bridled internally at this statement, but did not let it show. "Maybe," I said.

"What the fuck you mean, 'maybe'? Ain't no question 'bout it. Them white cunts ain't never had nothing good as this nigger can give 'em."

"I mean maybe," I said. "Maybe you will, maybe you won't. Maybe none of us will. We could be so far out in the boondocks, we'll never see a skirt." I looked at the mountainous wall of water rising just thirty feet away, and felt the shudder running through the ship as she reached her limit and started the return roll.

"Yeah," he said. "Okay, they's a maybe in there. But they must be gonna let us into town now'n'again. Then us 'Merican Indians will whoop it up and show them girls what a good time is all about."

"American Indians?" I asked.

"Sure. That's what we tell 'em. That's what summa our guys already tole 'em. They believe it. We're genuine wild red Injuns, just a little dark around the edges."

"And you think telling them that is going to get you what you want?"

"Worked so far, with some of the guys already there. We got letters."

I squashed my butt and put it away. "That's interesting," I said, and turned to go inside.

"That all you got to say about it?" he asked. He looked at the wall of water, now receding as we rolled back. "Where you from, anyway?"

I told him.

"Hm. Things must be different there than what they is in Mississippi. I oughta go visit Massachusetts some day, though that's prob'ly another one of them 'maybes'."

I went below, and got into the line to use the head (toilet facilities on a ship). When I thought about it, as I was doing again now in Normandy, I had to compare that antagonistic character aboard the Pasteur with George at Aberdeen. If I'd said something wrong, something out of line in the view of a young black man spoiling for a fight, we could both have ended our lives in that wall of North Atlantic seawater. George, however, was someone with whom I'd have felt comfortable in almost any circumstances.

You had to think about this whole thing, and think deeply. It represented something basically wrong in our society. That much was obvious. It wasn't so much that blacks had descended from slaves who had never wanted to be brought to America. Every white person, every black or brown, every Asian or Native American, every inhabitant of this weary old world could trace his or her ancestry back to a time when his family had been slaves. It was a recognized and accepted condition at some point in every person's history. Humanity had grown and prospered by the labors of those who had never known freedom. Even all the mitigating circumstances of better conditions for some, with a longer life expectancy, improved diet and health care, were not enough. When slavery was the price of progress, both were impossible to justify. At least, that's how I saw it in this "modern" age, when millions were doing their best to kill, maim, and impoverish millions of others, all for no reason any better than their differences in political and religious beliefs. These were simply not enough. It almost seemed that anarchy and atheism might have provided something far better for our world's suffering masses.

Three of our fighter planes, P47s from the nearby field, flew over. It was always good to see them.

We could not say the same for our bombers, or our fighter-bombers. Theoretically, we were all a part of the same effort to kill Germans and destroy Germany. However, theories needed a reality check from time to time. In this case, it came down to a matter of attitude.

The Air Force had its own strange (to us) code of ethics. A group, or squadron, or whatever, could be returning from a mission in which they had successfully butchered or mutilated thousands of defenseless infants, children, women and old people, yet it was doubtful that those in the bombers felt little beyond the satisfaction of a job well done. Remorse was difficult to imagine, because from thousands of feet in the air, it was impossible to see at close hand the results of their work.

In all fairness, it had been the Germans who had first targeted civilians, their cities, towns, and homes. As has been so often the case, such an action initiates a response in kind. We bombed their people, their cities and towns, but at a higher level of proficiency. Terror begets increasing terror. The lowering of moral standards is inevitably followed by the abandonment of all pretenses to the "high ground" from which honest and critical judgments might be made.

Our Air Force losses were heavy at times. They might run into enemy fighters or anti-aircraft fire. Planes could be hit and go down. Pilots and crew, if fortunate, would bail out and float to earth under their parachutes. This was all well and good, unless they were falling into enemy territory. In that case, they could, and often did, receive fire from the ground while they dangled, helpless, under the chute.

To members of the Air Force on both sides, such actions were examples of unspeakable depravity, unlawful under the rules of civilized warfare. We had violated these conventions when our machine-gunners killed that German kid over Normandy. We'd do it again, because we saw things differently from the way the Air Force did. Reprisals were normal human behavior. A pilot who shot up our people on the beach should not have expected any degree of clemency.

This attitude was not limited to the military. We received reports of German civilians using their own form of unauthorized retribution against our flyers. If a plane went down in Germany and the pilot and crew reached the ground alive, their first hope was that they would be picked up by enemy soldiers and escorted to a special POW camp (Stalag) for Air Force personnel only. If it were necessary to travel through a town, or part of a city, to reach that destination, survival itself depended on this escort. German housewives, many of whom had lost a child, a parent, a brother or sister or close friend to American bombers, ran into the streets, screaming and waving meat cleavers or large knives. They approached the American or British pilots and examined the insignia on their uniforms. If they were fighter pilots, they were allowed to pass unharmed. Members of a bomber crew were attacked with mayhem in mind. Only the protection of German soldiers saved any of them.

There were a few thousand members of the Ninth and Thirtieth Infantry Divisions who shared the feelings of the German housewives. They'd have gladly manned the anti-aircraft guns, if they'd been permitted to target our own and the Royal Air Force planes. More than once, ground commanders threatened to do just that.

The problem was that the Air Force seemed to be engaged in a different war, and we were unsure on whose side their loyalties resided. They placed themselves miles above the troops on the ground, not just physically but in the value of their contribution to the overall war effort. The crew of a heavy bomber probably felt they were equal in effectiveness to a division of infantry. They were not. This was an illusion permitted and possibly encouraged by the generals who ran the Air Forces. Perhaps it was necessary. Their casualties were high, although never as high as the infantry divisions most used in combat. Maybe pilots and their crews needed an extra measure of hope, expressed as bravado, to believe they could survive the war.

One of the first examples of the Air Force "attitude" was on D-Day in Normandy. Beachhead commanders asked that an air strike be launched against the German coastal gun emplacements, using the heaviest bombs available. As we had seen on our first day ashore, the guns on the battleship offshore had accurately targeted these emplacements, but had been unable to put one out of action. The Air Force agreed, sent their planes, and bombed cow pastures and apple orchards three miles away. Air had its own way of doing things, and refused any orders or advice from ground commanders, even though radio contact was usually available. The cows had been unarmed, but this still counted as another "mission" for the bombers. It was left to the infantry to neutralize those big coastal guns.

The situation with Air became much more serious when the Ninth and Thirtieth attacked Cherbourg, the French city with port facilities much needed to replace the primitive ones on the beachhead. Defense of Cherbourg was fanatical, with every German soldier aware that he would die soon if he fought well against our troops, or his own officers would shoot him if he did not, or attempted to surrender.

Dragging artillery along those country roads and through the marshes approaching Cherbourg was brutal and time-consuming work. Close tactical air support was needed. When requested, Air mounted an offensive of many hundreds of planes to strafe and bomb the German defenses just ahead of the infantry assault. Even before H-Hour, when the infantry was to launch its attack, ground commanders were screaming into their radios to call off the planes. They'd bombed and strafed our own troops, inflicting heavy casualties and upsetting the timetable for the assault on Cherbourg. Air had refused to take orders from ground commanders, and expressed little regret about causing this catastrophe. "Friendly fire" and "collateral damage" were just things that happened. We should get used to it.

We did, but not in the way that Air had intended. The fighter strip close by on the beachhead was nothing but a cleared area covered with metal mesh. The plane selected to occupy this base was the P47, probably because it had superior short-field capabilities. It was an ugly craft, with a huge radial engine in its nose, but we welcomed the idea of having it available on a moment's notice.

Late one day, they were still patrolling the beachhead when a distress call came from a Brit pilot in a Spitfire. He was headed home after an engagement, but was not going to get there. His Spit had been hit, and the engine was losing oil much too rapidly to take him across the channel. He radioed his problem to all who might be listening, saw our fighter field, and headed in for a landing.

There were quad-mount Bofors guns (small automatic cannon) lining both sides of the landing strip. The gunners saw a strange plane headed for them. Hastily and sketchily trained in aircraft recognition, they knew only that it was not one of their P47s. They opened fire. What landed were parts of a Spitfire and the mangled remains of a young Brit pilot, an ace we learned later, who had shot down fifteen enemy planes in his brief career. The incident was apparently hushed up, the news media denied any knowledge of it, or at least forbidden to make it public.

A few days later, we suspected something even more unusual was about to happen. It had been announced that General McNair, a well-known figure to both our own and the German high command, was coming to Normandy to take charge of a new army group.

This didn't quite add up. Although more divisions had landed by now, we were still greatly outnumbered and hardly ready to turn over command to someone new and unfamiliar with the situation. In addition, an army group indicated the creation of at least one more army. It would be a boost to our morale, certainly, and we hoped it would worry the Germans sick. But why would McNair be its commander? Few enlisted men had ever heard of him, at least not in the way we knew Bradley and Eisenhower.

There were too many unanswered questions, but on July 23, McNair and his headquarters staff were in Normandy. They settled in near the Perriers Road, which ran from St. Lo to the shore of the Cotentin Peninsula, about twenty-five miles south of Cherbourg. Our information was sketchy at best, most of it derived from accounts in the Stars and Stripes, plus stories told by former walking wounded from the Ninth and Thirtieth divisions, returning to their units through our company.

Enlisted men were, as a rule, kept uninformed or deliberately misinformed about major troop movements or the location of important commanders. We were not stupid, though. We were aware that the Thirtieth was close by, filling out its ranks and preparing for its next offensive. We'd sent them a large number of replacements, so nothing else made sense. General McNair didn't make sense, either, but we'd eventually learn what that was all about.

All such questions were put on hold when medium bombers and fighters roared over our heads. They were often used to knock out enemy anti-aircraft in advance of the heavy bombers.

Ernie, our truck driver, came into the supply and armorer's tent. "Something's up," he said to me. "Want to take a ride a mile or so down the road to see what's happening?"

I grabbed a carbine and climbed into his truck. We could hear the heavy bombers coming.

Ernie pulled off the road into a field he knew had been cleared of mines. We sat on the roof of the truck's cab and watched. The weather was less than best, with broken clouds, some threatening rain.

He pointed straight ahead. "Over there is General McNair's headquarters," he said.

"So he's real?" I asked. "There'll be an army group soon?"

"McNair and his staff are real enough, at least," Ernie replied. He sat up straighter. "Holy shit! We're getting the hell out of here."

He jumped to the ground and opened the door of the truck. I did the same on my side.

Any further conversation was fruitless, as we clambered in. The thunder of exploding bombs and the rising plumes of smoke and dirt filled the air, all of it originating in that field ahead of us. Ernie slammed the truck in reverse and backed onto the road. We headed for "home."

I turned to look at him. "Shouldn't we..."

"What?" he asked. "Go back there? There's nothing at all that we could do, and I seriously doubt there's even one survivor. Army HQ will know about it soon enough, probably already does. They'll have someone on the way. Our best bet is to stay clear and let them do whatever they think is necessary."

I shrugged. "But what happened there? Our Air Force just bombed our own headquarters. Why?"

Ernie shook his head. "They're just repeating what they did at Cherbourg. They're showing how arrogant and stupid they can really be."

"Stupid, I doubt," I said. "They've got to be smart to become a pilot, or any other member of a plane's crew." (I had a cousin who was a Navy fighter pilot in the Pacific, and I knew he wasn't at all stupid.)

"Okay," said Ernie. "They're not really stupid. They have to be smart. And we have to be even smarter to stay alive when they're flying over our heads. But being arrogant does something for them, something they seem to need. For us, an attitude like that would likely get us killed."

Reports varied. The one that we heard the next day, from those almost as close to the scene as we had been, was that McNair and his entire staff had been killed. Some said that his son was a member of that staff, and had also died. The official news release, days later, stated that the general had died alone in his foxhole. We never really knew who had it right, but even with McNair gone, the deception surrounding the creation of a new army group, with all its phantom increases in Allied strength, was played out as long as it would serve a purpose.

Propaganda, we began to realize, was a decided part of this war on both sides. Skillfully done, it became a weapon of immense power. The Germans refined it and used it to the fullest. We followed, and gradually became more skilled in its applications. The Russians, we heard, also tried, but never with great success. Their outlook was more apt to be "Why bother? A few well-aimed bullets are much more convincing."

The next day lieutenant Markinson came to the tent to see me. It's rarely good news when an officer wishes to speak to an enlisted man, but I was comfortable with this one. As our gunnery commander, he seemed to respect my knowledge and abilities when it came to weaponry.

Weapons were not the topic of conversation this time, though. "You remember deBourbon, from our camp in Ireland?" he asked.

"Sure," I replied. "He was in my hut, had the cot next to mine. What happened to him?"

"Nothing bad. He's been given a battlefield commission and is now a lieutenant. I thought you'd like to know."

"That's great," I said. "What did he do to get that?"

"When he left us, he went to England for some special training. About two weeks before D-Day, he parachuted into Normandy one dark night, found some resistance members, and organized them into an effective unit to help prepare for the landings."

"I'm not totally surprised," I said. "There was something about him that gave him an air of authority."

"And, of course," said lieutenant Markinson, "he is French royalty. If France ever returns to a monarchy, he'll likely be the king. But even as a private in our army, he was someone the natives would listen to and respect. He spoke their language and knew their problems."

"But what, exactly, did he do?" I asked.

"He brought several resistance groups together, gave them some quick training, and proceeded to raise merry hell with German communications just before, and during, D-Day. That was his assignment, and no one could have done it any better."

This was fantastic news. Any of us who learned about it felt a sense of pride in deBourbon's accomplishments. After all, he'd been one of us for a short time. I could imagine the frustrations of German coastal defense commanders who tried to phone Berlin for instructions on lines that carried messages anywhere except where they were supposed to go.

There was also some wonder about how deBourbon would react to his new rank as a second lieutenant in the American army. He'd been a private when in Ireland, as were all of the European nobility there. Some complained about the indignity of this, but deBourbon was never one of them.

Despite all that the Germans had probably looted and stolen from him, he was still the potential king of France, with estates and wealth measured in many millions of dollars. Could becoming an American army officer really mean anything at all to him? I thought it might, because he was likely one of the few Frenchmen who realized just how insignificant his native land had become under German domination, and how vital to the rebirth of French national pride the Americans were. I'd known him, and personally considered him one of the most capable and trustworthy men I'd ever met.

# 10

## *Breaking Out and Moving Up*

The bombing of McNair's headquarters was a mistake, of course. The explanation was that all of the participating aircraft had been radioed to abort the mission and return to base. The weather was far too unpredictable. For some reason, that one group had not received the message, had thought they were over enemy-held territory, and had dropped their bombs. There was also a generally accepted story that only the lead plane in each group had a bombsight, and all the others dropped when that one did. This may have been true.

In any event, that incident was already history, and by the morning of July 25, we knew with certainty that something major was about to happen. The city of St. Lo had been bombed into oblivion by this time, but the rubble was still in German hands. It represented a gateway out of the beachhead, now closed by German artillery, tanks, and infantry.

Nearly every Allied soldier on the beachhead was aware that we could not remain in our present position much longer. At any hour of any day, the German High Command could decide to end it by simply moving fifteen first-rate infantry and panzer divisions from Calais to the beachhead. We'd be overwhelmed, our few survivors pushed into the sea. We had to get out of this confinement, into the open country beyond, where our tanks and artillery could be more effective, and our Air Force given targets far enough removed from our own lines to eliminate the errors that had plagued us so far.

Our Sherman tank, with its 75-millimeter gun, had worked well in close support of the infantry, especially since one smart ordnance sergeant had devised a "hedgerow buster" that was welded to the front of the Shermans. Made of rail steel salvaged from underwater obstacles built by the Germans, it added a pair of "horns" to the front of our tanks. These, driven into the hedgerow barrier, held the front of the tank down and let it grind right on through what had been an almost insurmountable obstacle. Without these horns, the Shermans simply rode up and up until they turned turtle and were as helpless as a June bug flipped onto its back.

Against German armor, we had not done as well. The Mark IV Panthers and Tigers were bigger, more heavily armored, and carried an 88-millimeter gun. Our 75s could do nothing to the Mark IV's armor, the Mark IV could shoot right through a Sherman. Our tank losses, along with the crews, were absurd and pathetic. It reached a point where newly arrived eighteen year olds, who had never driven a car in their life, were given twenty minutes of instruction and made tank drivers. They died almost as quickly as did the infantry replacements we sent to the line.

Yet with all their weaknesses in design, the Sherman did have some advantages, if they could find space enough to use them. They were faster than a Mark IV, and they could traverse their gun turret much more quickly. In an open field of forty acres or more, the cat and mouse game played by tanks took on a new twist. The more nimble Shermans could become the cat instead of the mouse. It might take two or three to outmaneuver a Mark IV, but working together, they could pound the enemy's treads until they dislodged one, turning that tank into a piece of stationary artillery. Fighter-bombers could then use it as target practice, something most of them desperately needed.

A final advantage our armored forces had over the Germans was in maintenance and supply. If we lost a tank, we could have a replacement on the line in twenty-four hours. If a Sherman had been damaged enough to make it inoperable, but not a total loss, a mobile ordnance crew could be on the scene with spare parts just as quickly, and have it up and running in hours. If the Germans lost a tank, it took them three months to get another. If it were damaged, there were no spare parts, beyond what might be salvaged from another tank. Their almost legendary 88 lost its accuracy after too many rounds had been fired from it, and there were no replacements. In other words, we were winning the battle of materiel, in spite of the necessity to unload most of our needs on a beach.

So we expected a major push in the St. Lo area. Maybe the Thirtieth would mount another attack. Maybe a major air assault would be used, but that was questionable, considering their miserable performance thus far.

We were therefore surprised when the first waves of fighter-bombers and medium bombers passed over. There were a lot of them. Just behind them were the heavies, and it looked to us as if every aircraft in Britain that could leave the ground was up there. From horizon to horizon, they filled the sky. The thundering drone of their engines made conversation impossible. The land itself answered with a steady, perceptible vibration. We watched in open-mouthed wonder. Never before, and never since, had such an armada of military aircraft been sent aloft. It was some time later that the numbers were made public. What we'd watched was a fleet of 1500 heavy bombers and 750 mediums and fighter-bombers, all in the air at once, all over that small beachhead at once, all going in the wrong direction at once.

There was almost no anti-aircraft, but supposedly non-existent German fighters were up, flitting through the formations like bees through a squadron of sparrows. Some fighters went down, trailing smoke. Some of the heavy bombers went down, one with all four engines burning. We looked for, but could not see, any parachutes. Maybe they were simply too high. The formations held and reduced the distance between airplanes. There was something unreal about it, a movie scene so completely impersonal and mechanical, it was difficult to imagine that humans were in any way involved. The planes, the people, we ourselves, far below them on the ground, were merely playthings for some malevolent being who found pleasure in the wanton destruction of his own toys.

Soon, the bombs became a known quantity in this theater of the absurd. Explosions on the ground contested with the drama above for primacy, until the whole show was a roaring, thundering chaos, much of it in the wrong place.

The target had been a three-mile strip, the other side of that Perriers road. Sixty thousand hundred-pound bombs were dropped.

The Thirtieth Infantry, against the road on our side, had been pulled back a mile or more, to let the bombers have some latitude in their target zone. It wasn't far enough. The Thirtieth, and parts of other Allied units, were pounded along with the enemy. When it was over, it took two days to pick up our dead. The Air Force had done it again.

While we waited for the line companies to recover and regroup, using the replacements we sent them, Bernie Vernal walked into the tent and asked if we needed some help. He was a relatively small man, probably about five six, and lightly built. It was difficult to picture him man-handling artillery ammunition, but that's what he'd done. In addition, he was too old to even be here.

"How old are you, Bernie?" I'd asked when he'd been with us briefly a little earlier.

He never minded that question. "Thirty-eight," he replied. "I'm also married and have three kids."

It was known that some draft boards, unable to meet their quotas any other way, had taken overage men. But married, and with three kids?

"Geez," I said. "What did you ever do to your draft board?"

He just smiled, more a lopsided grin, as if life itself were a joke, and he was one of the few who knew the punch line. "My wife said they just liked my mush. I really don't know why. How about it? You need help in supply? I'd really like to get away from the KP duty for a while."

He was put to work immediately. With his irrepressible good humor, Bernie was a nice guy to have around. For an old guy, he was no shirker, either. He always did his share of the work, and then some.

What was probably most ironic about his presence in Europe was that it was never really needed. The job for which he'd been so carefully trained no longer existed. He'd come overseas as a member of a 57-millimeter four-gun anti-tank battery. Like some of our other equipment, the 57 was obsolete, except as single guns trailered behind trucks for use against dug-in enemy positions. Against tanks, they were of no value whatever.

Bernie's one battle experience destroyed his pride more than anything else. "We set up the battery on this small hill, just a sort of rise in the country road," he said. "Two guns on each side. We had them positioned so they could all fire at once without putting any other gun in danger—you know, typical enfilade. The Kraut came along right when we expected him—a Mark IV Tiger. We opened fire as he hit the rise, all four guns blasting away. You know what he did?"

"Sent you scurrying for cover with his machinegun?"

"Nope. He didn't do anything—just drove that big old tank right through our battery as if we didn't exist. Our rounds just bounced off his armor. We might as well have been chucking rocks at him. We imagined we could hear him laughing at us as he passed, and it was humiliating, that's what it was. What good were we, after all that training? What good were our guns?"

"So you've been without an assignment since then?" I asked.

"Yeah, I'm a perennial casual. Bounce around from one unit to another, but never settle down anywhere. I'm too old for the infantry, what I know about artillery is now obsolete, and I have no training for anything else. Hell of a way to spend a war, isn't it?"

Bernie was still with us three days later, when lieutenant Markinson walked in. "We're moving up," he said, without pre-amble. "You'll have a truck here in two hours. Strike the tent and be able to load everything as soon as it arrives."

He looked at me. "Corporal, you're responsible for the ammo, the machinegun and mount, and any other weapons you have on hand. Get them all on that truck. Find some volunteers to help load here and unload when we get there."

"Get where, Sir?"

He laughed. "Get wherever we're going. That's all any of us needs to know. We're moving east, out of this miserable beach-head. It's a new day and a new world, Corporal. Go find your volunteers."

There was an SOP (standard operating procedure) for doing this. It was to walk up to any group of five or more, point at as many as you needed, and inform them they'd just volunteered to load, ride, and unload the ammo truck.

I didn't need to do that. Bernie offered to take care of it for me while I made whatever preparations were necessary to start the loading. Sergeant Parsons was doing the same with supply.

It was late afternoon when the truck arrived, and it had started to rain. Bernie returned with four volunteers, men he'd known who would willingly work with him. We began loading, the machinegun and mount first, supplies packed around and over it, and at the rear of the truck, a sort of bench made from ammo boxes, on which we sat. This was a two-and-a-half ton truck, a standard "Jimmy." We loaded about nine tons, then climbed aboard. With considerable groaning of the engine and with all six wheels driving, we moved out of our hedgerow-enclosed field onto the road. We had no opportunity to bid farewell to Jacques, but he'd understand. The kid was sharp, and very aware of what was happening to his little corner of the world. The French farmer would continue to care for his three-legged cow, and the dog would live or die, depending on how generous his human acquaintances were with their food. There was little sadness in our departure, with the possible exception of our lack of any goodbyes to Jacques.

Our truck found its place in the convoy, we pulled shelter halves over our heads against the rain, and I did what First Sergeant Grollin had advised me to do when this move happened. As soon as the truck began to roll, I opened a carefully hoarded bottle of calvados, mixed it with some previously prepared synthetic lemonade in a canteen, and passed it around. Slipping and sliding down a country road in pelting rain, listening for the drone of enemy aircraft overhead, in an ammo truck seriously overloaded, we talked, drank, laughed a little, and decided this trip wouldn't be so bad after all.

# 11

# *The Smell of Death and A Billion Flies*

It was still light when we rode through what had been St. Lo. This was our first close view of what modern war could do to a once beautiful and thriving small city. No building of any kind was left intact. Our truck, the next to last in a convoy of eight, lurched and bumped and swayed in low gear, shaking us and threatening to upset our load of ammo. It was not a road over which we moved, but the rubble of a city, with a swath pounded through it by tanks using bulldozer blades. It was passable, but no more. With waves of their hands and pointing fingers, the Military Police kept us moving. People had lived and worked here, but there was no sign of any life now. It was a desolate moonscape, dusty and still smoking in places.

As the senior non-com in our group, Sergeant Parsons rode in the cab with the driver. Sitting next to me on the ammo-box bench was Pete Janson, a rifleman in the First Infantry Division with more combat experience than any of us. "What happened to the people?" I asked him.

"They're here," he said. "Any Krauts who lived through the bombing and the shelling have pulled back, probably to organize a defense somewhere farther along. We'll meet them soon enough. The civilians? If they didn't leave town and get out when they had a chance, we're riding over them now. They're dead, and no one has time to stop and properly bury the dead in the middle of a situation like this."

"What about survivors?" I asked. "There must have been a few, at least."

"Damned few. If they didn't get out of the way, the tanks would have run them down and buried them in the rubble where they fell. The only thing important here is to get through this bottleneck and into open country as fast as we can, with as many tanks, guns, trucks, and as much manpower as possible. Nothing can be allowed to get in the way."

It was something to think about as we slammed and jounced across a couple of miles of trashed city. Once beyond, we picked up speed on a paved road.

Fully dark now, it was our supreme hope that our driver could keep this Jimmy on the road. He didn't, at least not all the time. At one point, we left the pavement and stopped in a field. The truck behind us followed. Someone, one of our officers we assumed, came to our truck's cab. There was a conference. Apparently this was the wrong place, because we started again and lurched our way back to the road, the other truck following.

We barreled down a hill, the driver braking and downshifting with what seemed like desperation. In the final fifty yards the brakes screeched, the rear of the truck fishtailed, and our ammo-box bench threatened to slide right through the side of the truck and take us with it. The driver had seen the bridge before we could, and tried to slow. It was an old iron structure by the looks, spanning a deep ravine, probably with a river at the bottom, but it was too dark to see. We got across, the other truck following, while we kept our heads down and watched metal girders and braces fly past, just inches over the high point of our load. After twenty more miles or so, we pulled off the road into a field with its typical hedgerow and an odor we could not yet identify. Working in the dark, gagging with the stink and holding a handkerchief to our noses, we managed to unload and settle down for the couple of hours remaining until daylight. The trucks left.

With the dawn came a silence so eerily all-pervasive, we had to wonder if we'd wandered into some supernatural landscape that, in its millions of years of existence, had never known a warm-blooded creature. We talked in near-whispers, not daring to offend whatever gods or demons still lived here. The early mists of morning vanished, and the flies came. There were immense swarms of them rising into the heat and humidity of another day in Normandy. They were everywhere, and they were sticky, clinging to our faces and hands, climbing into our ears and up our noses, clustering around our eyes, and forever doing their best to get inside our mouths. We accumulated beards of living flies. I recalled seeing pictures of this in old National Geographic magazines, but that was in Africa. That was where there were always dead animals, or parts of animals, lying around. We realized this was the case here, too, and the odor was the sick-sweet stench of dead and decaying flesh.

It was a place without a name, as far as we could learn, but still Normandy. This was eastern Normandy, though, where the fields were larger, the hedgerows smaller, and the land more varied with small hills and valleys. Yet, it was still dairy and orchard country. This accounted for some of what we could smell. Dead cows, dead sheep, dead chickens, and an occasional dead farm dog or cat lay all around us. As far as human remains, the major pieces had been picked up before we arrived. What bits remained were infested with maggots.

It was nearly August now, the ideal season for flies. There was no use trying to escape them, or the odor. We ignored our living beards, brushed the flies away from our eyes frequently, and tolerated the sickening smell of massive death. Eating was a problem without swallowing dozens of flies with every bite. My trick was to exist on the hard, dry "dog biscuits" from our K rations. Practice made me an expert in forcing a biscuit (they were about an inch wide and three inches long) between tightly clenched lips that would strip off most of the clinging flies. Liquids were from the canteen only, with the mouth and lips tightly locked around its neck. With all these precautions, we still spit out or swallowed flies every hour of every day.

Our officers took several men to nearby farms and borrowed shovels and axes, or simply appropriated them if there was no one around. The men worked in teams, and dug a hole beside each animal, large enough to bury it, then used the axes to chop holes in the carcass and release the accumulating gases of decomposition. Cows usually lay on their backs, legs straight up in the air, their abdomens swelling almost by the hour, until it seemed they'd soon reach the size of a barrage balloon. A few blows with an axe and the fetid gases poured out as the carcass deflated, until it would fit into the burial hole. When it was available, gasoline was then poured over the animal and set afire. Burial followed cremation.

Each disposal of a dead animal deprived the flies of one more place in which to lay their eggs, where maggots would thrive and fatten. Maggots became flies. Flies laid eggs, eggs became maggots, and so on. On some of the bodies, the maggots were a thick white blanket, alive and endlessly writhing.

I walked around when I had a chance, to observe this cycle of death, decay, and the birth of billions of flies. Other than the carcasses that were chopped, burned, and buried, there were endless body parts, most impossible to identify. Pieces of blackening meat and bleaching bone, they, too, bred flies, and the worst part of it was that some of those sticky insects doing their best to crawl into our every body opening had fattened and metamorphosed on the remains of some kid's leg, arm, internal organs, or splattered brains.

I wondered why and how such slaughter had happened in this place. The large trees at the edge of the fields gave a partial answer. Most of the upper branches were shattered or gone, large limbs and smaller ones in a chaotic tangle reaching for the ground. Apparently, artillery of both sides had used "tree bursts." Death had rained from the treetops, showers of shrapnel impossible to evade.

In the open fields were countless round burnt marks, streaks of blackened grass radiating outward from each. These were the signatures of mortars. A mortar round looked like a small bomb. It had tail fins and a bomb-like body that held the explosive. It was the deadliest of all combat weapons, accounting for over half of the military casualties in this war.

As soon as we had a straddle trench ready to use, the flies invaded this, too. With a large group of men in the field, straddle trenches were the most common method used to dispose of human waste. We'd lower our pants and place a foot on each side of the trench, which was no wider than a shovel. If available, toilet paper was on a stick within reach. If not, we did without. An army in the field stinks after a few days.

The flies seemed to gleefully accept our straddle trench as another home and breeding ground. We spent as little time as possible using the facility, and before pulling our trousers up, swatted and brushed away as many flies as possible from our butts and from around the anus.

Flies were not our only concern here, though. Booby traps were much used by the Germans, whenever they had time to prepare and plant them. In the small villages of coastal Normandy, such things as fountain pens and wristwatches were often left lying on a table in some of the houses, waiting for an American or Canadian or English soldier to discover them. Turn the cap on the fountain pen, and the explosion was enough to blow off several fingers. Put on the wristwatch, tighten the strap, and when the smoke cleared, that hand was left dangling by a few tendons, totally useless. They did not, at first, do this with their armament, such as grenades or rockets, but here, they had taken time to prepare a surprise or two for us.

In the ditch where most of us dug in, one of the new men found a German potato masher grenade. He was an experienced soldier, and knew how to deactivate it. The trouble was that it didn't work as expected. He walked into the field, put the grenade against his thigh, and turned the handle to loosen it and pull out the fuse. This was standard procedure. The grenade exploded. For the rest of us, it was well that he'd had enough sense to go out into the open first. He walked to the aid station, where the medic spent a couple of hours picking small bits of sheet metal from his leg and hands. It was not a serious injury, simply because it had exploded in the open and not in a confined space.

Our medic had been gaining practical experience all the time since our early days on the beachhead, and had become proficient in dealing with injuries such as those caused by the grenade. The doctor, however, was new with us. His predecessor had been shipped forward to a line company. We got a replacement, and it was the short end of this tradeoff.

Good doctors, as a rule, were sent to where the need was greatest. This was also where they were most likely to become a casualty themselves. Our new doctor was Bavarian, another refuge from German occupation forces. He spoke very little

English, and tended to treat every complaint with a bottle of aspirin. He did that with a broken leg on one occasion. He deeply resented his service in the United States Army, and was not shy about letting others know of his displeasure. He seemed to hate Americans, and could rarely bring himself to touch one of us. Fortunately, our medic was good. He did all that the doctor should have done, and generally did it well.

There was nothing any medic could do about what had happened here, though. Mortars were completely impartial in the way they treated human flesh, and just as uncaring about the after effects, such as the flies and odors. A mortar round was like a grenade. It could not penetrate anything, the way a bullet could. The mortar just landed, and after a couple of seconds exploded, making those burnt marks on the ground.

Someone who knew more about the effect of mortars than we did arrived the next day. He was Private Leonard Grant, fairly tall, lean, brown-haired and nineteen years old. He'd spent a couple of days with us earlier. He was remarkable only in that he'd been another section eight case, was treated and released, then sent back to the First Infantry Division when he left us. At least, that's where we thought he went. He'd seemed stable enough back then, although he now shook his head and muttered unintelligible things to himself when he got off the truck and realized where he was.

"I was here before," he finally said, "just a few days ago. Before the stink started, back when...back with what made all this stink. When can we get out of here?"

Sergeant Parsons turned away to continue whatever chore he'd been doing. It was up to me to answer, if I could. "Who knows?" I said. "Personally, I've had enough flies and polluted air to last me a dozen lifetimes. But maybe you've got even better reasons to move on."

Lenny Grant looked at the killing field, brushed some flies from his face, and said, very quietly, "Yeah, I think I have. You know what I've been doing since I left you guys back on the beachhead?"

I shook my head. "No idea. You seem okay now, though."

He stared at me for a while. "You know how they cure us whackos now? How they turn section eight cases into usable soldiers?"

Again, I shook my head, with the feeling I was about to hear something I'd have preferred not to know.

Lenny was not to be stopped, though. "You get a psycho evaluation first. The really bad ones—the guys twitching, jumping, screaming, and trying to take their own body apart with their teeth and fingernails—they're sent somewhere else. For the rest of us, it was quick and simple. Two or three days of off-and-on conversation with a shrink, or maybe only an hour or two, depending on how many they were trying to 'treat,' a few pills, and reassignment. That was it. It didn't cure many, maybe not anyone, but it worked just well enough to make it feasible."

"Okay," I said, and knew right away I shouldn't ask questions, but we'd gone this far, so I might as well let him tell me the rest of it. "So what, exactly, worked well enough to be feasible?"

"Shock treatment," Lenny replied, and waited.

"What kind of shock treatment? Electric shock? Immersion in ice water?"

He stared at me again. "You know," he said, "I'm not telling you this because I enjoy it, or even want to tell you. It's purely because I feel someone should know, and it should be someone who's got a better chance of surviving this insanity than an infantry rifleman. You're a specialist, and qualify. So listen up. The shock treatment used was reassignment to Graves Registration. You know what that is?" He turned to look at a spot fifty yards away in the field.

We all knew what Graves Registration was. They were the guys who picked up the dead. At a collection center somewhere not far in the rear, they pulled off the pair of dog tags from the chain around the neck of the body, put one with whatever personal effects they found in the guy's pockets, and put the other dog tag between the teeth. The notch in every dog tag was pushed between the two front lower teeth. It was there to keep the tag in place, after someone used the heel of his hand to slam the jaws shut and force the dog tag to remain upright and readable.

I looked in the same direction, until too many flies had gathered around my eyes. I bent my head to brush them away. "You were here, weren't you? You were here in this field, or the next one."

"Both," he said. "We worked in pairs, of course. It takes two to carry a litter. We followed the medic litter bearers when they picked up the wounded. It was usually a couple of hours later, to give them all the time they needed. Then we went out, with our litter and rubber sheets. Some were still bleeding a little. Most had leaked—blood, urine, body fluids, brains even. We'd pick one up, put him on the litter with the rubber sheet under him, fold it over him, strap him on, and deliver him to the nearest collection point. Then do it again, and do it over and over until the area was cleared of anything that resembled a human body."

"Not a pleasant job," I said.

"No. And it was why we were assigned to it. If there's anything in the world worse than being a combat infantryman, it's going out after a battle to collect the dead. You find them in any and all conditions, some whole, others blown apart, barely enough left to identify. And it was right out there, in this field, that we had our worst experience."

"Which you're going to tell me about now?"

"Which you've got to know, like it or not."

"Okay, Lenny," I said. "I've a feeling this is something I'll always remember, and might even hate you for telling me about it. But do it if you must."

"My partner was Tommy Wales, a decent enough guy who carried his share of the work load whether he felt like it or not. We were nearly done for the day when Tommy spotted one more, right out there." He pointed at the spot fifty yards away. "We carried the litter over there, looked down at what we expected to be a very dead American kid, and saw that the kid looked back at us with eyes wide open. He moved his head a little.

"Understand, we never blamed the medics. They'd found him first and assumed he'd be dead before they could carry him to the aid station. He should have been. The kid should have died long before we got there.

"Tommy and I both knelt on the ground, to be closer to him. He was too weak to speak much above a whisper. And we looked at the rest of him. He must have fallen on a mortar round just as it exploded. From the bottom of his rib cage to his crotch, there was nothing but a bloody opening with his shattered backbone showing. No intestines, no kidneys, none of the small parts that help keep a living body functional, just a pool of blood and vertebrae.

"He spoke to us. 'Hey, guys, take it easy with me, okay? I know I'm hurt real bad. Just put me on your litter real gentle-like, and I'll try to be no trouble for you.'

"The explosion must have cauterized all the blood vessel ends and nerves. He obviously had no feeling below the rib cage. I looked at Tommy; he looked at me. What the hell were we supposed to do now? We weren't medics. We didn't even have morphine with us. Dead men don't need it."

Lenny shook his head and brushed away more flies. I stared at him, and thought he was crying, but even if that were true, the flies were drinking the tears as fast as he made them.

"Christ," I said. "I'd never wish that situation on anyone. So what did you do?"

He put a fist in his right eye and twisted it, killing at least twenty flies. "We stayed there. We talked to him, stalled him when he wondered why we didn't put him on the litter. We asked him questions about his home and family. And we silently begged whatever gods might be to please let him die. He did, finally. When we lifted him to the litter, he fell apart, into two pieces."

Now I was crying. I put an arm around Lenny's shoulder and squeezed.

"Okay," he said. "That's what I had to tell someone. Sorry it had to be you. And I know that in the big picture of this, or probably any other war, it's too small a thing to matter. But it's also too big a thing for one man to carry. I'll go back to my company soon, and I'll be with them for the next offensive. And it's not likely I'll ever be a section eight again. They knew what they were doing when they sent me to Graves Registration. It's an answer to the worst fears of any infantryman, simply because, in a situation where we're unlikely to be killed, it's something worse than front-line combat. It's also something we need to talk about, but not with the folks at home. They couldn't possibly understand." He looked at me. "Thanks for hearing it," he mumbled, and walked away.

The author's dog tags, two-thirds size. Note the notch in the lower end. This is the part that was forced between the lower teeth of a body. With rigor mortis usually already set in, the jaws needed to be pried apart, a tag inserted, then the lower jaw given a hard rap with the heel of the hand to jam it together enough to hold the dog tag firmly in place. The second tag was placed in a cloth bag to accompany personal effects.

The tags were originally issued with a narrow cloth tape, but the majority of new recruits bought a chain, such as this one, to replace the cloth, which became dirty altogether too quickly, and was soon apt to rot and break. The army PX sold the chains.

# 12

## *Feeding The War Machine*

Lenny left us two days later, without explaining whether that mortar round that had blown the kid in half was one of theirs or one of ours. There were so many "splashes" in that field, I couldn't tell. Did it really matter? Dead is dead. Walk into an area targeted by either side, and you were unlikely to leave it alive.

A lot of others left when Lenny did. There were rumors and stories everywhere, about something big happening not far ahead. The name "Falaise Gap" was a part of it. We had no idea whether that was a geological feature of the terrain, or an opening in our line or in the German lines. Maps were forbidden to enlisted men, so it wasn't until we read accounts in The Stars and Stripes that we started to put it all together.

Falaise was a town held by the Canadians northeast of us, twenty or so miles away. Mortain was a town held by Americans to the east, or maybe a little south of east. Almost forty miles separated the two, and this was the "gap." It was through this that an entire German army was trying to escape eastward. Our side was trying to close the gap and encircle the remainder of German forces in Normandy.

Details were slow to reach us, but we did learn that a battalion of the Thirtieth Infantry was holding the high ground at Mortain, and doing so against vastly superior German forces, including two Panzer divisions.

Casualties were heavy, and we were needed there as soon as we could move. Another reinforcement company was already on the scene. We loaded up and went to Mortain.

We set up around the edges of a large potato field that had already been harvested—a good idea for the French farmers, but not so good for us. The most diligent search turned up no more than two or three small spuds. We tried to eat them raw, but that wasn't the best idea in the world. They had a rough, alkaline taste that puckered the mouth and caused gas and an upset stomach, at least for me.

Our supply/armorer's tent was on the side of a hill, with my personal space on the lower part of it. Almost anything was an improvement over that "land of flies" we'd just left behind. Our .50 caliber anti-aircraft gun was outside the tent, close to the flap. It was now my responsibility, to keep it clean and oiled, to have the ammo ready at hand, and to fire it if that were needed. Once more, we had assurances that the Luftwaffe was no more, but we'd heard that song before. With its armor piercing, incendiary, and tracer ammo loading, our .50 would be effective against any truck or armored car, but probably worthless against tanks. The mount, however, was designed for use against aircraft, not ground vehicles. It would be awkward to depress the barrel enough to use it against armor, but possible.

From the nature of the replacements we received, and the kind of ammunition issued to them before they arrived, it was obvious that armor of all kinds would be a large part of the action here. We soon learned that the Third Armored Division had moved in, to relieve what little was left of the Thirtieth Infantry battalion that had held so doggedly to what now appeared to be the "hinge" of a door that should have been slammed shut on the escaping German divisions.

The Germans, their officers well aware of the possibility of being trapped, hammered away constantly at Mortain, holding the "gap" open. They probably did the same at Falaise. Ninety percent of the armor, and a major part of the men of our Third Armored Division, were lost. Ordnance supply and the replacement systems were strained to their utmost to fill the never-ending need. Our own security was stepped up, because German patrols were operating all around us, squads of Kraut infantry apparently "written off" and sacrificed in the ongoing effort to keep roads and communications open long enough to get their main force out of the threatened encirclement. We began to see this battle at Mortain as part of a huge mechanical beast, ever hungry for more human bodies on both sides.

Our sentries were experienced infantrymen, whose nightly calls to anyone lighting a cigarette were to "put it out before I shoot it out." Most of us gave up smoking after sunset.

It was during this time that Jim Grollin, our First Sergeant, made a late call to the supply tent, to talk with Sergeant Parsons. I listened and said nothing. In truth, I could hear only snatches and pieces of their conversation, because they both asked me to stay away from them, at the other end of our combined tents.

Both regular army, Grollin and Parsons were, in a way, the backbone of our company, the only two who had the rank, the experience, and the seniority to sometimes question decisions of the officers, and to offer their own opinions when these were needed. No matter what they said or did, neither could be broken in rank by any company officer. They were first three graders, and only a court martial could do that. That's why Grollin came to our tent late at night. He came with a bottle, which they passed back and forth between them, and cigarettes, which they chain-smoked, rather than use a lighter or strike a match that might be seen outside. He also had a plan that would make him a candidate for a court martial.

The fact that our First Sergeant and Supply Sergeant had shared the Icelandic experience gave them a bond that neither could ever have with the rest of us. We respected it, and respected them.

Grollin, as nearly as I could understand from what I overheard of that midnight conversation, planned to leave the company, to go AWOL. This was in protest against what he saw as the incompetence and failure of the company commander.

"How long do you expect to be gone?" Parsons asked him.

"I've no idea," Grollin replied as I sidled a little closer. "My French is good enough to get by with the civilians. My mother was French, you know, and she insisted her kids know it. I could find some sympathetic locals and stay with them almost indefinitely."

"You'd be taking a hell of a chance, Jim. This is a combat zone, you know. That means your absence could be interpreted as desertion, not simply AWOL. That's the death penalty."

"That's one reason I'm telling you this before I go. I do plan to come back. You're my witness to that. And I know it's a hell of a gamble, but there's no way I can live with that bastard any longer. If I do this, it will force the issue, all the way to a court martial, if necessary. I'm willing to do that. I'll do almost anything, to put some distance between him and me."

Parsons made a comment I couldn't hear, then added, "How did he ever get as far as he has? He's regular army, too, and a first lieutenant. Yet, a juvenile clam has more real brains."

"Politics, I think," Grollin replied. "I heard a few remarks made to the other lieutenants about family connections. It's the only thing that makes sense. But I don't care how or why he wound up commanding our company. I've just plain had it with him. He's destroyed my authority, to the point I'm no longer able to give an order without him countermanding it. I've done my best, Frank, and I could have made this a great company, but not with a commander who's never known where he stood on an issue, or if he did know, decided his personal image was more important than rules, good sense, and justice. So I'll be gone tonight. Just remember, when you're asked, that I did plan to return, but I want to know there will at least be an inquiry, if not a court martial. Someone with higher rank than company level, and more authority, needs to set the record straight."

"I'll remember, Jim," Parsons promised.

Jim Grollin slipped out the tent flap and was gone. We never saw him again.

After, I wondered if some part of the reason the Top Kick did not want me to participate in that discussion was for my own protection. I was a lowly T5, a corporal, and could be punished in ways that could not be used with them.

Events moved quickly—too quickly to dwell on uncertain possibilities involving a fine First Sergeant and a good man, now no longer with us. I'd had my own differences with our company commander, and now harbored even more resentment over his crude handling of what should have been no more than minor problems.

With or without Jim Grollin, we had to function as a company, and do it efficiently. Staff Sergeant Trent Edgars stepped in as acting First, with the approval of Lieutenants Markinson, Cicciloni, and Larson. Lieutenant Bailey refused to participate. He wanted only to find and prosecute Jim Grollin.

The need for replacements became more critical daily. The Third Armored Division clamored for more and more as their casualties mounted. Several hundred had arrived in our company and the other. A pickup by division trucks was scheduled for the next day.

At the appointed time, our replacements had just finished eating a meal far from favored by the majority of servicemen there. It was known as SOS—"shit on a shingle." It was creamed corned beef on toast, nourishing enough, even if intensely disliked. The trucks arrived, a convoy under the command of a new lieutenant, himself a recent replacement in the Third Armored. One of own lieutenants was on hand to meet him as he swung down from the passenger side of the lead truck with the orders in his hand. He checked his watch. The truck drivers gathered around, and asked him if they could have some food. They'd not eaten in 48 hours.

He checked his watch again. "Damn," he said. "Well, it may be another 48 hours before you're this close to food again. Take twenty minutes, no more. We'll get the trucks loaded while you eat. Hurry, hurry!"

They wolfed down some of the S on S, drank a quick cup of coffee, and returned to their trucks. The convoy left, ten minutes late. They carried three hundred replacements for the Third Armored, but never got there.

The road to the Third's position was used in places by both sides. One of those places had been targeted by division artillery, with an intense barrage planned for just after the convoy had passed. The purpose was apparently to prevent German armor from following and attacking the trucks.

The convoy arrived just in time to run directly into our own artillery fire. Eighty percent of the replacements were killed, all because a new lieutenant did not have the heart to refuse food to some half-starved truck drivers. It was a lesson for all of us, in following orders exactly, regardless of any temporary cost or discomfort.

Other things were happening, and we had little time to think about it, little time to grieve, when a group of French resistance fighters arrived. There seemed to be dozens of these groups, each with a different name. We never knew half of them. Here, they were the FFI and the RFF, and probably a dozen more. In the south of France, there was the Maquis. Each group seemed to be under local control, with little or no attempt to coordinate with other groups. This was the problem that deBourbon had been sent to correct, and after his notable success in Normandy, we wondered why he'd not been given wider authority.

Sergeant Jinks had also been regular army, like Grollin and Parsons, but without their outstanding service records. Jinks invented his own name for these French groups, especially the RFF. He said they were all "Rat Faced Fuckers." This fit the initials, but he also used the term indiscriminately for all French resistance forces. He did not think highly of them. Of course, when one of our own did something that did not meet his approval, that person also became a "Rat Faced Fucker." If nothing else, Jinks was impartial in his classification of RFFs.

A dozen RFF Frenchmen came into the supply tent, all highly excited and all talking at once while Lieutenant Markinson tried his best to interpret. A wedding had taken place in a nearby village. From the church to the reception and the home of the newly married couple was a long walk, up a hill and through some woods. One of those German patrols was in the woods, and stopped the wedding procession. They took the bride with them and raped her, according to what we could gather from the babble of a dozen excited Frenchmen, all talking at once.

Resistance members gathered and came to us for help. They wanted to capture or kill the Germans. They had rifles that had been dropped to them by parachute months earlier. These were Enfields, the excellent World War I arm of the British forces, with some issued to American troops. The difference was in the cartridge used. The British was different from ours. The Enfields dropped were British rifles, and the ammunition dropped for them was ours. They did not match, so the weapons were useless.

I had ten M1s on hand. They were battlefield recoveries, picked up and turned in to me by whoever found them. These were critical to me if I were to perform my armorer's duty properly. Any time a replacement arrived with a defective weapon, I often had no more than a few hours to repair or replace it. Spare parts, ordered from the nearest ordnance depot, could take a month to arrive. In addition, field regulations forbid me to make the most common repairs, all of which I'd been well trained to do, and for which I had the necessary tools, some of them improvisations I'd built myself.

There was no excuse if a replacement could not move up because he lacked a functioning weapon, of the type specified for his MOS (Military Occupation Specification) number. Any failure was my fault. Yet, if I repaired or replaced his weapon, I was breaking regulations. That, also, was my fault, a dereliction of duty. I was damned if I did, and damned if I didn't. Where army regulations were involved, there was never any way to win.

I chose to make repairs whenever possible. For this, I needed battlefield recoveries. When they'd been stripped of the most needed parts, I sent them to Ordnance, to be repaired or discarded at their discretion. Every soldier who came through our company had his proper weapon when he left. It was in working order, and if it happened to be a recovery, it was one I had personally test fired. Trying to understand army regulations was an exercise in futility. We did our jobs, and hoped that was enough.

Those ten M1s on hand had been stripped of the ejectors, the part that flipped the spent casings from the rifle, and the most frequently missing part in the hands of replacements. They were always told never to remove the ejector, because it needed no adjustment or repairs. Also, when released, its small but powerful spring sent it flying with a force that could easily put out an eye. Naturally, many replacements removed the ejectors, then came to me, sheep-faced, and wanted to know what I could do about it. If the part were found, I could re-install it. If not found, I needed a spare.

The M1s ready to be shipped to ordnance would, if loaded, fire a single shot, then jam. The empty cartridge, still in the rifle, prevented another from loading. This is what I explained to the lieutenant. He shrugged and ordered me to give them to the Frenchmen anyway. They left their Enfields as security and a highly voluble, and volatile, band of RFFs went on the prowl for German rapists, armed with single-shot rifles.

They were unsuccessful, and at day's end a dejected and disillusioned group of resistance fighters returned to claim their own weapons, for which they had no ammunition. No shot had been fired.

Another disaster, as grave as our lost convoy, struck that night in the other company. We were only about a mile apart, so we were generally aware of what was happening over there, as they were aware of our problems.

This time, it was their turn for unreasonable losses.

The rifle ammunition issued to the replacements before they arrived was three armor piercing and one tracer, repeated, in an eight-round clip. New arrivals were instructed not to fire at any aircraft with their rifles, especially at night. Tracers did more than act as an aiming device for those using them. They also announced the source of ground fire to observers in a plane. This do-not-fire message was given to the replacements several times, by officers and by the sergeants.

Not all were impressed by it. They were fresh in from the States, full of piss and vinegar, ready for a fight. Some had been just waiting for a chance to kill Germans. They didn't believe the orders about not shooting at planes. It couldn't possibly apply to them. Those were the enemy, right? The planes came. They fired at them.

Experienced German airmen were not stupid. They knew perfectly well the sort of orders that would have been issued to the newcomers. They also knew that if a few of them were down there, firing their rifles at the planes, there were probably a lot more. They swung out and around, and came back for a bomb run. They dumped everything they had on the presumed assembly of replacements. They were right on target.

It was worse than our Normandy beachhead experience with the truck drivers and exploding ammo. There were more men involved here, they had arrived after dark, and they had not really had time to dig in properly, although many were in the ditch next to the hedgerow.

There were four hundred casualties that night. One of that number, and a severely felt loss, was our medic, who had been covering both companies at the time. The story reached us the next day. He'd been working most of the night and was bone weary. He saw a pair of legs on the ground next to the ditch. They bore several wounds. He bandaged, and pulled the rest of the man out of the ditch, bandaging as he went, until the whole body lay flat on the ground. Only, it wasn't a whole body. This one had no head. The medic lost it right then and there, and raved about how the time wasted might have saved someone else, who did have a head. People without heads, he shouted, should not demand medical services. He was taken back with the next load of wounded, another section eight case. As far as we were ever able to find out, he never recovered. He'd given everything he had to the job, and it finally demanded more of him than he had left to give. He was probably sent home, but he would never again be the young man who had left family and friends a year or two earlier.

The Third Armored Division, still taking heavy casualties, had no time to commiserate. More and more men were needed. More trucks were found, more replacements sent up. The beat went on. Eventually, the German counter-offensive weakened. They, too, were running out of armor and manpower. Many escaped, to fight again in another place and another time. Many others did not. The prisoner catch was huge, thousands for whom this war was over at last.

We had three staff sergeants, Parsons in supply, Tomkins, our mess sergeant, and Trent Edgars. Edgars had joined the company with his rank, just as Grollin and Parsons had. He was not regular army, though. A heavy-set man with a voice that could roar like an angry bull, he was conscientious, and led the company well as our new Top Kick (First Sergeant). Before we moved again, Lieutenant Bailey, the company commander, left in a Jeep sent for him by a Board of Inquiry. Lieutenant Cicciloni took over, at least temporarily. We were a different company now, but functioned and did our job as before. Sergeant Parsons and I knew what had precipitated the presumed questioning of Lieutenant Bailey, although we'd heard nothing about Jim Grollin. In this situation, our sympathies were completely with our former First Sergeant. We hoped that some day we'd find out what had become of him. We didn't care what happened to Bailey.

This was still Normandy, calvados country, and Sergeant Jinks saw an opportunity just waiting for someone to take advantage of it. He located a good supply of the liquor, filled a couple of jerricans used for water by the cooks, and took a position beside a well just down the road, where many in the company filled their canteens. An old-fashioned hand pump raised the water in the well. Jinks convinced many who went there that the calvados might be a more appropriate beverage, and would entail none of that laborious pumping. He sold each one of them a canteen full for a modest fee, calculated on how much he thought the buyer might be willing to pay.

Calvados was a fluid of many uses. Highly flammable, it could start small fires for heating water. It was an excellent fuel for cigarette lighters, because it burned with a blue, almost invisible flame. It was probably a better water purifier than our halizone tablets. In colder weather, there was little doubt it could be used as antifreeze in the truck radiators. Plus, for those with a cast iron stomach, it could serve as an intoxicating drink. However, there was a drawback that soon put Jinks out of business. The cooks refused to allow him to use any more of their jerricans. Calvados ate the enamel off the insides, and would soon etch holes in the metal walls of the cans. Jinks pocketed his profits and closed shop.

With a suddenness that caught us off guard, the fighting at Mortain, and the need for replacements, stopped. The Falaise gap was no more. Prisoners had been taken back to holding areas, and much of the German army in France was now the other side of the Seine River, beyond Paris. American divisions followed, and so did we.

The way through, and out of, Mortain left little to the imagination about the severity of the battle that had been fought here. Blown-up tanks, trucks, and armored vehicles of every description littered the sides of the road. Ours and theirs were often side by side. Casualties, as we already knew, had been many thousands.

Perhaps worst of all, for animal lovers such as some of us, were the horses. The German army still relied on these animals to pull their artillery, both cannons and caissons. They'd scoured Europe for the best available, and these were without exception beautiful creatures. Large draft horses that had worked the farms of Europe for generations, they included Belgians with hooves the size of barrel ends, and Clyesdales, probably second or third generation from the originals sold to Belgian and French farmers by the Scots who had raised them.

Like their mechanical counterparts, these magnificent animals lay shattered and broken by the side of the road. There were hundreds of them. We learned from a former walking wounded, now returning to his company, that before the battle was finished, horses had become prime targets for our artillery. If they could disembowel a lead horse in a four-horse team with a well-placed artillery shell, that piece of German artillery was quickly put out of action, and the road blocked. The German driver, often a man who loved his horses, was forced to end the misery with a rifle shot to the head of his dying animal.

That would not be the last of it, though. The road had to be cleared, and done so quickly. Unless the driver acted immediately, a tank would soon arrive to push the horses, alive and dying, into a heap off the road. The animals, tangled in their harnesses, screamed and flailed their hooves. The artillery piece they'd been pulling might be shoved right on top of them. There was rarely enough time to cut a horse out of its harness. There was sometimes just enough time for the driver to use his rifle on the other three before the tank arrived. More than one German did that. He killed his horses, than sat beside his dead team after they'd been bulldozed out of the way, and wept. He would not leave them until he himself was killed or captured. This love of his animals by an enemy soldier was possibly the only sign of sanity in this corner of hell called Mortain.

# 13

## *The Breakdown in Supplies*

From Mortain to our next location was a long, wearying haul across much of northern France to the bank of the Seine River, a few miles south of Paris.

We were not allowed to go to Paris. General Lee, head of the Services of Supply, made sure that only those assigned to that service would be allowed in the City of Light. Paris, we heard, was filled with SOS officers and enlisted men living the good life, sleeping in the finest hotels, eating the best food anywhere, enjoying the attention of Europe's most beautiful women and, for many, becoming rich with the illicit sale of army goods to the black market. Cigarettes had become the new medium of exchange, legal tender for anything that could be bought or sold. We wondered who eventually smoked them. A pack, or even individual cigarettes, might change hands dozens of times, until they were as worn as old paper money.

In defiance of Hitler's express orders, Paris had not been burned by the retreating German army. It was, for the most part, intact, although missing many of its art treasures.

We settled in on the pestilential flood plain along the river, where we swatted mosquitoes, ate the worst excuse for food in any modern army, and became sick. At least, many of us did. "C" rations were never designed for anything more than a few days of use in dire emergencies, and a healthy profit to the per-petrators of this crime against humanity. There were only three kinds. They were stew, hash, or beans. The stew was brown glop with bits of unknown meat and unfamiliar vegetables lurking in it. The seasoning was unfamiliar, the flavor mainly parsnips, which I'd always detested. The hash was a dry, gray matter that might have been almost anything before it was "processed."

Defective dog food, most likely. The beans were edible, but the cooks usually reserved those for themselves. All of it was in cans, from which all identification had dissolved in the hot water used to warm them. A "meal" was a warm can of something unknown until it was opened, with another can of dry, tasteless round crackers and a few pieces of hard candy, also tasteless.

We read the humorless account of a group of German prisoners in Italy, who petitioned the Swiss Red Cross to stop the Americans from practicing inhuman torture by trying to feed them "C" rations. The Geneva Convention stated quite clearly that soldiers who surrendered would be fed the same food as their captors. Not one of the Germans would believe that Americans could, and did, survive for any length of time on this.

In two weeks, I could not hold down another bite of any of it. Weakness and nausea were constant companions. I tried. I tried mightily to force just a little down my throat at least once a day. Within twenty minutes, I always vomited the mess into a nearby gravel pit. Satisfied I was not going to get better, I staggered to the aid station, using the small trees and saplings along the way for support.

Our own Bavarian doctor was missing, possibly attending a course in the use of English for communication. In his place was a fresh-faced child wearing one of our uniforms and second lieutenant's bars. A medic took my temperature. It was 104. With wisdom gathered during a brisk jog past some stateside pre-med institute, the "doctor" pronounced my condition was due to a lack of decent food. Not to worry, though. He also stated in no uncertain terms that this war was over. We'd all be home in just a week or two, where I could eat whatever I needed and feel lots better in no time. He handed me a bottle of aspirin, and told me to take them as needed to control the fever. What I, and nearly everyone else here, needed was someone to control the qualification standards of these morons who were posing as doctors, and in many cases might soon treat men who were seriously wounded.

Supplies of all kinds became difficult to obtain. We heard that in the Third Army divisions somewhere ahead of us, the men were getting one meal of "K" rations per day and all the ammunition they wanted. The trucks that carried everything forward often did not have enough gasoline to reach their destination. What was available was used to deliver ammunition. Tanks, which needed eleven gallons of gasoline to travel each mile, ran dry and stopped.

It became rapidly worse. Tires were the next to go. Beside the highways were at first a few, then hundreds, then thousands, of trucks, pulled off the road with their axles on logs or large stones. The wheels were gone, stripped to use on other trucks. Pushed to the limit to keep up, there was no time to change a tire. A truck with only five of its ten tires remaining was useless. Any wheels still equipped with a tire that held air were simply removed and put on a truck that could still roll. The wheel and tire they replaced were tossed aside. It did not take long before the entire drive across France was stopped, not by the enemy, but by a lack of tires.

Rumors abounded. Some said the dock facilities in Normandy were far from adequate, which was probably true, but we'd made do with nothing but makeshift facilities on the beachhead, and surprised the world at what could be accomplished under the whip of necessity. Of course, the distances traveled by the trucks had dramatically increased, but the port of Cherbourg was operating now, which added more dock capacity. The cause of the tire shortage had to be more than that. Maybe too many cargo ships had been lost, but that didn't ring true, either.

The answer finally proposed was based partly on reports from those who had recently left the States, and partly on articles in The Stars and Stripes, when we received a rare copy. It was that the good people of Akron, Ohio, rubber capitol of the nation and the world, were on strike. They had refused to make more tires until their demands were met. There was something phony about this. The tire makers, like every other manufacturer doing war work, were given cost-plus contracts by the government. After all costs were covered, including administrative expenses, ten percent could be added for profit. Ten percent was a much larger profit margin than many of them had ever enjoyed previous to the war. The beauty of it, from the viewpoint of industry, was that the more an item cost, the greater would be the profit. There was no motive whatever to deny workers any increase in pay that was acceptable to the government and approved by the

War Labor Board. Yet, they went on strike. It simply didn't add up.

Neither did the lack of replacement tires, but it was an ongoing and too obvious fact of life. There was a legitimate, if farfetched, explanation. Communists had infiltrated the nation's labor unions. This seemed to be established fact, although it had not yet been proven in any court. There was certainly enough precedent, and enough circumstantial evidence. The strikes against the automotive, aircraft, and heavy equipment industries in 1941 were all thought to have been communist inspired. Government seizure of the factories and the use of the military as strike-breakers had followed, without the apparent need to pursue the matter further.

American and British armies were tearing across western Europe at a rate much faster than the Soviet armies were moving from the east. The Soviet Union could be fearful that they would not finish this war in a position to dominate the eastern half of Europe. Therefore, they needed to slow down the Allied advance in the west, and one sure way to do this was to disrupt production of gasoline, ammunition, and food supplies, or perhaps an easier choice—rubber tires. This answered all the nagging questions about a breakdown in the impetus of our advance. Of course, it permitted many German divisions to reach relative safety in their homeland and prepare for the bitter fighting and possible stalemate to come.

Nowhere in any of this did rationality play a part. On the other hand, all motives in this war (and all wars, possibly) were, at their base, political. The Soviets recognized this. We seemed unable to do that. Perhaps this was because American servicemen, as a whole, were naïve in the extreme. We looked for any excuse to avoid stigmatizing our fellow Americans at home with accusations of disloyal behavior. Yet, a small backward glance at recent history was more than enough to substantiate the lowest opinion of the majority of civilians.

There had been an accumulating body of evidence that spoke clearly about the lack of concern exhibited by many segments of American life. Waste and corruption were widespread. Greed and devotion to the philosophy of "me first" and "get it while you can" had extended far beyond the politicians who were normally accused of this sort of behavior. Back in February, while we were in Northern Ireland, reports had been made public about the necessity of the federal government, under direct, signed orders of the President, for the WLB (War Labor Board) to move in with armed troops and confiscate seven textile plants in Fall River, Massachusetts because management and the labor unions could not agree on wage scales. Workers had walked out, leaving unfinished the materials needed for military uniforms and other articles.

The same thing seemed to be happening across the nation. In Cleveland, WLB lawyers walked in on a meeting of the Mechanics Educational Society of America (a labor union) and served subpoenas on the president and secretary. They were summoned to testify concerning a call for a massive walkout of their members, involving 2500 to 3000 workers. A strike by the Molders and Factory Workers' Union had already closed 35 iron foundries and idled 3000 workers, most engaged in war work.

Go forward to June 17, just 11 days after the first landings in Normandy. The Central States Drivers' Council, a union of truck drivers, voted 98 percent in favor of a walkout, according to the council's director. This would affect 1800 trucking companies and idle 250,000 other workers in addition to the drivers.

So our trucks had no tires, we had few supplies, our front line troops plenty of ammunition but little of anything else.

In the micro world of our supply tent, all reasons for our existence slowly vanished. Of the total items requisitioned, we were likely to receive less than ten percent. Socks, the ever-present need of every soldier in the field, were reduced from the thousand or more ordered to a couple of dozen, all of them too small to fit anyone but a deformed midget. Field jackets, underwear, shirts and trouser, were simply unavailable. American cigarettes, formerly sold through a traveling PX, nearly vanished from the list of things available. As company supply, we were chosen to dispense what few were received, at first one pack of off-brand smokes per man per week, then, when that was gone, one sack of Bull Durham roll-your-own.

Some of the men who came for their rations were less than pleased. They looked at the Bull Durham and said, "I'll be damned if I'll smoke those things." Three days later, most returned and humbly asked if there were any left. It was too late. The last of the Durham, the last of almost everything, had been issued.

Another problem that exacerbated our whole position was that we continued to receive replacements, until our one company grew to two thousand men, sleeping in the field, wearing socks and other clothing that were worn out, poorly fed and often sick. Malaria always threatened. Scurvy became a new possibility. The little boys playing doctor had nothing to counteract or treat any of it. The rule of the day became denial. Deny that we were badly fed and sick. Deny that our clothes were becoming little more than rags. Deny that a sort of sickly submissiveness infected everyone. The army and everyone else had abandoned us. We might as well just sit down and die.

Properly caring for all the replacements was impossible. We needed to send hundreds of them forward, to the units that needed them, and we couldn't. There were no trucks available. There was no bridge across the Seine here, even if the men had been well enough to move fifty miles on foot. Just ahead, waiting at the river's bank for a way across, was the Thirtieth Infantry. We could only wonder if the same lethargy and uncaring attitude were infecting them.

Bernie Vernal, our former 57-millimeter artilleryman, came in with a truckload of what we assumed was C rations, water, and other items. He was still unassigned, still bouncing around Europe from one impossible job to another. He quickly learned where supply was, and came in looking for something to do. There wasn't anything, so he and another combined their shelter halves and pitched it behind the supply tent.

I was becoming weaker by the day, and thin enough to be termed "emaciated."

Bernie noticed. "You're sick," he said. "Have you been to the aid station?"

I nodded.

"Didn't they do anything for you?"

I took the bottle of aspirin from my pocket and showed it to him. "Gave me this," I said.

He put a hand on my forehead. "Have you taken any?" he asked.

"A few. They may have helped some, but not a lot."

"Yeah, damn right not a lot. Look, I speak good French, and there's a village only about a mile from here. You could well be coming down with scurvy, or some other deficiency illness. I doubt there'll be a doctor anywhere, but most villages have a healer of some kind. A midwife, maybe, who knows enough to treat a few common sicknesses. My guess is that you've been on "C" rations much too long. That can be cured. What have you got for trade goods?"

I shook my head. "Not much. Most of a bar of bath soap, sent from home. A bag of Bull Durham. How about a couple of pair of socks too small to fit any American here?"

"Whatever. Give it to me and I'll see what I can get for it."

Bernie returned in a little over an hour. He had a fresh egg. One egg. To get that for what little I'd been able to give him must have take a lot of fast talk on his part. An egg was worth about seventy-five dollars, over a full month's pay for an American private waiting in the fields here. Bernie put it carefully aside.

"First," he said, "you've got to be cleaned up. You're filthy, and you smell sick. Part of getting better is usually first getting clean."

He and his friend had already fashioned a crude fireplace, a ring of stones within which they could burn dead wood and heat water for instant coffee when and if they found some, or for shaving if they were so inclined. The nearest German soldiers were far and away the other side of the Seine, so we had nothing to fear from an open fire. Bernie took my steel helmet and his own, filled them both from a Lister bag beyond the supply tent, and put them on stones in the fireplace. Less than twenty minutes later, he had warm water. While we waited, he ordered me to get the cleanest clothes I owned and have them ready.

I stripped, and Bernie Vernal gave me a bath, using an undershirt and a piece of yellow GI soap intended for laundry. While I stood by the fire and let him do this, I put my hands around my waist, thumbs and middle fingers aimed at each other. They touched. My waist size was down to about eighteen inches, my weight probably no more than ninety pounds, but he'd been right about getting clean. I already felt better.

While I dried and dressed, Bernie boiled the egg in some clean water. He put it in half of my mess kit, gave me a spoon, and told me to eat it. We had no salt, no seasoning, but it was the best tasting egg I'd ever eaten. The next day, my strength was returning. I thought I owed Bernie my life, but he dismissed that idea, and with a serious look, sat on a log and told me something unsettling.

"That truck I came in on," he started. "You have any idea what was on it?"

"No," I said. "It came in after dark, and left before I even knew it was here. I don't suppose it had any of the clothing we'd ordered, or someone would have let us know."

"Nope," he said. "No clothing. Something a whole lot more important to at least half the guys in these fields, you included."

"All right. What was it, then?"

Bernie stared at me for a half a minute. "Two thousand fresh oranges," he said at last. "Army knew the shape you were in. They knew what was needed—fresh fruit loaded with vitamin C. Oranges. They bumped a load of ammo to send it to you, one for every man here."

I stared back at him. "Okay. Then where are these oranges?"

"That's exactly what I'd like to know. I haven't seen one of them anywhere. They seem to have vanished during the night. I can tell you a couple of things, though. First, we're pretty close to Paris. Second, in Paris an orange is worth six bucks, wholesale, probably twenty retail. Someone here made himself a fast twelve thousand or more last night."

I no longer felt as good. Sergeant Parsons and I had always understood each other perfectly when it came to any dealing with the black market. We simply did not do it. It would have been easy enough at times, but we'd need to live with ourselves later. The possibility was never mentioned, never discussed. Even with the Bull Durham, we'd issued ourselves exactly the same ration as everyone else. I believed the rest of our company possessed the same sense of fair play and honesty. Apparently someone, a cook or someone working with the cooks, saw things differently.

# 14

## *The Argonne*

Two days later, the Thirtieth was gone. Someone said he'd heard them moving, on a road along the river, during the night. We loaded up and followed after another two days, to a pontoon bridge the engineers had put across the Seine.

We crossed and headed northeast, passing through several places that had made history in Word War I. Chateau Thierry was one, the scene of several brutal battles in that old war. Part of it was the Belleau Woods, where Americans received their baptism of fire, and acquitted themselves nobly, according to the stories. With the exception of those one-in-a-million events when some soldier expressed his ultimate altruism by sacrificing himself to save his companions, I wondered how anything about a war could be called "noble."

Our destination was in the Argonne Forest, on both sides of a dirt road that led from the paved road to nowhere in particular. We could hear artillery firing, and hoped it was ours. It turned out to be the Thirtieth again, information that made us, if not happy, at least relieved to be with a known and experienced division.

The locals walked past us on the road every day, going to and from their fields. As in much of Europe, a family might live in a village, but their land and crops would be a mile or more away. They carried hoes, shovels, and containers in which to carry their produce home at day's end. Most also had a lunch of some kind with them while on their way to the fields. They worked from first light until nearly dark.

We began to realize something that we should have known, if we'd paid attention to history and social studies in school. The people in France wore the last rags of what had once been good clothing. They wrapped their feet in whatever was available, or wore wooden shoes. They existed at a level beneath our understanding of poverty. Yet, they ate regularly. France was truly the "bread basket" of Europe, producing enough for themselves and more to export to their European neighbors; or, in the case of the German occupation, to have confiscated by the enemy. French factories had produced most of the manufactured goods they needed, but the French people had not received any of those products. Everything went to Germany, or the nations occupied by the German army. The French railway system served all of Europe, but in no way benefited the French people. All of this illustrated, in the most graphic way, what it had meant to lose a war and become an occupied country.

Bernie was still with us, and his language skills became a valuable part of our daily existence. He talked to, and befriended, one family in particular. They were a father, mother, and two children. The boy was a skinny, frail youngster of about thirteen years, the image of his mother, for whom life appeared to be a wearisome affair, more of a struggle than it was ever going to be worth. The daughter was sixteen, and a visual banquet for eyes that had seen no beauty in far too long.

Strangely, the father was German. He'd fought here in World War I, and remained to marry his French sweetheart when it was over. A question never asked by us was if he had deserted when it became obvious Germany was losing the war. His could not have been an easy life, nor hers, during the immediate postwar years, but they persisted, and eventually fit into the community. He was ruggedly built, although lacking any hint of fat, and obviously well able to handle the rigors of life imposed by the back-breaking labor of a small family farm. They grew potatoes, onions, and a few other crops.

It was doubtful that he'd been favored by the occupying German forces because he spoke their language and shared a heritage with them. Some may even have looked upon him as a traitor, especially if he had, in fact, deserted over twenty-five years earlier. He'd kept his German surname, Manchard, an indication he had never tried to hide his past. That may have caused some friction with the locals at times.

Throughout France, there was one crying need above all others. That was shoes. Since 1939, every pair of shoes made in the country had gone to Germany. So, it was not more than a couple of days until Fritz Manchard appeared at the supply tent and made it clear that he would be grateful for any old shoes we had. They need not be anything an American soldier would be able to use. The soles and uppers could be, by our standards, beyond repair. He would fix them, he insisted, and showed me the dilapidated relics he was currently wearing, the leather cracked and falling apart, with course twine wrapped around them to hold the remnants of the soles in place.

We usually had fifty or more pairs of old shoes that had been exchanged for new ones. The army insisted we send old footwear back to our base supply depot for salvage. We complied, but it had now been over two months since the supply lines had functioned with any sort of reliability. We'd received no new shoes, so there were few old ones. From the dozen or so pairs on hand, I let Manchard choose one that he thought would fit him. "Danke, danke," he repeated, and seemed grateful, but frightened.

It had been Bernie who'd told him to see me in the supply tent. It had also been Bernie who'd told him I spoke German. I did, a little. I'd had it in high school, but Manchard spoke so rapidly, I had trouble catching the meaning of what he said. It was this that frightened him. I probably scowled, trying to translate, in my mind, the gist of his speech. The scowl he may have interpreted as a sign I was about to shoot him. I had no intention of doing that.

Simone, his daughter, was something of a problem. Just arrived at the threshold of womanhood, she was the stuff of every young man's fantasies. We always knew when the family was near. Whistles and catcalls from the sides of the road marked their position. We feared some of our guys, carried away by overwhelming desire and lust, might drag her into the woods and do what the Krauts had done to the new bride at Mortain.

The likelihood was remote as long as enough of us kept an eye on her. We did that anyway, but we wanted everyone else to know how severe the penalty was for such an act. The army had classified rape as a capital offense. Already, several former

American soldiers had been court-martialed for this. When the evidence was strong enough, each of them faced a firing squad or the hangman the next morning. There was never any appeal. Take a girl by force, and you were dead.

We wanted Simone to have no part in any of that, so Bernie and I warned those closest to our position to put a damper on the enthusiasm of their remarks, and to pass that word along. Amazingly, it worked. A few relatively harmless whistles remained, but most of the lewd and suggestive calls stopped. We said nothing about this to the family, but were certain Fritz suspected what we'd done, and was grateful for it. We wondered if Simone ever realized how much danger she'd been in. That wasn't likely.

Jack Williams showed up, and became a member of our little band. Jack was tall and thin, with a seriousness about him that belied a real sense of humor whenever the occasion allowed.

It was perhaps an odd thing, but we almost never knew, or asked, another's middle name. Even first names were reserved strictly for those with whom we worked closely, or considered friends. Everyone else was on a last name only basis. This was typical of the military, of course. One of us, maybe Fred, made a casual remark one day that if Jack's last name did not end in an "s," there'd be a lot of confusion about which name came first. This was the sort of meaningless comment that could keep some of us engaged in conversation for a good part of an otherwise deadly dull and boring day.

"You don't know the half of it," Jack said. "Most of my life, I've lived under a name curse."

"What does that mean?" Fred wanted to know.

"The curse of the terminal 's.' If my middle name had it, and my last name didn't, I'd be someone else, someone you might like, or not, but at least would waste a whole lot of time riding me about it."

"So what is it?" Bernie asked. "If you don't mind."

"Oh, I mind, but that's never helped much. I'm Jack Daniel Williams. So, I've been called "Bourbon William." I've been called "Sippin' Jack." I've been called "Barkeeper Billy," and too many others to remember."

Sergeant Parsons had sidled out from a supply tent that had no supplies, and added, "I like Barkeeper Billy. Could you pour me a double right now?"

Jack replied with a weak chuckle. "Truth is," he said, "I don't even like bourbon. Would rather have a Canadian Club any time. I don't suppose you've any of that tucked away at the rear of some box that should be full of new socks?"

Parsons shook his head and Jack became serious. He was a new replacement, an infantry rifleman, and he made us an offer in exchange for a promise.

It turned out that Jack was a former hotel chef, and a good one, if we accepted his own self-appraisal. He offered to prepare one tasteful and nourishing meal each day for us if we, with Bernie's special assistance, could supply him with a few necessities, and if the rest of us, now five in number, brought back to him anything we collected in our mess kits at chow time.

The promise demanded from us was that we reveal to no officer, or anyone else in authority, that he had been a chef. He lived in constant fear that he might be reclassified as an army cook, and was certain that if that happened, his life would be over. He would never again be able to create the culinary masterpieces that were so much a part of his civilian occupation. We all agreed, to both the reason for his fear, and to the promise he asked.

Fred, who had followed Bernie to supply, and become a general handyman, was placed in charge of the cooking fire. He was incredibly strong, and quickly built a ring of stones, such as we'd had in our previous location, then scoured the nearby woods for dry deadwood. We were still close enough to the enemy to make any smoke a danger to us, but with dry wood, carefully tended, a cooking fire could be limited to a minimum of flame and almost no smoke. Fred managed that quite well.

Fritz Manchard helped. He brought an ax one day, and stopped long enough to chop several large tree limbs into firewood. He let Fred do some of that, but kept warning him about the dangers. The wood here was filled with relics from that older war, shrapnel and bullets, and each piece could dull the edge of an irreplaceable cutting tool. We found how true that was. We could have collected a small pile of metal souvenirs from that time of hardships, terror, and death that characterized this place a generation ago. Like most wars, it had never solved the problems of a world longing for something better.

Time and again throughout human history, people who believed themselves deprived, or accepted the half-truths of those who told them they were, decided war was the solution to their problems. The result was invariably more deprivation, more suffering, death and destruction. War, once unleashed, grants no immunity to once-cherished memories of more peaceable times, and soon diminishes the value of any reminders of them. The toys of children become so much rubbish, to be consumed along with the remnants of older moralities. Ethics are generally treated as worthless antiquities.

One of the more insidious effects of war is that every combatant sooner or later is forced to mimic his adversaries, then concoct various fantasies about how much more righteous he is than those evil "others." Each time it happens, the things of war, the weapons, become more horrible. Witness the advent of poison gas in that older war. Once used, everyone had to use it.

War is a hungry beast that must grow or die. In major conflicts, that growth is measured in escalating destructiveness. If we did not avail ourselves of gas this time, we did use flame-throwers that rivaled gas in the horror of their effect on human flesh. Invented by the Germans in World War I and quickly copied by the French, we "improved" them for use in our war. Air power grew from simple wood and fabric constructions to enormous metal giants that could loose millions of tons of explosives on civilian populations, and could create firestorms that would roast alive living women and children by the hundreds of thousands. We had these things, and used them, knowing that if the enemy had them, he'd not be one bit reluctant to return the favor. Modern warfare becomes a series of examples of one-upmanship, until nothing is too cruel, nothing too obscene to become a weapon.

In our present circumstances, we were more concerned with the small things of life, though. Jack Williams had made us an offer in exchange for a promise.

The offer could enormously enhance our appreciation for life. We eagerly accepted, and all agreed to keep the promise.

# 15

## *French Kids, Some Edible Food, and Bobby*

Jack Williams kept his word, and was everything he'd claimed to be as a chef. We stopped eating in the field where the cooks had set up their kitchen. We collected our food, covered our mess kits and immediately returned to our own area, where we handed everything to Jack.

We all contributed what we could to Bernie for use as trade goods. With soap and a little candy from home, he bought potatoes, onions, sometimes a few carrots, and anything else available. Mrs. Manchard even brought some herbs that Jack used to good advantage.

On the days we were issued K rations, those went to Jack, too, after we removed the little pack of four cigarettes in each meal box. These, if we could refrain from smoking them, were hard currency, just as in Paris. They were never prime brands, though, so if we did use any, we learned to tolerate Wings, Congress, Players (an English brand name), and others that had never been seen before, and would likely never be seen again. It seemed that anyone who could get his hands on a cigarette making machine with enough tobacco and cigarette papers could get a cost-plus contract from the government to manufacture smokes.

Most days, we ate well. I regained some of the weight lost back on the Seine, although I still wondered what had ever happened to those oranges. We even shared our good fortune with a few of the kids who showed up. Like the Manchards, they came from the nearby village of St. Gobain, province of Aisne. There were two brothers who became "our" kids, and visited every day. Claude was twelve, and René ten. It was not the food that brought them. France rarely suffered shortages of basic food-stuffs in the small villages and farming communities. Shortages in the cities were from a lack of fuel and transport, rather than the food itself. Nor was it the cigarettes. We had no candy, nor any chewing gum. These kids simply seemed to like our company. Having Bernie on hand as interpreter was a huge bonus, of course.

There was no possibility that we could keep our good fortune altogether quiet. Our sergeants noticed, and one day Jinks stopped with a very young soldier he introduced as "Bobby." Bobby had recently arrived, and would now stay with us, Jinks announced, because no one else was able to care for him as well.

We didn't know what to do, but accepted this strange assignment with as much equanimity as we could manage. Jack looked at the kid and shook his head. "Guess I can do my part," he said, "but sure as hell, I can't do it all. No one can."

Jinks took sergeant Parsons aside and explained to him. Parsons told the rest of us, when an opportunity presented itself. Bobby sat on the ground and stared at nothing. He moved only when he was told to, ate when he was told to. If he needed to relieve himself, he said simply, "Gotta go." One of us would lead him into the woods behind the supply tent for that. He said nothing else and did not offer any evidence that he understood more than a few simple commands.

Bobby was another section eight case, who had been given the "standard" treatment with an assignment to Graves Registration. He looked to be about seventeen, which meant he'd probably lied about his age to join the army. No one bothered to check much when that happened. The draft boards simply used kids like him to fill their quota for the month, while the politicians talked of patriotism and glory.

The problem was that the "treatment" had not worked with Bobby. Perhaps he'd been too young. He'd shut out the world and now existed in a place of infinite horrors within his own consciousness. Nothing outside this registered with him for more than a few seconds. We fed him. Bernie, our self-appointed nurse, saw that Bobby kept reasonably clean, and that was the extent of our ability to care for him. He sat there, day and night, and stared at things none of the rest of us could see, or wanted to see. Claude and René just looked at him and slowly shook their heads.

It was at this time that our supply lines completely broke down. Even K rations failed to show up. The French kids were smart enough to realize what was happening, and René worked the road on his way to us, begging from any GI he saw smoking. He showed up one day with five cigarettes, which he gave to me.

The opportunity to gain a few smokes this way didn't last long. We all searched the ground for discarded butts, from which we removed the tobacco and rolled it in old newspaper scraps to smoke. Some joker, remembering the signs on the roadsides in Normandy that the engineers had posted, saying "mines cleared to hedges," made cardboard signs, tacked to sticks, that read "butts cleared to hedges." At the least, it was evidence that some sense of humor remained.

A few days later Jinks stopped by, ostensibly to check on Bobby, but more to vent his anger with anyone who would listen. He arrived muttering to himself, and when asked what the problem was, declared that one of the men in his charge was the worst "rat faced fucker" he'd ever run into. The guy, he said, had approached him with the saddest eyes and most downtrodden look we could imagine.

"Sergeant," the man had pleaded, "I haven't had a smoke in three days. Do you suppose you could let me have enough tobacco to fill my pipe just once?"

Jinks took out his little Bull Durham sack of carefully hoarded and once-used tobacco remnants. With utmost concern and pity, he'd handed it to the soldier. "Okay, fill your pipe, though I'll be damned if I know where I'll find any more of the stuff." He looked at us. "You know what that miserable excuse for a human being did? Do you know?"

We didn't, of course, so Jinks explained. "He hauled out a thing that looked like a fifty gallon oil drum on a stove pipe. He took more than half of all my tobacco. Then he smiled and thanked me. I'll thank him to stay a mile or more away from me in the future, just in case I remember how I was conned."

He looked at Bobby. "How's the kid doing?" he asked Parsons.

"He's what you see. Not doing much of anything. What's going to happen to him?"

"Damned if I know. There's a rumor around that the Thirtieth is going on the offensive again. They'll need more replacements. I hate to see it happen to the kid, but our hands are tied. We do what we're told to do, and so will he, if he's capable of under-standing what that is. Work with him a little, if you have the time. Maybe you can help." He looked at Bernie, and at me.

We were out of food, but someone, knowing that, had located some abandoned German emergency rations nearby. There was nothing about them that could be called "good," but it was prob-ably better than nothing at all. There was a story around that the German army was the best fed in all of Europe. We learned that this was true, for the front line soldiers. German cooks set up field kitchens right where the fighting was heaviest, and saw to it that their soldiers received hot, nourishing meals, right from the stoves that cooked them. German cooks were frequent casu-alties, but the survivors persisted, and even improvised when the stoves were shot full of holes. A circle of stones and firewood did what was needed, just as we had learned. We didn't have the steaks and roast chicken, the mashed potatoes, vegetables, and freshly baked biscuits that was standard fare for the Germans, but we'd been doing okay while our shredded corned beef and dehydrated potatoes lasted. All it took was something fresh and a guy like Jack Williams to convert army issue slop into edible rations. Even Jack needed the basics, though.

We soon learned that the German army might well have been the best fed in Europe on standard rations, but their emergency food was the poorest. It consisted of a thin, black, watery "soup," that looked as if it were composed of ink from a public school inkwell, back when I was young enough to have one of those in my desk. What little flavor existed in this "ersatz" matter could also have been that of ink. Tins of hard, nearly indigest-ible crackers supplemented the so-called soup, with that in turn supplemented by ersatz "coffee" that was related to real coffee in the same degree that a rotted and broken piece of deadwood might be related to a good baseball bat.

We ate the soup and the crackers and drank the coffee, but there was nothing Jack could do with any of it. Our glory days of good eating were finished, but a couple of days later, we were surprised by a bit of totally unexpected good fortune. Claude and René came in carrying a hot cooking pot, covered with a metal lid and a thick cloth. They grinned when they put it down, and told Bernie "Maman" had sent it. That would be "Mama" in English. We gathered around, and held our mess kits while Jack spooned it out of the pot. The aroma alone was like nothing we'd experienced in a year or more. Jack gave some to Bobby, who poked at it with his spoon.

It was the most delicious stew we could imagine. Bernie and I wolfed down our portions while Claude and René grinned and watched. We did something mean then, something for which we were later ashamed. Claude had told us the meat in this wonderful meal was rabbit. That was okay. We already knew that rabbits were raised throughout this part of Europe as food animals, and were more common than chicken back home.

Bobby had tentatively tasted a very small bite of it. Bernie turned to me and said "You know, this is the best cat I've ever eaten! Wonderful cat."

"Yeah, I've never in my life had better cat," I agreed.

Bobby looked at both of us and put his mess kit on the ground. He was done eating.

Bernie dove for it, and divided the contents between his mess kit and mine. We filled up on our ill-gotten gains while Bobby continued to stare at nothing.

We realized a little later that this was the point in time when we started to lose our values, when what was ethical or moral became confused with what satisfied our bellies or our animal instincts. We did not attempt to excuse such behavior, but we did know, even if marginally, that we were becoming something we would have detested in an earlier time, yet we did not really care.

The rumors about the offensive were true, and Thirtieth Division trucks appeared, with a lieutenant carrying orders for replacements.

Jack picked up his pack and rifle and left. They came for Bobby next. Bernie and I tried to talk to him, but at first he only returned a blank stare.

"You've got to get up," Bernie told him. "You're going back to your company, Bobby."

He shook his head. "No. No gun."

That was true, and it was my responsibility to see that he had one, except I'd been unable to get any. One more failure in our supply system.

I squatted beside Bobby. "Yes, I know you have no gun. There's nothing I can do about that, though. They'll have one for you at division, or at your company. They haven't sent back any battlefield recoveries, so they must be using them there. You'll have a gun, Bobby. I just hope to hell you have it aimed in the right direction when you squeeze the trigger."

He looked at the ground and shook his head. "No." He looked up at me, quite suddenly, with a gleam of rationality, or understanding, in his eyes. His eyes widened. "You know what I did, don't you?"

It was my turn to shake my head. "No, Bobby, I don't know what you did, and I don't think it matters now. You need to get up, grab your pack, and go get on that truck waiting for you right now."

"I shot one of them," he said. "He was close, coming right at me. I didn't aim. I just pointed the gun and shot. I shot him in the mouth." Bobby shook his head. "Horrible. He sank down on his knees, tried to scream, but couldn't. He was suffering. I hate suffering. Couldn't let it go on, so shot him again. Meant to do it in the heart, but didn't aim again, and guess it went through his left lung, kind of high up. Now there was even more bleeding. Bleeding all over the front of him."

Bobby stared at me for a minute. "Had to finish it. Couldn't let it go on. Put the end of the barrel close to his right ear. His helmet had fallen off. Closed my eyes and squeezed. The other side of his head opened up, brains sprayed out. But it was over. I got sick and threw the rifle on the ground. Sat down and cried. That's where they found me."

I could imagine now just a small part of what he was suffering when he withdrew into that inner world of his. He must be seeing, over and over again, that enemy soldier's brains spraying out the other side of his head. Bobby was a child, and children should never have to experience such things. I waited, not wanting to pressure him.

"What?" he asked. "What more do you want? That's it, the end of it. Now you want me to go do it again?"

"No, Bobby," I replied. "I don't want you to do anything. Tell me, though—how old are you?"

His eyes were glazed again. He was losing it, going back into his denial of reality. "Seventeen," he whispered. "So what? It doesn't matter. Nothing matters. No one cares."

"Some of us do, Bobby. But you're going to go with the lieutenant now, see what they can do for you at your company."

He glared at me for the briefest time, then got to his feet just as the lieutenant and two soldiers walked into our area. "Ready to go, soldier?" the lieutenant asked.

Bobby nodded. He wasn't ready for anything, but he did move. "Was that really cat?" he asked me.

"No, Bobby, it was rabbit. Forget about it, will you?"

He nodded, and glanced back once as he stepped out onto the road beside the truck waiting for him. There was room for just one more.

Our own orders came two days later. We expected them. There was no way we could be useful this far back when the division was moving steadily ahead.

Claude and René knew almost as soon as we did, maybe a little before. René told Bernie that Maman would make us a pie, that he'd bring it in the morning.

That afternoon, I sat on a log and wondered what I could possibly say to these kids that might make life a little easier for them in the future. I'd known for some time that they had no father. He'd died a few years ago. I didn't know the cause of death, but that never seemed to be very important. The kids had their mother, and they had each other, and that was it. René had attached himself to me, and I believed he looked at me as a sort of father/older brother figure, or maybe just a father. Claude was two years older than René, and seemed to fill that role adequately. I just didn't know what to do.

René jumped up into my lap, put his arms around my neck, and sobbed. My French vocabulary consisted of about ten words, but even those seemed unnecessary. I knew how he felt, and he knew there was nothing that could be done about it. I just held him close and rocked back and forth until he was able to control his crying and stop.

We were roused at four the next morning to load up. Since we'd been expecting it, most of our few supplies were already packed and ready. We struck the tent, loaded what we had, plus the machinegun, and made our usual bench from the ammo boxes.

Just as we pulled out of the forest road onto the paved highway, Bernie and I saw a small kid trudging toward us, with a covered pie pan in his hands. We waved to him.

# 16

# *Non-combat Casualties*

This move, like the last one, was a long haul. We were well inside Belgium when the trucks pulled off the road to a spot on the side of a small hill. At the crest, about a hundred feet above the road, the dirt track turned right to parallel a stone wall. An opening in the wall let us into our new "home."

It was the end of October. Back in the Argonne, autumn had come on with a gentleness we now missed. Here, there was a raw dampness in the air, maybe because we were both farther north and closer to the frigid North Sea. The trucks stopped, and we manhandled the folded supply tent halfway down the hill and set it up. The cooks set up a hundred yards away, closer to the paved road and at the foot of the hill. Company HQ was near the stone wall, and we were soon surprised by the arrival of battalion HQ, which shared space with our company. We had communicated with battalion supply many times. All of our orders went through them. Now, for the first time, we shared the same physical space. It was, in general, a good experience. They understood our problems, as we did theirs.

The entire First Army, it seemed, moved forward in fits and starts. Replacements continued to arrive, but transport was unavailable to take them farther. Rainy days, freezing nights, and sucking mud became the norm, bringing with them an all-encompassing misery. Each of us, in his own way, did his best to stay dry and find a little warmth, something nearly impossible. Every day magnified the discomforts of the previous day.

There was little to do as far as my weapons work was concerned. New arrivals had theirs, along with the basic ammo load. The detritus of war lay scattered about the area, and my prime concern was in how to dispose of an enormous variety of unexploded shells, grenades, and miscellaneous ammunition, for which we had no matching weaponry. With the help of some "volunteers," we made a natural pit in the woods deeper and wider. We dropped all the potentially dangerous materiel in the hole and covered it with dirt.

I spent much of my time with Parsons, doing what we could without dependable supplies in the matter of blankets, coats, and dry socks. Shoes were a major concern. Because they were always wet, the leather soon began to rot and fall apart. We could not get enough replacements for them.

We reached a point where there were two thousand of us, just as it had been on the bank of the Seine. All those feet tramping back and forth turned our entire area into a sea of viscous, sloppy mud. It became deep enough to reach above our knees and halfway up our thighs. Only with great effort could we drag one foot after the other to reach any destination.

Our food was better than the German emergency rations, but not by any great measure. It got so we'd eat once every other day. The work involved in going to the mess area and returning was simply more than the food was worth.

A messenger came down from the HQ tent one day, and specifically asked for the armorer. I was told to report to Colonel Hansfeld at battalion supply. I'd never heard of him, but slogged and squished my way to the tent and reported. Daniels, our battalion supply sergeant, was standing next to a desk—a real, genuine desk—on a floor of wooden planks a step above the mud.

He smiled at me. "This is colonel Hansfeld," he said, and nodded to a lieutenant colonel seated at the desk and smoking a cigar. He was a big man, although not the least bit fat, with deep blue eyes and close-cropped blond hair.

Sergeant Daniels turned to him. "Corporal Spooner, armorer for the 480th," he said.

The colonel stared at me as if I were a small stuffed trophy animal. "Armorer, right?" he asked.

"Yes, sir," I replied.

"Got an assignment for you, corporal."

"Yes, sir?"

"I need a pair of handguns—special handguns. I want you to get them for me."

"The only handguns I can get, sir, are the M1911 Colt .45. And I can't get those now. Supply has been out of them for several weeks, as Sergeant Daniels can tell you."

"Hell, corporal, that's not what I want. I've got one of those things. What I need is a pair of pearl-handled revolvers, with holsters, just like General Patton wears all the time. He's got them, so they must be available. And I want them chambered for the .45, same ammo as the M1911, with a good supply of the half-moon clips so they'll fit the revolver. Got that? When can I have them?"

I shook my head. "There's no way in the world I can get something like that, sir. I'm sure General Patton bought his privately."

He blew cigar smoke in my direction. "The hell you say. You know where I just came from, corporal?"

"No, sir."

"Just got here from Burma, where I served on Vinegar Joe Stillwell's staff." He pointed the cigar at me. "In Burma, when I asked an enlisted man to do something for me, he damn well did it, and without any pissant excuses. You get my point, corporal?"

This guy was beginning to remind me altogether too much of the "mad major" of Southampton. Except, he was a rank higher, and the mud here was worse. It was pretty obvious that sergeant Daniels had been totally buffaloed by the colonel's bullying. I wasn't, and really didn't much give a damn.

"I'm not making any excuse, sir. I'm only stating that what you're asking is impossible."

"Is it, now? You don't have any direct connections with the Colt company? You couldn't pull a few strings and have them send you a pair of those beautiful pearl-handled pieces? What the hell kind of an armorer are you?"

The guy was really beginning to irk me. "I'm a well-trained armorer, sir. I'm just not one who has any special connections, as you put it."

He waved the cigar. "You people around here are pitiful. You don't have any conception at all about how to fight a war." He pointed the cigar again. "Get the hell out of here, before I decide you need a transfer to the worst and most dangerous assignment I can find."

I left, stepping off the wooden floor into the mud once more. I hoped the colonel would find a place, very soon, where he'd be able to test his "conception" of warfare at very close quarters.

The weather worsened, just when we thought that was impossible. Rain poured down steadily during each day. At night, it froze, so by morning everything and everybody had a coating of ice. Our first sergeant came to the supply tent with a length of stovepipe and a five-gallon tin that had held dehydrated potatoes. He and sergeant Parsons converted the pieces into a makeshift stove. There was, however, no fuel, nothing anywhere around that was dry enough to burn. They settled for old rags soaked in gasoline stolen from the kitchen. It burned too fast and too hot. The "stove" exploded, blowing off the door. But the stovepipe got warm from the glowing remains of the rags, and we hung our boots near it during the night. By morning, they were still damp, but not as cold.

From a hay field at the top of the hill, I gathered material on which to lie down and try to sleep. It, too, was damp, but body heat helped to partially dry it, just as it did our socks. Those were never removed, until they were practically welded to our feet. Any spares we'd once had were long gone, used up and discarded. The hay in time sank into the mud, as did everything else not buoyant enough to float in brown earthen soup.

Sickness came soon enough. We had no doctor here, but the medic and litter bearers did what they could. They walked the area each morning and looked for men too sick to stand. These, they put on litters and carried them to the dirt path at the side of the area. No ambulance could reach us. We heard that even the tanks had stopped, defeated by mud. Only a two and a half ton "Jimmy," with all six wheels driving, could get through. The sick were loaded into the back and taken to a field hospital. Before long, two trucks came every day.

You'd see the sick ones in the mornings, some lying in ice-covered water on the ground, some sitting, wrapped in a blanket that was soaking wet and glazed with ice, the man shaking, shivering, and in many cases near death.

Basic sanitation became history. Rain-filled straddle trenches dug uphill overflowed, making streams of urine-colored ice water that ran down past, and frequently into, the shallow foxholes. Turds and toilet paper floated down with it. Litter bearers picked men out of the filth and took them to the next available truck.

Our small company truck, with food supplies, bogged down one night at the break in the stone wall. Four of us worked until three in the morning, shoving logs and stones under the rear wheels, all to no avail. The four rear wheels, even when all were in gear, were no match for the mud. One reason was that the tires were only singles. The Jimmies had duals on all the rear wheels, giving them double the traction, plus front wheels that also could be put into gear. Our driver eventually called for help. A two and a half Jimmy came, with a winch and steel cable on the front. He drove past our truck and over the stone wall, hitched a tow cable to our truck, the winch cable to a large oak tree, and with six wheels driving and a winch pulling, and our own driver doing what our small truck could do to help, the Jimmy pulled it out. We went back to our tents covered in mud and thoroughly soaked.

There was just one benefit from the daily rain. The Germans were sending their V1 "buzz bombs" past us and on the way to England or other targets every day. They did not allow for the loss in "lift" from damp air, and we watched many V1s lose altitude until they hit the ground and blew up. It was a large explosion, because what the V1 amounted to was a three hundred pound bomb fitted to a jet-propelled small drone airplane. Going past, or over us, it sounded like a Model T Ford with its engine firing on three cylinders instead of four.

Someone somewhere up the chain of command decided we needed, more than anything else, a little something to boost our morale. It couldn't hurt, at least. So each day another truck came grinding its way through the mud, with a unique offer to any who wished to take advantage of it. We'd be taken to the nearby city of Huy, where a special company had set up a laundry and hot shower installation.

I went at the first opportunity, and found out that a hot shower and clean, dry clothes were something that belonged in a soldier's vision of heaven, once lost and now recovered. We'd had no shower or bath in five months. We'd been wearing the same clothes for three months. We were sick, exhausted, filthy, and we stank.

The "drill" was that we put any personal stuff in a cloth bag supplied, to take with us but keep away from the water. After that, we stripped—everything, including shoes. We were handed a bar of soap and a towel, then pointed at a shower. They were all within individual stalls, and we walked to them on "duck boards," narrow strips of lumber fastened closely together on crosspieces to keep them above the concrete floor. We showered, we dried, and went to the end of this unit, where clean, warm clothes waited for us. They were not our own, but that didn't really matter. Care was taken to give us the correct sizes. Clean and dry and warm were the properties that made them pieces of magic on a world unfit for human occupation. We went back in the same truck, knowing that a degree of sanity did exist here. Our showers and clean clothes were a sign of it.

We now had to get out of the weather, out of the mud and rain and ice and, very soon, the snow. There was nothing unique in our situation. All along our front, the same conditions existed. Winter was on us, and to meet even a minimum level of effectiveness, the army needed to find shelter.

The toll in sickness climbed steadily. The combat divisions on the line were losing as many men from disease as from enemy fire. When, at long last, we were informed that we were moving into winter quarters, twelve hundred of our two thousand had been hauled off to a hospital. Pneumonia was the most common problem. Trench foot was a close second, with many suffering from both ailments. Some died here, some on the way to the field hospital, some after they arrived there, but almost all who received treatment early enough recovered. We were never informed of the final count. Eight hundred quiet, exhausted survivors gathered what we could salvage and rode the trucks to, hopefully, something better.

We had several different destinations, some going to join a division as replacements, we ourselves headed for an unknown, but surely better, place to live for a while.

Many of the trucks were new. Nearly all of the tires were. Obviously, the problem with the rubber workers had been settled, and they must have been going straight out, twenty-four hours a day, to catch up.

We'd been in that place just thirty days. When we left, our casualty rate was sixty percent, without a shot ever having been fired at us or by us.

# 17

# *Rest and Recovery*

We huddled in the back of the truck, shelter halves drawn over us against a cold wind, and did not at first see the long, steep hill down which the truck rolled. Curiosity took command, and we poked our heads out to take a look around.

This was the town of Stavelot. The road was paved and reasonably good, even if it threatened to be treacherous in ice or snow. At the bottom of the hill was another good road that went left or right. Beyond, we could see glimpses of a small river. It seemed a pleasant little place, projecting a sense of welcome and friendship. We hoped this was true.

We did not go all the way down the hill, although trucks ahead of us did, or nearly so. Ours turned right onto a side street and stopped after just a few feet. We were in front of the basement of a two-story red brick school. This was a hillside community, the buildings constructed with the lower levels facing a side street, the upper floors looking at the main road on the hill. The school appeared solid and comforting after the time we'd spent outside in far from ideal conditions.

Parsons was in the cab with the driver. Three "volunteers" rode the ammo boxes with me in the rear. Bernie was not one of them, and I missed him. He'd been shipped to a different destination when we left the place of mud, ice, pneumonia, and trench foot. We were now attached to the Fourth Infantry Division, an outfit with which we'd served briefly back in France. They were here now, in eastern Belgium, not more than fifteen miles from the border of Germany. We were getting close, getting very close. The Fourth was a good division, one of the best. An infantry-man was waiting at the door to what could only have been the janitor's quarters for the school. He handed Parsons a set of keys and left.

When we went inside, we found paradise. There was a comfortable office with toilet facilities, another smaller room beyond, with a window through which we could look at the street. In both rooms there was a small cast iron, potbellied stove. The faucet worked and the toilet flushed. God, what luxury! From a few articles left behind, it was apparent this had been used as an aid station by the Fourth. Across the entrance hallway was a garage, empty now. It had large doors on the street, and was ideal for our ammo storage and a place to unload supplies, if we eventually received them. At the rear was another large room where I could keep any weapons on hand, and do my armorer's work, if I could manage to rig some sort of light. There was no electricity, the one drawback.

We unloaded and my "volunteers" went down the street to join the other replacements. Parsons made the larger room his office and bedroom. I was given the smaller one, ample for my needs. We settled in and organized our schedules, created a makeshift desk for Parsons and a similar workbench for me. We looked around for something to burn in the stoves. Fuel was scarce, and we settled for torn up cartons and whatever else might work. We'd have no lasting fires, but the two stoves, even burning paper, would quickly reduce the morning or evening chill. A large bucket was found and used to heat water for washing, shaving, and laundry. We'd discovered "home" and were as happy about it as possible in the circumstances.

Farther down the road, on the other side, was another, larger school. It was here that company HQ set up, on the first floor. Classrooms in the floors above became a temporary home for the replacements. Another building, across a courtyard, was a multiple garage, four units plus an area at the end for maintenance work. This became the kitchen and mess hall.

It took only a couple of days for the kids to show up. Three of them came around, curious at first, later looking for candy or gum, if we had it, and later still just stopping in and talking to us, as had the kids in the Argonne. These were all a little older, though. The boy was Ivan, which he wrote as "Yvan." He was thirteen, and lived just three houses down on the hill road, which we now knew was "Rue de Spa." Léone, also thirteen, lived across the street. Hèléne was twelve and lived a few houses away on this same street.

We learned from these kids. Belgium was a nation with two languages and two cultures. This part of the country was Walloon, the people descended from French refugees who had fled their country during some ancient war and settled here. Walloon was also a French dialect, and their primary language. The other was Flemish, related in some ways to Dutch and other tongues of the northern countries. I recalled reading somewhere that Flemish had once been considered for use as an international language. It was easy to learn, and had almost no irregularities. In the voting, it lost by a very slim margin to Esperanto, an artificial tongue created to serve as the "lingua franca" of world commerce.

The three kids spoke Walloon, but knew Flemish well enough, and all of them were studiously learning English. Yvan also spoke German. It was pure joy to talk to these kids, and rarely was there any difficulty in making ourselves understood, or in understanding them. That was true for me, at least. Others, who had no aptitude for languages, or just never wanted to learn, might have a few problems.

We quickly realized that Belgium, or at least this part of it, was the most openly friendly place we'd seen yet. There was a movie theater in town, where ancient American films were screened, most old cowboy shoot-em-ups. We could go there any evening for a show, and the proprietor insisted that we were not allowed to pay. We could use almost any public service without charge, such as buses, but they were rare. The single exception to this open-handedness was a drink in the local pub or barroom. Here, it cost us five cents for a full pint of great beer.

Supplies began to reach us regularly, and worn out clothing was soon exchanged for new. Even the PX truck appeared, with cigarettes, tobacco, candy and gum for sale at ridiculously low prices, although there had been a recent increase in cigarettes from five to six cents a pack. We made our young friends happy with chewing gum. This was a novelty throughout Europe, and something every kid seemed to want and enjoy more than anything else we could offer them.

More important than any of that, and a boost to our morale at least equal to the shower and warm clothes in Huy, mail arrived, some of it over a month old. I had many letters from home, most expressing wonder why they had not heard from me in such a long time. There were two packages, containing home-made cookies, bath soap, and small items such as a new comb and, in one, a thoughtful gift of two packages of cough drops, something the army never considered as anything other than a luxury.

Best of all, there were five letters from Kay. In the one dated last, she had moved to England, but as yet had no permanent address. There was a temporary one I could use for a letter, something like our own APO (Army Post Office) numbers. There was so much I wanted to tell her, and so much I couldn't because the censor would not allow it to pass. She'd filled her letters with expressions of love and hope, and in about every other one a beautiful poem. I'd not been exposed to nearly enough verse in school or at home, and determined to correct that situation as soon as it was possible. I did try my hand at it, and managed a few lines I thought Kay might like, but was it poetry? There was so much to learn!

Kay's letters brought home to me a feeling of almost irreparable loss, a longing so great it hurt physically. This could be soothed only by her presence, only by holding her in my arms once more and trying to find words for something we knew was real, yet at this time lay far beyond our ability to express in terms that had current meaning.

Every woman on earth, I decided, was beautiful. There were simply different kinds and degrees of beauty. Some had beautiful features, others an attractive body, still more a great personality, or sense of compassion, or numerous other different qualities. Personal attractiveness, that magnetism we called love, was a combination of these, in varying amounts and in a blend that exactly suited our personal conception of the ideal. That's what Kay was to me: the perfectly balanced blend of all that I believed was ideally suited to my own character. The wait for this war to end and the opportunity for us to become one would be filled with anxieties and sometimes irrational hopes. I wanted time to pass much more quickly. Meanwhile, the best

I could do was to develop this friendship with some wonderful kids, just as I had in the Argonne with Claude and René.

As we settled in more fully, it almost seemed that the war was a thousand miles away and of little consequence to us. This was a nice feeling, but the reality was that the front line was only a mile distant, just the other side of the river. All was quiet, though—no artillery banging away, no hurried efforts to get more truckloads of replacements sent forward. We guessed that the Germans must be settling in for the winter, just as we were.

Now and then a V1 "buzz bomb" flew over, just to shatter our complacency and remind us of where we were and why we were here. If it were raining, as it sometimes was, one of them would hit the monastery on top of the hill behind us. The monks who lived there had adapted to this, and we understood that they lived only on the other side of the large, stone building. The damage done was usually a few windows shattered in the town, from the force of the explosion. Those huge stones with which the monastery itself had been built were nearly impervious to harm from such crude weaponry. When the weather conditions were right (or wrong) we expected a few booms and rattled windows. Our usual comment was, "another one that won't find its target."

The kids began to visit daily, at almost any hour, and Yvan was there one evening when First Sergeant Edgars stopped in with a bottle to share with Parsons. Edgars was not a "fishhead," as Sam Grollin had been, but first sergeants usually made an effort to stay close to their top three graders, if they were in any way compatible. In our company, these were Parsons in supply, Tompkins the Mess Sergeant, and Furman who ran company headquarters. The rest of us were of lower, company rank. Enlisted men in a company needed to trust their first-three-grade sergeants, and the sergeants needed to both trust each other and know the problems each might be having. A lot of this could be learned in a quiet evening with a shared bottle.

I stayed in my room, washing out some socks and hanging them near the stove to dry. Yvan was here this evening because he'd brought us a bundle of firewood. Parsons called out and asked me to help them with something. I went to his room. He and the First Sergeant were trying to make Yvan understand what they wanted, but not doing a good job of it. Edgars had learned that there was a bakery in town, and that it made bread every night for distribution the next day. He and Parsons had decided that a loaf of freshly baked bread would be a good accompaniment to the bottle they were trying to drain. They wanted Yvan to go get one for them.

Yvan was clear enough about what they wanted, but the bakery made several kinds of bread, and he couldn't seem to make the sergeants understand that. "Quelque coleur?" he asked in Walloon, and got nothing but puzzled looks in response. That's when Parsons called me. Yvan looked at me and switched to German, "Welche Farbe?" and I understood immediately—"What color?"

"White," Parsons and Edgars answered together.

"Weiss," I told Yvan. Problem solved.

I picked up a rifle and followed Yvan out into the night. The bakery was about a half mile away, and we passed through a blackout screen when we went in. The place was busy, with seven or eight men working to make the next day's bread. Yvan explained to one of them what we wanted. He wrapped a fresh, warm loaf in a sheet of yesterday's newspaper and handed it to me. There were a few Belgian francs in my pocket, and I tried to pay for it, but Yvan said they would not take any money. With a smile and a nod, I told them "Merci," which I guessed was the same in Walloon as in French, and we went back to Parsons and Edgars. They enjoyed the bread.

The First Sergeant seemed to be satisfied that supply and the armory, such as it was, were in good shape. He left about midnight, and the next day a new replacement showed up to help us. Sent by Edgars, he was qualified for the supply work, and enough of a handyman to assist with anything on which I might need help. He was Ed Lammond, a tank driver whose unit was attached to the Fourth, just as we were. His tank had been knocked out, and he'd been wounded badly enough to spend some time in a field hospital, then came here, to Stavelot.

Ed had a great sense of humor, reminding me of Bernie in that respect, although Ed was tall. In civilian life, he'd worked with his father in a family business that installed and serviced vending machines. Most of them dispensed soft drinks, but Ed told us they were not averse to doing a little work on slot machines that some of the illegal gambling houses owned, or on the new dispensers of packaged food. Anything that would make a buck and was reasonably honest, he said. We became good friends.

For the moment, Ed was stuck here. He seemed to enjoy working with us and being temporarily away from all that reminded him of his recent wound and loss of the tank. Slowly at first, he talked a little of his experiences.

Although it was not the encounter that had destroyed his tank, and nearly him, he related an earlier affair when he thought he was as good as dead. The lead tank in his group had punched through a hedgerow and he was close behind, with the others following him. It was the kind of situation extremely dangerous for our tanks. If the Germans could knock out the lead tank, or even the next, while half way through the hedgerow, they'd have created a "stopper" that would bottle up the others while they were exposed and vulnerable. From a good position and with the right gun, each tank could be destroyed in turn.

The gun, Ed and his crew discovered, was a Gerlich gun. It was located at the top of a small hill, from which it fired, then vanished beyond the crest, out of any line of fire from the clustered tanks. I was perhaps one of the few here in Stavelot who knew what a Gerlich gun was. I'd studied it for a day at Aberdeen. The Gerlich was a Swedish invention, first offered for sale to the U.S. Army, and when they refused it, to the Germans, who bought a number of them.

Basically, this was a heavy, two-man rifle. It was a single shot weapon, and the second man on the team normally carried the ammunition. The barrel of the gun was tapered inside, from 28 millimeters to 20 millimeters. The projectile it fired had fins around it, which compressed as it traveled down the barrel. There was a hardened steel core, to make it armor piercing. It had a tremendous "punch," derived from its muzzle velocity, the highest known of any widely used firearm. That "bullet" traveled at eight thousand feet per second. That's over a mile and a half while you count "one."

Ed's tank was broadside to the position of the Gerlich. The Sherman had three inches of steel armor, and along each side near the bottom was a large plate measuring another three inches in thickness. This was designed to protect the tank's ammunition, which was stored there. Ed said he looked down, and with each "thunk" of a Gerlich projectile hitting, that extra three inches of armor bulged in, menacing their own 75-milli-meter shells. In other words, from two hundred yards away, the Gerlich was almost penetrating six inches of steel armor plate. Any safety margin was frighteningly small. All he could think about was that if the Germans simply raised their sights a foot or two, his tank would soon have enough holes in it to qualify for use as a gravel screen. This was not at all reassuring.

The gunner turned the turret and tried to get a fix on the position of the Germans, but they kept moving. When the other tanks, from slightly different angles, started firing, the Gerlich gun and its crew vanished for good.

This was the one "war story" Ed was not reluctant to relate. For the rest of it, he was as reticent as any battle-weary infan-tryman.

The quality of our food steadily improved, and one day a spe-cial truck arrived. It carried all the "fixings" for a traditional Thanksgiving dinner. The next day, the cooks presented us with a much-appreciated reminder of home, and the majority of us thought about things for which we might be thankful. There were enough of them. Just being alive probably topped the list.

# 18

## *Time Out*

The front remained quiet, and Army HQ, in an inexplicable burst of sensitivity to the plight of the average soldier, reached a unique decision. On a rotating basis, a few at a time would be allowed twenty-four hour passes to visit any community of their choice within a reasonable travel distance.

Ed and I each applied for one of the passes, and they were granted. We decided to go together to Verviers, fifteen miles away and the nearest city of any size. We had no idea how we'd get there, what we'd do, or how to get back. That was secondary to the fact that we'd be allowed to get away. Not since my company had left Ireland, seven months ago, had I been given a day, or even an hour, off duty. It had been nearly as long for Ed. We existed, day after day, beneath a smothering blanket of duty and regulations.

Soldiers in a combat zone, or close to one, lived in a virtual prison, never permitted to move beyond a designated area. The psychological effect was enough to make borderline psychos of all of us. Ed and I started walking. The Ardennes Forest on each side of the road looked endless, a thing of vast, somber beauty with its evergreens accented by snow on the ground beneath them. Ed looked at me, and I looked at him. We grinned foolishly as tears streamed down our faces. This was an altogether unexpected reaction, and made us aware of just how long and to what an extent we'd been held captive by our own organizations. Now released for twenty-four hours, we were as giddy as a pair of teenage girls on their first date.

Sergeant Parsons had expressed his displeasure about our decision to take the passes. He'd outlined a formidable list of duties he could not hope to manage alone, and let us know we'd be placing an impossible burden on him when we left. We still took the passes, and urged Parsons to take one when we returned, but he was completely unresponsive to this idea. Both Ed and I felt an inner desperation to escape, if just for a day, the monotony and the pressures of military life.

Grinning all the way, we hiked to Malmedy, the next town. We never felt the road. Between it and our boots was a foot of crisp, clean air. We did not go into the town, but followed the road as it turned left toward Spa and then continued on to Verviers. Traffic was light, but it did exist. Now and then a truck passed us.

"Want to try for a ride?" Ed asked.

"Sure," I replied. "It's going to be a long walk if we have to hoof it all the way." When the next truck approached, I held out my thumb in the hitchhiker's request for a lift. The truck stopped, the driver asked where we were headed, and said he could drop us off on the outskirts of Verviers. We climbed aboard, in the back. The canvas sides were rolled up, the slat benches along each side were down. We pulled up the collars of our jackets against the wind and watched the scenery slide past.

A strange thing about soldiers in, or near, a combat zone was that the war itself was rarely a topic of conversation. We lived very much in the moment. The future was far too uncertain to talk about it, and we never knew what the generals might be planning anyway. It was almost as if there were two wars: the one with all the plans and little colored blocks representing divisions that the commanders pushed around, and the one lived by the enlisted men and company officers. Ours was the real war. Everything above and beyond us was make believe, a piece of fantasy created by the powers-that-be, and never real until a few thousand soldiers had died so that those little blocks on the great plans could be moved a trifle. It was grossly unfair, but it was the way things were. We would never change any part of it. We didn't know how.

So, it was with genuine surprise that I listened to Ed when he asked what I thought about the war as a whole.

"What do you mean?" I asked. "Like why we're here, and what we're supposed to accomplish before it all ends?"

"Yeah, something like that, but more about the forces that combined to create this situation in the first place. It was all political, you know."

"Isn't everything, when you come right down to it?" I responded. "It's a problem I have sometimes, even on a local level. I don't think any government works as it should for very long. They all need change. If that change is in the right direction, all people benefit. But if it's not going as it should, it's very often too late by the time we realize what's happening. Still, I don't have any good answer to it all. Do you?"

Ed thought for a minute. "No, I don't suppose so. I've probably seen more graft and corruption in government than you ever did, and it makes me pretty mad sometimes that I'm over here, getting ready to die, to preserve all of that. My Dad's business ran on kickbacks and bribes. He expected it, and I came to expect it, too. But why in hell should that be the case, when all we did was install and service vending machines?"

"And a few illegal slots, if what you told me was true." I added.

"Oh, that was true, but it never amounted to a large part of our work. We did it because it gave us a little added cash to pay the bribes and kickbacks. You can't grease a politician's hand and then write it off as a business expense. They don't want records of everything they do. What I want, and would like to see if I live through this madness, is some basic changes in the way things are done. We have a democracy, and that's one of the better systems around today, but like all the rest, it becomes a victim of the people who take charge and manipulate everything to their own advantage."

"So," I asked, "what would you suggest to make things better? Anarchy?"

"It's a possibility, but not likely to happen. Have you read Thoreau?"

This whole conversation was awakening a new appreciation for the way Ed thought and the depth of his character. We lived in a world far too shallow, knowing only that we had to follow orders and do the best we could if we were to eventually get out of this situation and go home. "Yes. I hadn't gotten around to Walden yet, but I read Thoreau's On The Duty of Civil

Disobedience," I said. "I liked it, but can't say I saw anything practical in it for our present times. I'm not even sure it would have worked when he was alive. The main purpose seems to have been to stir things up, to make people think a little, and with that I can agree. I also agree with his maxim, 'that government is best which governs least.' In a very small way, I practiced civil disobedience when I was drafted into the army."

Ed looked interested. "How?" he asked.

"I never took the oath of allegiance to the military."

"How'd you get away with that?"

"I didn't believe in the war, although I was not the least bit impressed by the antics of the isolationists, those 'America First' people. So, when the sergeant at the induction center read the oath, and all the others in the group, about thirty of us, repeated it after him, I said nothing. No one noticed. I did hold my hand about halfway up, but I never said the words."

Ed laughed. "And what difference has that ever made?"

I shook my head and laughed a little. "Not one damn bit, and the army was actually very good to me, as far as sending me where I wanted to go and giving me the training I asked for."

We rode in silence for a few minutes. Eventually, Ed spoke again. "What do you think of socialism?"

"From the little I know about it, I don't think it's so bad. Communism is something I could never buy into. The idea of the government owning all means of production seems to just open the doors for more and greater political corruption."

"Like the Soviet Union," Ed added.

"Sure. What are they trying to prove? Back off from that extreme, to a socialist system, where the government controls basic industries, but owns nothing, and it might work, maybe better than a democracy that's riddled with self-serving politicians and corruption."

"So you'd favor what Germany has under Hitler?"

"No, of course not. Look at what the Nazi party has brought them to: a two-front war they can't win, hardships for the civilian population, and a brutally repressive system of secret police, home invasions, and, by our standards, lawlessness."

Ed smiled, but it was not a happy smile. He shook his head. "Don't you know what 'Nazi' stands for?"

"I didn't know it stood for anything but itself. And come to think of it, I've never seen a Nazi, and never met anyone who has. If they rule Germany, and are such a danger to the rest of the world, where are they?"

The truck slowed and stopped. The driver got out and came back to talk to us. "You guys just need to take the road on your left here, and walk about a mile to the center of Verviers. We're going straight ahead. Glad we could help, and good luck."

He returned to the cab, where he watched in the rear view mirror while we climbed down and began to walk. At least half of the road was a gentle incline, leading down into a valley between wooded highlands. Just beyond the city, we could see a river, until we were closer to the center of Verviers, when buildings blocked that view.

There was a sort of central square, with roads forming a large rectangle. We saw, on the short street at the right end of the rectangle, a barroom or pub. We needed directions and suggestions, and went there first. It was filled with locals, drinking beer at the bar. I asked if anyone spoke English.

One man turned to us. "Oui, monsieur, but joost a liddle. You want speak to man at Woolworth's."

Woolworth's? Where were we, back home? I thanked him and we went outside to find a Woolworth's. This was not difficult; it was on one of the longer streets, no more than fifty yards from the pub.

The manager saw us enter the store, and while we gawked around at the things for sale here, he approached. He spoke perfect English. "Welcome to Verviers," he said. "You have just arrived in town?"

"Yes," we both said at once.

"Then you will wish to know where you might stay, what there is to see, and where you might purchase some food. Yes?"

"Yes."

"You have Belgian francs?"

"Some," I said. I looked at the lunch counter, where a few customers were sitting and drinking—coffee? That would be good. "A coffee and sandwich is possible?"

"Certainly. The young lady at the counter does understand some English, but I'd be glad to place your order for you." He did, and told us not to leave until he'd had a chance to speak further with us.

This was so totally unexpected, we were flabbergasted. A Woolworth's, with an English-speaking manager, in the middle of a war-torn country recently occupied by German troops? And with food and drink to sell? We shook our heads in disbelief.

The coffee was ersatz, but it was hot and not too bad. The sandwiches were adequate. We finished with a doughnut, probably the best part of the meal.

True to his word, the manager appeared as we finished. "Was everything satisfactory?" he asked.

We nodded. "Yes, yes."

"Now, let me tell you what you might consider for the rest of the day. How long will you be here? Overnight?"

We nodded, but with just a tiny bit of misgiving. This guy, as friendly as he was, had recently been serving German troops, and probably making them feel at home, too.

He might have been reading our minds. "The Germans are all gone," he said. "And happily, for us. There is a small club just down this street, where you might enjoy the entertainment and have a drink. Featured is a young woman who does a strip tease. Americans are welcome there. Unfortunately, some of them become overly boisterous and must be asked to leave. Please do not become one of those."

We assured him we would not.

"Now," he continued, "as to accommodations for the night. You should see Madame Fleury for that. She is diagonally across the square, at number seventeen, on the second floor. Ring the bell at the front door, but not yet. She is at work, and will be home after seventeen thirty—that's five thirty for you—or in about an hour. Tell her I sent you over. Her English is not so good, but say to her that Monsieur Jacobs sent you. She'll understand. I wish you bon chance, and hope you enjoy your visit here." He shook hands with us, turned around, and went back to an office at the rear of the store. He'd been very helpful, maybe too helpful. We suspected, and looked for, some ulterior motive. Maybe it just wasn't there—didn't exist. If so, was all of Belgium as friendly as the people here and in Stavelot?

We went back to the pub for a glass of beer, then crossed the street to find Madame Fleury. She was just unlocking the front door when we walked up the steps. We told her Mr. Jacobs had sent us. "Oh, oui," she said. "Please to come inside." She led the way up a flight of stairs and unlocked another door. Inside was a small but immaculate apartment.

While she put her coat away, we stood and looked around, a little nervous and with our weapons still slung on our shoulders. This was the kitchen. In front, before a window facing the street, was a tiny sitting area with two chairs and a table. At the end of a hallway to the rear was the toilet. On each side of the hall was a door opening to a bedroom.

Madame Fleury was a middle-aged woman, probably forty to forty-five, with gray hair, a trim figure, and a nice, if somehow sad, smile. She was well dressed, and I guessed she may have lost her husband in the war, but managed to find a place for herself in some local business office.

"You go to club?" she asked.

"Yes," we replied.

"Leave fusi here. You not need." The "fusi" were our weapons.

Again, we had some misgivings, but left the rifle and carbine standing in a corner near the door. I removed my cartridge belt and held it over one of the chairs. "Ici?" I asked.

She nodded. "Oui." She looked at Ed. "Oui. You also. No need." She smiled and handed me a key. "Please to come back soon," she said. "I sleep not late in morning, go to bed soon. Please to come before half twenty-two...um, half past nine. I have for you small wine and little pan."

Pan, I knew, was bread. She must be planning to give us a bedtime snack of some sort, maybe biscuits and jelly, with some wine.

We used the toilet and prepared to leave. Ed and I looked at each other, at the weapons in the corner, and shrugged. "I'm okay with this," I said. "Are you?" He nodded and we left.

It was probably against all regulations to leave our weapons at Madame Fleury's, but if we couldn't trust her, there was no point in staying at her house for the night. We went to the club and found it crowded, about half of the customers American servicemen. None of them had a weapon, so we relaxed a little, found a small table against a wall with two chairs, and ordered beers.

It wasn't long until a piano player, a middle-aged man, sat and ran through an introductory piece for the feature attraction. She was young, nineteen or twenty, and a little overweight by our standards. This appeared to prove that not all places occupied by the German Army suffered from food shortages. Still, she moved well, and went into a dance routine obviously intended to be provocative. Ed and I ordered another beer and watched, interested but hardly enthralled. Perhaps we were too close to the tiny stage on which the girl performed.

What we noticed, that may have escaped the attention of others sitting farther away, was the total lack of any expression on the girl's face. Stony-faced and silent, she went through her paces while the piano player looked only at his music. She would bump and grind and shimmy as she removed her clothing one piece at a time, with never a hint of a smile, even an artificial one. She never pretended to like what she did. The Americans sitting at other tables hooted and yelled. "Take it off," they screamed, and graduated from that to shouted obscenities. It was not pleasant to hear, and we recalled what Jacobs at the Woolworth's had told us about Americans becoming boisterous. We also remembered our promise to him, and remained silent throughout the girl's performance.

At the end, the girl stopped with tiny panties and a filmy bra still in place. She scooped up the rest of her clothes and disappeared through a door at the rear of the stage, her expression one of infinite sadness. Howls of protest erupted from the Americans, many of whom apparently felt they'd been cheated.

We stayed until quarter past nine. It had been a tiring day, and the idea of a good night's sleep was appealing. Besides, Madame Fleury had asked us to be back by nine-thirty. I unlocked the front door to her apartment and we went up the stairs, where I knocked lightly, then opened the door. She sat at the kitchen table, reading a newspaper.

It was impossible not to wonder if Madame might expect one of us to express interest in sharing her bed for the night. True, she was twice my age, or Ed's, but she was an attractive woman, living by herself, and probably lonely at times. I didn't know what, if anything, I should do if she made any overtures. I was innocent as a babe in these matters, and believed Ed probably was, too. We'd grown up in an America that by-and-large adhered to the principles of Victorian conduct. Compared to almost any European kid, we wallowed in ignorance and the restrictions of an age long past.

As it turned out, all Madame Fleury offered was some biscuits, some cheese, and a glass of red wine for each of us. We sat, ate and drank, and went to bed in the room she'd prepared for us. It had a double bed, with thick comforters that defied the chill of a winter night. We slept well and rose early.

She was already up and dressed. She indicated that we should sit at the kitchen table while she made two fried eggs for each of us, with toast and jam, and a cup of tea. It was satisfying. We thanked her, donned our cartridge belts, slung our weapons on our shoulders, and went down the stairs.

At the landing, and before we opened the outside door, Ed asked, "Should we offer to pay her something?"

"How many Belgian francs do you have?" I asked him.

"About fifty cents' worth. You?"

"The same. We don't have enough between us to pay her a fair price for all she gave us. It might be an insult to offer less. Maybe she doesn't expect it, anyway. Nothing was said, by Jacobs at Woolworth's or by her at any time, about payment."

"That's true," said Ed. "Maybe it's best to just leave now. If either of us ever gets back here, and we have a reasonable amount of money with us, we should look her up and offer something."

"Agreed," I replied. "Right now, we'd better hit the road. Our passes are only good until noon, and we have no idea whether or not we'll get another ride. If we don't we'll be running that last four or five miles."

We did manage to get a ride for much of the distance, and walked into company HQ at eleven, with an hour to spare. Thus ended our few hours of temporary freedom and our adventure in a foreign city we'd never seen before. It was not a world-class tour, but it ended that despondency into which we had crawled like some fugitive beast of the Ardennes woods. It had also given us a reason to believe the world was not doomed, and maybe the war would someday end. We needed to get out of these uniforms and discover a way to find a sense of personal power, a means to control our own lives and create a purpose for our existence. We needed to go home.

Our HQ was a busy place, people going and coming, some actually running, phone lines jammed, the clerk hardly glancing at the passes we turned in.

"What's going on?" I asked Sergeant Furman.

He looked up from a pile of papers he was sorting. "Oh, you were away. How was Verviers?"

"Great," I said, "but what's happening here?"

"We caught a German infiltrator yesterday." He chuckled. "Kind of a freak thing, something you'd never expect. You know those little colored tickets Tompkins uses to keep everyone in order and fed at the right time in the mess?"

"Yeah, sure. I never could figure out how he made that work, but what happened?"

"Turns out those little colored tickets were responsible for the capture of an enemy spy. You and I never needed a ticket. We're part of the company and Tompkins knows us all. But he's always fed the replacements in groups, and to keep order, they're not allowed to eat until their particular group is called, and then they have to show their tickets to the guys serving the chow."

"And so? A Kraut wanted to eat and didn't have the right ticket?"

"Basically, that was it. He had no ticket at all, and this Kraut was dressed in an American uniform and spoke perfect English. He saw the chow line and simply joined it. The server asked for his ticket, and the guy didn't seem to understand. Someone called Tompkins, and he sent a guy over here to HQ. Lieutenant Markinson went out to investigate. He marched the Kraut in here with a .45 aimed at his back. I called the MPs, they sent a car around, and they hauled the Kraut away to be interrogated."

"Quite a story," I said. "What will happen to him?"

"Oh, he'll be executed. Wearing the uniform of the enemy is a capital offense in military law. It ranks with spying and treason. First, they'll question him for a few days, try to find out if he was part of a larger group, and if we need to be on guard for more of them. The MPs commended Tompkins."

This was something to think about. What if the German they'd captured was only one of many? Did that indicate some new kind of warfare was about to take place? And if they all spoke perfect Americanized English, and all wore our uniforms, how could we know who was one of us and who was the enemy?

I walked up the hill and picked up my mess kit. Parsons hardly spoke. He was still angry that we'd left him for a day. "There's some stuff in the garage," he finally said. "It all needs to be sorted out and put on shelves, ready to issue. You going to get started on it?"

I stared at him. "Frank," I said, "I'm still technically on leave. I'll do whatever you want after I have lunch. Ed will probably be back with me then, too."

"The kids were looking for you yesterday."

"They knew we were going away for a day," I replied.

He turned his back on me, and I went down the hill again to stand in the chow line.

Ed came out of the school building with his mess kit and joined me. He had his colored ticket in one hand. "Never did get a chance to tell you what 'Nazi' stands for," he said. "You really ought to know, because you'd said you thought a socialist system of government might be a good thing. 'Nazi' is a shortened form of 'National Socialist,' the political party that put Hitler in power. Originally, 'Nazi' was also a form of contempt by the majority of Germans, but Hitler's Brown Shirts adopted it as their own name for themselves. You think you'd like a socialist party at home?"

I shook my head. "Not if it's going to turn out like the one in Germany. So what's your answer, Ed? Politics are a part of life, all over the world, I guess. Isn't there anything that we can look forward to for honesty and truthfulness for more time than it takes to get elected?"

"We'll need to start something ourselves, if we get back."

Others in the line were starting to look at us now, in ways that held no promise of friendly understanding. We moved along and said nothing more.

Back at supply, Parsons did little more than point at items that had arrived since yesterday. We opened cartons and made them into compartments that were part of a wall, where sizes could be sorted and made ready for issue. My ammo was at the rear of the garage, and I insisted that an aisle be kept open to it. This was only the usual precaution, taken every time we stopped for more than a day. I held no expectations that I'd actually need to use, or issue, any of it.

Later in the day, Ed talked to Parsons and actually had him singing at one point, old bawdy songs, some from World War I that neither I nor many others had ever heard. Ed must have learned them from his father. We ended the day on a happier note.

The next day, an old friend stopped by. He was Tom Willis, a platoon sergeant in the First Infantry Division, now located a little north of us, in and around the town of Malmedy. The First and the Fourth combined held a twelve-mile front. Tom had come through our company a couple of months back, in France, after he'd recovered from a sickness. He was a technical sergeant, which meant he outranked Parsons, but he'd volunteered to help in supply, and did a good job. He followed orders from those of us who were experienced in the work, and his presence, especially when replacements filed through to pick up their new socks, pants, or whatever, was a big help in keeping order. Authority just naturally emanated from Tom, and this was accepted without reservation by nearly everyone who met him.

"Just thought I'd stop in for a visit," he said when he first showed up. "We're only about five miles away, and when I heard you guys were here, I hitched a ride over. My company's in regimental reserve right now. The front's pretty quiet, too. So how have things been going?"

Parsons made a few comments that were nothing specific, and both Ed and I told him things were great, and that we'd just returned from partying in Verviers.

Tom left before dark, and we settled down to business as usual. The kids showed up right after Tom left, excited and chattering about Christmas, not too far away. Ed walked down the hill to the school, and I did what I could to talk out the tension between Parsons and me, again urging him to take a twenty-four hour pass for himself. He just shook his head to that.

# 19

# *Start of The Ardennes*

Three days later, Tom returned, haggard and exhausted. "Got to wait a few days now," he said. "I've got no company any more."

"What happened?" all three of us asked him.

He took a deep breath, swallowed hard, and said, "Division decided to mount a small probing attack—just my company—to see how solid the Krauts were settled in for the winter.

"We made it to the next village—Elsenborn, I think it was called—and all hell broke loose. We were up to full strength, two hundred and fifty-four men. But the Krauts must have had a regiment in the area, and they wanted no part of us poking around there.

"They had us surrounded within an hour. We fought back from houses and barns in the village center, but there were so many of them, we had no chance to try a breakout. Our radio operator was still alive, and with my platoon, so I told him to get on the horn to regiment, or division, or anyone who would listen, and let them know what was happening.

"The Krauts must have picked up our signal. They sent more infantry in, to squeeze us down to a few buildings. They were hopped-up crazy, and taking no prisoners. They killed every one of our guys who ran out of ammo or was wounded."

Tom was the best of the best, the toughest, most resourceful, and one of the most experienced platoon sergeants in the Big Red One, possibly in the First Army. We were sure he'd done as much as anyone could have done, but now his eyes glazed, he shook his head, and he stared at the floor.

"Did regiment send in some relief?" Ed asked. Tom nodded. "Yeah. They fought their way through and reached us on the second day."

He raised his head and looked at Ed, then Parsons and me. "Four of us were still alive," he said. "All of the others—two hundred fifty guys—were dead. I'd been with some of them since before D-Day, since Sicily. I still can't figure it. Why? The Krauts were never that murderous before. They always wanted prisoners to interrogate." He shook his head again. "Not this time, no, not this time. I've got no platoon, no company. I'm just going to sit things out for a while, I guess. Any of you guys got a drink?"

Parsons reached into a box under his makeshift desk, and brought out a whiskey bottle, half full. He handed it to Tom, who sat on the nearest carton of new shoes and took a healthy swig.

"Every one of us has limits, you know," he said as he looked at each of us. "I think I've reached mine. I don't think I'm any good to the army or myself any more." He took another drink, then held up the bottle. "No, I'm not losing myself in this stuff." He handed the bottle to Parsons. "That's no real answer, and never was. I just needed a little to drain off the tension and let me look at what options I have left. There aren't many, are there? While this war goes on, I mean."

"No," sergeant Parsons said, "there aren't many options, Tom. But neither you, I, or either of these," he indicated Ed and me "really need to make that kind of decision. It'll be made for us, by those in authority. Unless you're planning to desert, they're where you need to put your trust, your beliefs, and your hopes for tomorrow. There are those who lead and those who follow. We each need to accept our personal role and live it. There's no point in denying what we are."

I wondered if this were some kind of roundabout criticism of Ed and me.

"And what are you and I, Frank?" Tom asked.

"That's obvious," Parsons replied. "We're both above company rank, so we're leaders, or at least part of the leadership team."

Tom stared at Parsons, narrowed his eyes, and asked, "When did you start to lose it, Frank?"

"Lose what?"

"I think you know what I mean. When did you lose your common sense and good judgment? When did you lose your grip on reality?"

Parsons spun around and left the room. "Bunch of friggin' assholes," he said as he went into the garage.

"What's out there?" Tom asked.

"New supplies, and my reserve ammo," I answered.

"Any weapons?"

"No, they're all in the room at the rear."

Tom stood and turned to leave. "You guys keep an eye on him," he said. "I doubt he's dangerous, and he sure does know the supply part of this army business, but watch him. He's got a few screws loose, and he could get worse. Hope I'll see you again before too long." He went out the door to the street.

That evening, First Sergeant Edgars came in with happier news. He spoke to both Parsons and me. "Just thought you'd like to know what finally happened to Sam Grollin," he said.

We both moved closer and listened carefully.

"It's taken a long time to find out," he continued, "but Sam made out okay. A week after he left us at Mortain, he turned himself in to the MPs. He was court-martialed, but only charged with being AWOL, and no mention of the fact that he was in a combat zone at the time. Sam was broken to the rank of private, but then given a carton of cigarettes, which is the army's way of saying this had to be done, but there were extenuating circumstances. He was then immediately promoted to staff sergeant and offered his choice of several assignments. So he's still a first three grader, with opportunities open to him, if he wants to go after them."

Parsons and I both expressed our appreciation for the news, and our satisfaction with the results of the court-martial.

"What about lieutenant Bailey?" Parsons asked.

"He didn't make out as well," Edgars replied. "He wasn't broken. I don't think they do that to officers, except in capital offenses. He was reprimanded, and a recommendation put in his record that he not be given a position of command in the future. Pretty rough, for a career soldier."

"But fair," Parsons added. "It was as fair as the army can get, and I'm glad for Sam."

"So am I," I said.

Edgars left, and Parsons half smiled at me. "You see, you leave things to the authorities and the system, and they work out."

He took the bottle from its hiding place and passed it to me. I drank a little and handed it back. He took a swallow, and our relationship immediately improved.

A few days earlier, the kids had asked me when my birthday was. It was a natural thing for kids to do, and I'd told them, then forgotten about it. I asked for theirs, and had forgotten that, too.

So Yvan surprised me the next day when he came in and said his parents had requested that the sergeant and I be their dinner guests on the ninth, which was tomorrow. At first, Parsons resisted the idea, but Yvan convinced him the meal would be good, and we would both be welcome.

The meal was more than good. It was excellent, quite possibly the best we'd eaten in all of Europe. Yvan's older brother, Raymond, was also there, but it was Yvan who kept the conversation going, as the one most skilled in languages. He kept busy interpreting for all of us. It was a thoroughly enjoyable evening, although Parsons would not stay for after-dinner conversation, and I felt compelled to leave with him. We both thanked the family and were back in our office/quarters before eight o'clock.

I was twenty years old, and found it difficult to believe how much had happened since I'd arrived in England, still just eighteen, a little over a year ago. President Roosevelt was then busy informing the mothers of America, through one of his "fireside chats," that "No American boy under the age of nineteen will be sent to serve on foreign soil." It was a lie, and I laughed about it, but it did illustrate how one hand (the politicians) rarely knew, or even cared, what the other hand (the military) was doing. Each group had its own agenda, and no effort was made to correlate plans or promises.

We had with us at this time a strange man named Zebulon Granger. He was from Tennessee, a mountain man in the older sense of the word. He could live indefinitely on game and wild plants, or roots at this time of the year, and possessed the instincts of early Native Americans. He would frequently disappear for three to five days at a time, walking into the forest with a carbine and a trench knife and returning apparently in good health.

He always returned, and his few close friends would cover for him at morning roll call by one of them answering to his name. Our officers were never the wiser.

Zeb came back this time quite agitated. "Something's going on out there," he said. "I've always been able to walk right through the Kraut lines any time I wanted to, but they've practically tripled their perimeter defenses and sentries. I have to stay back in the hills now. They've got work gangs out there cutting trees and making log roads through the low areas. In other words, putting down corduroy tracks for tanks. They're up to something, and it's no small thing."

"Shouldn't you report it?" I asked.

He flashed me a look of disgust. "How in hell could I do that?" he asked. "It would be an open admission that I was AWOL. I don't have the cleanest record in the world, you know. I'd probably be charged with desertion, and spend whatever was left of my life in Leavenworth, if they didn't hang me. No, I can't report it. And if anyone else tried, it would be the same story. At the very least, there'd be an investigation, and you, or whoever said something about it, would be a prime witness in a court-martial hearing."

"You sure about that, Zeb?" I asked. "I don't know what there is in your record, but I bet if you told Lieutenant Markinson, he'd try to get word back to Army HQ."

"They'd never listen to him. Not even by-the-book Markinson, because you don't have an officer in your company who'd get the time of day from the lowest clerk in Army HQ. If he couldn't be heard, he'd never get the message to them. I'd be even less likely to make them listen. They'd ask 'How do you know all this?' and then tell me G2 hadn't reported anything like it. So, if G2 doesn't know it, it doesn't exist. And where would that leave me, after admitting I'd been off in the hills without permission?"

He was serious, I was sure. I was equally sure he was right that something was about to happen. It all added up. The English-speaking German in one of our uniforms was the first tip-off, followed by the extermination of Tom's company before they could learn much of anything, the unusual silence from the Kraut lines, and now this, Zeb's discovery.

What added greatly to the seriousness of the situation was that on this day, both the Fourth Infantry and the neighboring First Infantry were pulled back to a rear area for rest and refitting, to bring the companies up to full strength once more. Tom was undoubtedly moving back. Ed was notified that he would be going, too. His tank battalion, still attached to the Fourth, would go with them. I was sorry to see him leave, and not a little worried about where he might be sent in the near future.

Our own future was equally a concern, for it was the Ninety-ninth Infantry Division that was brought up to replace both the First and the Fourth. Although a seemingly good outfit, the Ninety-ninth had only one month's experience on the line, and this at a time when all was as quiet as it had ever been. Now, they would be stretched out to cover the twelve miles formerly held by two veteran divisions. This was a mistake, and we knew it. Our generals didn't know it, though, because G2 hadn't told them. We bit our lips and prepared ourselves psychologically for the worst.

It came soon enough. Just a week after my birthday, the bottom fell out and the sky came crashing down.

It all happened in rapid-fire succession. The Seventh Armored Division rolled through Stavelot, crossed the old wooden bridge over the river, and moved on, into the German advance. We stood at the side of the road and waved them on with words of encouragement, shouted over the din of heavy armor clanking past. "Where you headed?" we asked some of the half-track drivers and tank commanders.

"Going to drive a spearhead into the Kraut advance and cut it off," was their answer.

It took them over two hours to go by, and from what we soon heard, about that long for the Seventh to be destroyed as a fighting unit.

The rest of the day was quiet, and we settled down for an uneasy sleep. At three-thirty in the morning, lieutenant Markinson burst into my room. "The whole company is on its way here. Open that big garage door and start opening ammo boxes. Every man is to have a standard issue."

I scrambled into my uniform and ran to the garage. I had some ammo boxes opened and ready when the line formed just outside. I grabbed the first three men and assigned them to issuing the ammo, with another helping to open more boxes. We gave a bandoleer of rifle ammo to each man with an M1, a box of carbine cartridges to each one who had that weapon, and an extra magazine if he needed one. Each one with a pistol received a box of fifty cartridges. The few with sub-machine guns got two boxes.

It was about at this time that we heard a tremendous explosion down at the river. A couple of guys grinned and told the rest of us. "The engineers just blew the bridge," they said. We knew there was an engineer company in Stavelot, but they'd stayed at the other end of town, and we'd had little contact with them. "Ten thousand pounds of TNT," our informant said. "They put it all under that little wooden span, set it off, then left."

Zeb Granger came through, and asked if he could have a few extra boxes of carbine ammo. "Sure," I told him. "but wait until the whole line is through. I'm sure there'll be some extra, and then you can have all you want. Or any of the other stuff, too."

He waited, and when he came in again, he had six others with him. I gave each of them whatever he asked for. There was still some ammo left after that, but not much.

"What are you planning, Zeb?" I asked him.

He grinned. "You know that old stone warehouse down by the river? You can see it real good from the school where we stay."

"Yes," I replied. "You and these others going to hole up there?"

"That's the plan. You'll be pulling out as soon as someone can find enough trucks for you. That's a pretty sure thing. These guys and I will stay in that warehouse. It's right on the edge of the river, and we can stop any Krauts that try to cross there. I've checked it out, and the river's no more than five feet deep. With the bridge gone, they'll try to ford it. Seven of us in the warehouse will hold our fire until they're at the midpoint, then we'll open up. It ain't likely any will live to get to this side."

Lieutenant Markinson came in. "The company from Malmedy just pulled in," he said. This, I knew, was one of the other reinforcement companies in our battalion. "They brought their MG and mount, so when you have a minute, figure out where to set it up and find a couple of men for the crew. By the way, do we have anything at all that might stop a tank?"

"We've got a rocket launcher—a bazooka," I replied. "And, I've got three rockets for it, all in their original cardboard tubes. We can't use them, though."

"Why not?"

"The bazooka uses batteries to fire the rockets. Ours have been long dead, and I've never been able to get replacements."

"We've got flashlights. Can't we use the batteries from them?"

"No, sir," I replied. "Flashlights use size "D" batteries. The people who designed the bazooka left their brains somewhere behind the barn and built it to use only size "C" batteries. No one has any, except maybe a division supply unit somewhere, if their line companies use enough bazookas. They'd never part with any, though, even if I knew where to ask."

"Any way to jury-rig a bazooka to use flashlight batteries?"

"Sure," I said. "Get me a few feet of electrical wire, a roll of friction tape, and a handful of D batteries, and I can do it in about two hours, after I have the stuff in hand."

"We probably don't have that long," the lieutenant said. "Is there anything else?"

"I've got a grenade launcher for the '03 Springfield rifle, the blank cartridges, and three grenades. I carry a Springfield myself, by choice, so we could fire the grenades, but I doubt they'd be of much use."

"Why not?" he asked.

"Because they're the old, World War I type anti-tank grenades. They'd probably knock out the radiator of a truck, but not much more. Certainly, no part of a modern tank."

"Damn!" Markinson said. "Okay, all we've got are the MGs, so do what you can. Some day, this army will get itself organized and join the twentieth century."

"Don't count on it, lieutenant," I replied.

He gave me a quick smile and left.

It was getting light when the other reinforcement company came in on the road from St. Vith. They, too, brought their .50 caliber MG.

Parsons was up and moving about, but with no real purpose. The situation, as it was quickly developing, was going to be my show. The training and knowledge to handle and use our weapons were entirely mine, with the possible help of lieutenant Markinson, who was still in command of his emotions, and keeping a cool head in the middle of it all.

False reports of German troops the other side of the river became common. They were not there, at least not yet. They were in Malmedy, five miles away, and they had crossed the road between that town and us.

A truck towing a 105-millimeter howitzer came down the hill and stopped halfway, at the intersection of our street and the Rue de Spa. Men bailed out of the truck and wheeled the piece around. They loaded and fired three rounds in the general direction of the German line. Test firing, I assumed, but immediately after that, they hitched up the howitzer, jumped in the truck, turned and headed back.

"Hey," I yelled, "where you going?"

"That's all the ammo we had," one of them yelled back. "Good luck, guys. We're out of here."

I went down the hill and checked with lieutenant Markinson. "I think one MG should be on the road from Malmedy," I told him, "with the one that just came in placed on the road to St. Vith. Our own, I'd like to place halfway up the hill, about where that truck and howitzer were for a few minutes."

"Sounds okay," he said. "Do it, but check out those other guns before you do. I'm not sure how much care they've had."

That turned out to be good advice. The Malmedy MG was in good shape, but the other, from down near St. Vith, was not. When I opened the receiver and looked down the barrel, it was thickly coated with rust, too much to safely fire it. I had three spare barrels, but this one was rusted solidly to the receiver. I couldn't get it off to replace it. With a few well-aimed curses at those who should have looked after this piece, I abandoned it on the side of the road. St. Vith was twelve miles away, and we had more to worry about from Malmedy, anyway.

With the other two MGs set up, we had nothing to do but wait. I'd still not had five minutes to round up a couple of crew members for the MGs. I asked around, but could find no volunteers. This one time, I was reluctant to appoint the men needed. The possibilities were too great that this would become a suicide mission. I spoke to lieutenant Markinson one more time, and offered to man the gun on the Malmedy road myself. He shook his head, but did not answer. From this, I assumed he'd try to find the men we needed himself, if he had the time.

The weather was miserable, snow on the ground almost everywhere, low clouds dropping freezing rain, visibility reduced to fifty yards or less. The entire U.S. Air Force was grounded. The Krauts had planned well to take advantage of this fact. We did see, if briefly, one heartening sight. A British Spitfire, at treetop level, went over, headed toward Malmedy. What the pilot could do that might be effective was debatable, but at least he was trying. Properly armed, and able to see his target, a Spit could knock out a tank on the road.

Father Victor, our battalion chaplain, ran up to me and asked, breathless, if I had an extra .45 pistol I could give him. He was a decent guy, from my point of view. He was also tall, athletic, and good looking. I liked him, although I'd never attended one of his services.

"Why would you ever want a pistol?" I asked him.

"Never mind why. Do you have one, and if so, can you give it to me?"

"Sorry, Father, but I haven't had a pistol in some time. They're hard to come by, and ordnance almost always substitutes a carbine. But you've had no training with one anyway. You'd never be able to hit the broad side of a barn. There's a bit more to firing a .45 than just pointing it, you know."

"Maybe so, but...never mind, I'll do something else."

He rushed off and I forgot about him.

Reports from other places were scattered and not always reliable. St. Vith appeared to be a major objective for the Germans, and they were massed in front of it with everything they could put there. The defense was the remnants of many units broken and scattered in the first day of the assault. Some of the Seventh Armored tanks had made it to St. Vith, and were surely welcomed. Remnants of the Ninety-ninth Infantry made it there, as did some of the One Hundred and Sixth Infantry. The Twenty-eighth, broken up and scattered, had switched to guerilla tactics, small groups harassing the Germans relentlessly in the Ardennes Forest. German Panzers had crossed the road between St. Vith and us, but there was no target of any importance in the woodland. It was the road network hub at St. Vith they were after.

The road to Malmedy was a different story. Now under German control, it eliminated all but the last way out for us in Stavelot. If we were going to go, it would be up the hill on the Rue de Spa road. Nothing else remained.

It didn't take a lot to figure out that Spa itself was a major objective of the Germans. The reason was simple enough. Spa was the site of First Army headquarters. It was also the location of over three million gallons of high-test gasoline, in five gallon jerricans and some fifty gallon drums. This was for our tanks, which used air-cooled aircraft engines, the same as in the heavy bombers.

It was a desperate scramble to get both army HQ and the gasoline out of Spa, because by now we knew that the Germans had altered their tank engines to use our fuel. They needed what we had at Spa to continue the drive on Liège, where our major tank farm was located. With that, it was reasonable to suppose that they hoped to push all the way to Antwerp, cutting the Allied armies in half.

That night, a gigantic flame lit the sky at Spa. It must have been visible from most of Belgium, or would have been if the weather cleared. It was high-test gasoline burning. What couldn't be moved in time was set on fire, to deny it to the Krauts. German commanders, unable to stop it, watched helplessly as their new Tiger Royal tanks, impervious to anything we had to stop them, ran dry and ground to a halt, now pieces of stationary artillery.

In the morning, lieutenant Markinson came to supply again. He spoke to both Parsons and me. "Bring your weapon, your cartridge belt and canteen. Nothing else. The trucks are arriving now, and we're leaving as soon as they're loaded. If you're not on a truck, you'll be walking out. Army has decided we can't possibly hold Stavelot."

"What about my MGs, Sir?" I asked.

"Leave them. Leave any other weapons you have here. Leave everything and get on a truck. With luck, we may return soon. Help is coming from the Third Army."

So we left Stavelot, not knowing what lay in store for the kids, the people, or anything else there, not knowing what we ourselves now faced. There were so many things I felt I should have done, but at the end, there was no time.

The Germans had taken into account every possible variable in their plans for this final assault. Nothing was left to chance, not even the weather. What was bad for us, because it denied us any air support, was good for them. Their soldiers had been treated to the best available propaganda to ensure confidence in their superiority over the Allied defenders of every critical objective. On our side, stories ran rampant of drugs used to enhance the performance of their combat troops. This was difficult to prove, one way or the other, but it supported what Tom had told us about the apparent German orders to "take no prisoners."

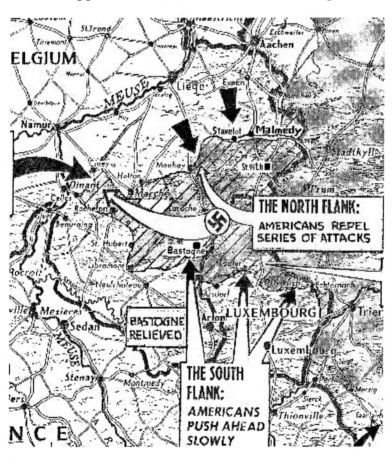

The media called it the "Malmedy Massacre." In the first hours of the attack, many men were separated from their units. A group of cooks and bakers, clerks, mechanics, and other non-combat troops surrendered to the first German troops they saw. They were taken to a large field, where a machinegun on the tailgate of a truck, and others in tanks, raked through them. Of the hundred and fifty originally part of the group, a few escaped into the woods before the gunfire started. Four others, all wounded, played dead and escaped detection as a German officer walked through the bodies firing his pistol at any who still showed signs of life.

The whole incident tended to corroborate all we'd heard from Tom and Zeb. The Krauts were probably juiced up on drugs and under orders to take no prisoners. The media, with the encouragement of our own headquarters, played it up, but most of us accepted it as one of the things that might happen under such circumstances. The rules and conventions of warfare are not always strictly observed, and this is not necessarily the result of mind-altering drugs. Propaganda can serve the same purpose, inducing an irrational hatred that soon becomes blood lust.

# 20

## *Escape from Stavelot*

For that day, the night that followed, and all of the next day, our four trucks played cat and mouse with the Germans. We were the mouse, running down country lanes, some little more than a cart path, our officers and drivers hoping these would be too difficult, and we too small a prize, for the enemy to follow. Some were not even on any maps. We stopped at times, and waited quietly for the sounds of motorized traffic on a nearby paved road to fade out. The total distance covered was not great, a good thing, because gasoline was limited to the contents of our truck's tank and a few jerricans carried with us.

We finally pulled into a Belgian farmyard. It was late in the day, almost dark. Lieutenant Cicciloni told us to get down from the trucks.

We'd not eaten since leaving Stavelot, two days earlier, and our canteens were now empty. We stood around on the cold ground, our breath fogging in the equally cold air. One truckload at a time, Cicciloni escorted us into the kitchen of the farmhouse. All the windows and the doors were covered with blackout material, but inside, it was warm and, with three oil lamps burning, bright enough.

The table was typical of a working farm, wide boards supported by trestles, with room enough to seat eight on each side. With the driver and another who rode in the cab, this was the contents of one truck. On the table was a platter of bread, cut in thick slices and fresh enough to have been made this day. A dish with some sort of fruit jam was also on the table, and we passed it around after we'd each taken a piece of bread. There were cups, of several different designs and varieties, and the housewife filled each of them with a hot drink from a huge coffee pot. It was not coffee, of course, but an herbal drink of some sort. It was hot, it was wet, and it was welcomed.

When we'd finished, we went outside and the next group entered. We waited while two of the lieutenants spread a map on the hood of a truck and checked it with a flashlight that had black tape over most of the lens, with just a narrow slit of light that illuminated one small part of the map at a time.

"Verviers" was mentioned, and some time later that night we arrived at the outskirts of the city. We climbed down from the truck and entered what appeared to be an old factory or warehouse. There were three floors, each one empty of any machinery or stored material. There was an operating flush toilet, and we were able to relieve ourselves after a wait in line. There was also water to refill our canteens, although we had no idea how pure it was. Most of us still carried halizone tablets. Added to a canteen of questionable water and shaken well, it could kill some of the more obnoxious bacteria. A few ounces of whiskey would do it, too, but no one seemed to have any of that.

Several of us went to the top floor and lay down to sleep. Any hope of doing that was soon eliminated. Verviers was presently a target for the Germans' new long-range rocket artillery. They were dropping all around us, shaking the building and blowing parts of neighboring buildings apart. The one next to us, similar to the one we occupied, took a hit. We heard bricks rain down on the street below. We all moved down a floor, to put at least that much space between us and the next round of rockets. They were not like the rounds fired from the hand-held rocket launcher, or bazooka, which could punch through armor with the help of a shaped charge of explosive. These new weapons and their projectiles were more like oversized mortars and, like mortars, unable to penetrate deeply. They came in bunches, and we had to assume the Krauts used those multiple-tube launchers, in which they could load forty rounds at once and fire them all in just a few seconds. Reloading was the slow part of the operation. That's when we'd get a break, and could move around or talk.

Other units shared the building with us, and a few new ones arrived at first light in the morning. Food came with some of them, in the form of large tins of shredded corned beef, the infamous "S" of the detested "S on S." There was no bread, so no toast. We ate a little of the stuff.

The day passed slowly, with the expectation that we may move on short notice. Explosions, many greater than the ones in our neighborhood, could be heard not far away, and rattled anything loose. It was not easy to know the exact cause, because the cities of Europe sat atop a multitude of often ancient pipes and tunnels. There were water pipes, sewage pipes or conduits, electrical service tunnels, and various sizes of gas lines. Each gas main was, under the right conditions, a deadly explosive, capable of destroying the buildings above it if detonated. Or it could, if the valves controlling its use in a house were damaged, fill that house with gas and become a bomb powerful enough to take out three or four other buildings with it.

Another night passed, and in the morning we experienced a miracle of sorts. Mail arrived. Letters and packages from home, piled up in some intermediate postal unit, had been forwarded to our last known location, which was here, in this ancient building. Anything edible, such as the box of candy I received, was shared and quickly eaten. The box itself became a container for letters, until such time as they could be read at leisure. There were three from Kay. She still wrote faithfully every week. I looked forward to a time when I had better light and a quiet place to sit and enjoy every word.

As soon as the mail had been distributed, the lieutenants ordered us to hurry—nothing unusual, but this time we obeyed with more than usual alacrity. Nothing around us seemed too stable or safe. The trucks were outside, waiting with their engines running. We climbed aboard and headed for the heart of Verviers.

It was a heart that no longer existed. I watched the endless rubble piles as we passed them, and remembered the time, so very recently, when Ed and I had spent the better part of our twenty-four hour passes here. The central square was unrecognizable. The same thing had been done here as at St. Lo in Normandy, when we needed so badly to get out of the confines of the beachhead. Tanks with bulldozer blades had smashed a path through the broken masonry, bricks, wood, and dust. Under the hammering treads of several tanks, all had been compressed into a rough but serviceable road for the trucks. With much swaying and yawing, we were able to get through.

The Woolworth's was gone, now reduced to part of the road over which we moved. The night club where the sad-faced young woman did her almost striptease was gone, likewise pounded into temporary pavement. I couldn't help wondering if she, too, were somewhere in the trash beneath our wheels, still sad and now maybe bleeding out her final moments of life. We passed the place on the other side where Madame Fleury's apartment once stood. It, too, was ground to dust beneath the treads of tanks, and did its small part to support the present retreat of an army. The people? No one could tell us anything. All things end, and perhaps they had, too. At the least, their hopes for a better world were now on hold.

No one knew whether it was German artillery, rocket propelled or conventional, that had destroyed Verviers, or if a Kraut Panzer division, tanks and infantry, had penetrated this far and drawn the fire of our own big guns. For once, it could not have been the bombers. The weather had not permitted that. All that could be said was that a war had passed through this place, and it was no more. I bit my lip, shook my head, and worried about the kids at Stavelot—the kids I felt I had abandoned. Were they still alive? Were they hurt, had their homes been destroyed, were their parents still okay? Did the town itself still exist?

It was a fifty mile run this time, all the way back to a place called Landers. A much used railroad track went through the town, with many sidings, on which stood numbers of box cars, coal cars, tankers, and others.

Our company HQ was set up in a first-floor store, the front facing a small open square. Supply and the mess were over a bridge across the tracks. I no longer had to be concerned with our reserve ammunition. We had none. Nor did we have our .50 caliber machinegun any more. We set up supply in, of all places, the office of a commercial print shop. I felt right at home, for I'd been serving an apprenticeship in printing when Uncle Sam, on countless posters at home, had pointed his finger and said "I want YOU!"

It was December 23. Christmas was coming up, food supplies were arriving, including turkeys, and the cooks had no stoves.

Our officers sent inquiries to every possible source within reach by trucks or rail, and located some second-hand units that had definitely seen better times. Field ranges operated on unleaded gasoline, and some of that was found, too.

The final problem was location. No suitable buildings were available, so the cooks placed everything in the open, between the rails of a siding. On Christmas day, they did the best they could, but it still wasn't much. The twenty-mile-per-hour winds blew out the flames before they had burned more than a few minutes, while we shivered in ten-degree cold. Our mess kits were filled with half-frozen vegetables and raw turkey. There was little to celebrate, and not much for which to give thanks, except that we were still alive.

The next day replacements arrived, and I did give thanks. Bernie Vernal, my savior of the Seine, walked in the door of the supply room. "You guys got anything for me to do?" he asked.

In reply to our questions, he told us he'd continued to bounce around from one place to another with no permanent assignment. "Hell of a way to spend a war, isn't it?" he said. "You'd think the army would just send me home and save a whole lot of senseless expense feeding me and moving me. I guess that's not the way the army ever does things, though, is it?"

Bernie fit right in and started working that same day. He lived across the tracks in a building being used to house replacements, so he crossed the bridge every morning and at the end of each day. All of the others did, too, because the mess area remained on our side, the cooks still struggling with beat-up and worn out field ranges.

Men arrived without weapons, and ordering them became routine for me. I also ordered and issued ammunition when it was needed for those moving forward. I never did receive any replacements for what had been issued or left at Stavelot.

The new men were a mix, not all combat replacements. One group of sixty was construction engineers. Their job would be to make bridges, most of them temporary pontoon affairs, but big enough to handle heavy truck and tank traffic. We were going back, regaining what had been lost to the Germans in their Ardennes offensive. That had ended with the German army's inability to capture the gasoline at Spa. Often, small things have turned the tides of war and changed the flow of world events. A million gallons of gasoline, burning on a night in December, had defined a new direction in the course of history.

I'd ordered M1 rifles for this group, but received in their place Enfields, still the standard shoulder weapon of the British armed forces. These were chambered to take our own ammunition, though. The engineers wanted no part of it. They wailed and complained loudly, and were certain they would all die from a lack of sufficient firepower. It was unlikely any of them would ever see a German soldier. Combat engineers would, for, as a friend of mine who was one told me, "It was ninety percent combat and ten percent engineering." Casualties in the combat engineers frequently equaled those of the infantry. Construction engineers moved up after the combat was finished, to build more permanent structures than were possible under fire.

I tried to tell these soldiers that the Enfield was actually a fine piece, and had served British forces well for many years, plus elements of our own army during World War I. This made no impression whatever. In their place, I'd have felt much the same, and been disappointed with anything less than an M1, but there was nothing I could do about this situation, and expected it would continue until this war was over, at least here in Europe. They climbed aboard the trucks a thoroughly disgruntled company. I sympathized with them, but was happy to see them leave.

The Ardennes had obviously been Germany's last gasp, its final attempt to regain the initiative and reverse the steady losses of men, equipment, and resources since Normandy. They'd failed, and the rest of this war in Europe would become a war of attrition, of gradually wearing down their remaining strength and their will to fight. It was going to cost many thousands of lives, because if the average German had fought with less than perfect zeal in France and Belgium, it must be expected that he could well become a cornered tiger when protecting his homeland. This was not a prospect to relish, but a thing we needed to face.

It was a reasonable conclusion that our Pacific forces had, until now, been the "poor relative" when it came to allocating resources. That, I was certain, was about to change. The evidence was those Enfield rifles. The arms makers at home had not stopped producing weapons. It was just that, from this point forward, their products would be going to the divisions in the Pacific theater. In Europe, we'd make do with whatever was on hand. If, at this time, that happened to be World War I Enfields, so be it. I was sure some discretion would be practiced in reserving the newer and better arms for those who needed them most—the combat infantrymen. If the bridge builders complained, they'd be just whistling in the dark, trying to soothe their own disappointment at their relegation to second choice in weaponry.

Our supply room had a pot-bellied stove, as we'd had in Stavelot, but fuel was just as scarce. We burned whatever we could find, and wore overcoats day and night. Dominic, a first-generation American with Italian parents, came in to help and pass some time. He was useful, especially when Bernie wasn't around, because Dom was fluent in French, and easily adapted that to the Walloon dialect. He was also good with the endless paperwork that supply entailed.

He was outgoing, and made friends with a local family, at first through their son, who was about Dom's age. He was soon staying the night with them, and asked me if I'd like to join him there. It was just down the street, less than a hundred yards away. We made sure Sergeant Parsons knew where we were at all times, in the event he needed us during the night, or orders to move came in.

Our bed was large, covered with layers of thick comforters, a wonderful way to spend a freezing Belgian night. It was customary to spend an hour or two with the people, downstairs in the tiny room they heated with a small coal stove. We had cigarettes to offer, always a stimulant to friendship. Their son knew a smattering of English, which made some conversation possible for me.

Dom and I retired to the upstairs bedroom as soon as the talk waned for the evening. Warmth was what I wanted, and it was there, if I burrowed beneath the coverings. I soon learned, though, that Dom had more complicated ideas in his head. On the third night, I was almost asleep when his hand crept across my thigh and moved toward disputed territory. I rolled over, away from him. Maybe he was asleep, and this had been an accident, I thought.

It was no accident, and he tried again. This time, I grabbed his wrist and forcibly pushed his hand and arm over to his own side of the bed. I heard him sigh and turn away. In the light of day, I now had a dilemma. Homosexual activity was not just frowned upon by the military, it was expressly forbidden. The penalty could be high for anyone found guilty—up to twenty years at hard labor, a dishonorable discharge from the army, and loss of citizenship.

I was supposed to report this incident, but nothing had happened beyond my rejection of Dom's advances. If I did report it, we'd both face a court martial, probably within three days, with sentencing the following day. Military justice never wasted time. I did not feel any blame attached to me, but who knew what a court martial board would think? Dom could lie to save himself, and to be sure they punished the guilty party, both of us could be condemned.

Before the day was over, I was relieved of any pressing need to take action. Dom left with a couple of dozen infantry replacements. He was probably going to a greater punishment than any court martial would impose, maybe going to his death.

What good could possibly have been served by following orders in this case? I told no one.

# 21

## *Turnaround*

Landers was the limit of our retreat. Our next move would once again point us at Germany. In the meantime, there was work to do and something akin to normalcy to regain.

A famous unit of the British army came to town. We didn't mingle with them, although a friendly greeting in passing was common enough, and acceptable. I thought Army headquarters was just a little overcautious in outlining permissible behavior with the Irish Guards. We respected them, something they'd certainly earned, and looked up to them. This latter was not difficult. They were all over six feet tall, a requirement for membership in this elite group, and unusual for the Irish.

They were unusual in other ways, too. They were an entirely volunteer unit, fighting for Britain, while their Irish friends and families at home directed German bombers to Belfast and any other British target of opportunity they could find. The old hatred of England and the English by most Irishmen was very much alive in Eire. With the lowest pay scale of any modern army, Britain had little to offer the Irish for their service, yet they took it and performed well. This may have been a measure of how desperately poor the people of Ireland were.

Back in September, an attempt had been made to establish a bridgehead across the Rhine, opening the way for later attacks on the German homeland. Twenty thousand paratroopers and fourteen thousand glider troops had landed in and around the town of Arnhem in Holland. It was a disaster almost from the beginning. The British First Airborne Division was quickly surrounded and threatened with annihilation. In a retreat, less than a quarter of the original number survived and reached safety.

Not far away, the U.S. Eighty-second Airborne and the One Hundred and First Airborne did little better. Surrounded, out of food and medicine, low on ammunition, they waited for reinforcements that never came. That was when the Irish Guards entered the picture. In a fierce attack that ended with a wild bayonet charge, they broke through the German encirclement and rescued the Americans. The Guards were now in the same town with us, and we couldn't help but treat them with awe.

We would have liked to go into a barroom they frequented and lifted a glass or two with them. We could not, for we'd not been paid in three months. As good as many Belgian people were to us, they stopped short of making a gift of their beer and liquor.

Dominic was gone, but I continued to spend my nights with the family down the road. Conversation was possible only when their son was home, but that was most evenings.

In the supply room, I poked around among some of the papers in a desk drawer and discovered something I thought could be important. It was a printed list of names, headed "Collaborateurs." To my mind, there was only one interpretation of that. This had to be a list of local people who had helped the German occupation forces, possibly to the extent of reporting political dissidents and others who would consequently be arrested and sent away.

I remembered something Yvan had tried to tell me once, back in Stavelot. I couldn't get the whole of it, and he spoke softly, as if afraid someone might hear what he said. Several times, he repeated the word "Buchenwald." I knew only that "Wald" was German for "woods" or "forest," but could not connect that to any present knowledge I had. Nor could I understand why it inspired so much fear in a thirteen-year-old boy. Further, it was nothing in the local area. From the little bit I did understand, "Buchenwald" was many miles away.

I took the list of "collaborateurs" to Sergeant Parsons. "Should we do something about this?" I asked. "It could be important to the local police."

He grabbed the papers from my hand. "This is what we should do with it," he said, and tossed them in the stove to burn. "Maybe you can get some wood in there, so we can have a little heat around this place." Whatever value the list might have had to authorities, military or civilian, it ended there and then.

Others who had been in Stavelot with us began to drift in. Some had gone far afield before they'd learned our whereabouts. A pair of truck drivers had their story well prepared. "Sarge," they said, "when we was told to get out of Stavelot, we got. And we kept gittin' until, what with a ride now'n then, first thing we knowed, we was in Paris. We figured, what the hell, long as we was there, we might's well have a good time."

"Did you?" the sergeant asked.

"Oh yes, sir, we surely did enjoy ourselfs. That is, until some MPs asked to see our identification and passes, which we didn't seem to have. That's when they told us we could either spend a whole lot of time in a stockade, or we could hop a ride here, to where you was. We come here."

Edgars smiled and sighed. "A wise choice," he said. "And what should I do with you, now that you're here?"

The pair looked at each other and shrugged. "Don't rightly know, Sarge. Guess we should do a little extra duty of some kind, but it weren't like we planned to do nothing wrong, so maybe you could go a little easy on us?"

"I'm thinking," Sergeant Edgars said. "I'm thinking that until someone calls and has a need for a couple of really smart truck drivers like you two, who have seen Paris and all, maybe the cooks could use a lot of help with their work. How does that sound?"

"You mean sort of permanent KP, don't you, Sarge?" one of them asked. "Until we get an assignment, that is?"

"You've got the picture. As I said, you two really do have something besides wet sawdust between your ears. We agreed on that, then?"

They nodded, a little glumly, and left to find the mess and the cooks.

A day later, another had a sadder tale to tell. His name was Alwin, and he arrived alone.

"And what's your story?" Edgars asked him.

"Seems I been hiking all over Europe and back again," said Alwin.

"And why would that be?"

"Well, I started walking, just like everyone else who didn't get on a truck quick enough. Carried my rifle and ammo belt and canteen, like I was told. Carried my barracks bag, too, 'cause I didn't want to leave nothin' behind for them Krauts to steal." He shook his head and looked at the floor. "Man, that barracks bag got heavy by the time I'd got to the top of that hill goin' outa the town."

"So what did you do then?" the sergeant asked.

"I throwed that goddawful heavy barracks bag into a field at the side of the road." He looked up. "That was a whole lot better, but I was still walkin' and not too happy about it."

"So?"

"So that there rifle, it got monstrous heavy, like the barracks bag done."

Sergeant Edgars sat up straight in his chair. "You saying you threw your piece away next?"

Alwin nodded. "Guess I did at that, sergeant. It wasn't that I was lazy, or nothing' like that. And it wasn't that I wasn't willin' to fight with them Krauts if'n they showed up. Believe me, I'd of done that. But you just wouldn't believe how heavy that there rifle done got."

"Oh, I'd believe it. Would you believe you committed a serious offense in doing that? An offense that could get you court-martialed?"

Alwin nodded. "I been tole that by the MPs what tole me where you guys was."

"Well, is there any more?" Edgars prodded.

"Oh, yes, Sarge, they's more. They's lots more. I done walked most of the night, and even my cartridge belt was gettin' heavy as a whore's load of sin. Couldn't see much use in keepin' them bullets. Had no gun to use 'em in, so I throwed it away, too. But a hour or so later, things looked lots better."

"What happened then?"

"Well," said Alwin, "what happened was a armored car come along, stopped, and asked me if'n I'd like a ride. Well, you can bet your sorry ass—oops, I mean you can just bet I did want that ride."

"And?"

"And we rode the rest of the night, until it started gettin' light enough to see. And what I seen made me yell out at those other guys in the armored car. 'Stop the car!' I told them. 'Stop the car right now.' We stopped.

"We stopped and they wanted to know what the trouble was. Sarge, the trouble was that there sign. It said 'Stavelot 1 kilometer' and it was pointin' the way we was goin'. After all that walkin' and after throwin' away all my stuff, I was right back where I started."

"What did the guys in the car have to say to you?" Sergeant Edgars asked Alwin.

Alwin took a deep breath. "What they said was that they was part of the Seventh Armored, and they was tryin' a flankin' maneuver against the Kraut Panzer division up ahead. I told them right away, I said, 'You guys got me all wrong. I ain't flankin', I is retreatin'. Goodbye.' And I got out of the car and started walkin' again."

Edgars leaned back and grinned. "Alwin, you've had quite a time of it, haven't you?"

"That surely is a fact, Sarge. What you goin' to do to me?"

"Well, I don't really think you'd like to do much hiking for a while. And, in spite of the fact that you committed a grave error in losing your weapon, maybe just standing in one place for a week or two will help you recover. Sort of like a soldier does when he scrubs pots and pans for the cooks."

"Every day?" Alwin asked.

"Every day until someone wants a smart truck driver who knows how to change directions twice during the same night. I'd surely be willing to give you a recommendation for any job that required that particular ability."

Others came in with a variety of reasons why they'd been lost, indisposed, or too weary to make much progress on the roads. The cooks had a lot of KP help for a while.

The Enfield rifles had been the first indication that things were changing, and quickly. Next was the group of replacements that arrived.

They were "retreads." That's what we called them, and it was a fitting description, although it was doubtful they appreciated it. They were now replacement infantry riflemen, even if they'd never before picked up a rifle. A carbine was probably the heaviest implement any of them had slung on his shoulder or fired.

These guys were accustomed to the luxury of beds with clean sheets, laundry service, hot showers, hot meals, and a wealth of other perks no infantry rifleman had ever known in this corner of the world. They were former ground crew members and field personnel from one of the Eighth Air Force bases in England. Before long, the great bombers would fly no more, at least not over Europe. There were simply not enough remaining targets that needed their attention. The Eighth had begun the process of "standing down." It was certainly a sign of things to come, even if no timetable was known at this time.

These men were no longer needed, but infantry riflemen were always in short supply. Far from happy about the dramatic change in their situation, and still wearing insignia with wings now meaningless, they were not a bit shy about letting everyone else know their displeasure. No one blamed them too much for that. We did blame them for the disagreeable manner in which they accepted it all. They were surly, foul-mouthed, and argumentative. They complained about everything, without end. Some came into supply and asked for directions to the hot showers. We laughed at them. Others wanted to know where they could buy cigarettes and bottled beer. That was even funnier. They stomped out with angry curses. We'd now seen enough retreads to last us a long time, and hoped that after these had left, we'd see no more.

I requisitioned rifles and ammunition for them, and wondered what would be sent. Not more Enfields, I hoped. As miserable and difficult as these characters were, they were destined to become infantry. They would need the best weapons available. They'd need M1s.

That's exactly what did arrive, but they were not the new rifles, packed in oiled heavy paper, that I'd been accustomed to receiving. Every one was a battlefield recovery, whose previous user was dead or hospitalized. I'd already had a lot of experience with recoveries, and had three on hand right now that I could personally guarantee were as good as any new rifle.

The hundred and twenty M1s that came in were not. Ordnance was supposed to have checked all of these weapons before sending them up to us. They hadn't even wiped off the mud and dirt. They'd done nothing but empty them of any live cartridges, dipped them in oil, and shipped them out. Maybe this was a payback for the fact that the only rifles I'd ever sent back to ordnance were the ones I'd stripped for spare parts. I didn't know that, but I did know that they were not hurting me by their sloppy work. They were hurting the replacements who needed dependable firearms.

They came through supply in a line. I handed each one a rifle, Bernie handed each a bandoleer of ammo. One kid refused to accept his rifle. It had two swastikas carved in the stock. The weapon was mechanically okay, and I refused to exchange it. I pointed out that for a short time, at least, it had been a lucky piece. Now he had a chance to extend that luck, to add another swastika or two himself. And, those already there did not mean the previous user had been killed. He could be recuperating in a hospital at this moment, with nothing more serious than a case of frostbite. The kid was not fully convinced, but did leave with the rifle.

I exchanged another, though. It represented the worst case of ordnance neglect yet. The kid had looked at the thing when it had been handed to him, held it out by the sling for me to see, and said nothing, but pleaded with his eyes. He had reason to plead. This M1 was covered with dried blood. There was no way I could refuse to exchange it, and I gave him one of my three spares. Later, I disassembled it, took it outside with a bucket of soapy water and wiped it down until no blood remained.

The retreads left us later that day. They were still unhappy, and we were much relieved to see the last of them.

The next day was New Year's Eve. Bernie came in, as usual, but left about midday. Sergeant Parsons had declared a half holiday, maybe to recover from the hassle of equipping former Air Force personnel to do some good in this war.

Bernie came back fifteen minutes later. There had been some sort of racket at the bridge over the railroad tracks. He walked in with his uniform dirty and scuffed.

"What happened?" we asked him.

"You didn't see it? No, I guess you couldn't from here. But you must have heard something."

"We did," I told him, "but we had no idea what it was."

"It was the German Air Force, out to get me," he said. "I've known for a long time they were someday going to try it. Today was the day. They didn't want me to see the New Year. But I escaped, if just barely."

Knowing Bernie, we expected some sort of exaggeration in his account, just for a laugh or two. "Okay," said Parsons, "what really did happen?"

"Well, I was just about to cross the bridge, when I heard it coming. Not only that, but bullets were bouncing and twanging and ricocheting all through the bridge girders and cables up there. I dove head first off the side of the road, rolled down the embankment, and watched him go past, shooting up some of those box cars on the siding. But he was really after me, you know. They were only his secondary target."

"And this was the entire German Air Force?" I asked.

"Well," said Bernie, "it was close enough. It was one of their fighter planes, and I guess he'd followed the railroad tracks, looking for me. Wait'll I tell my wife about this. She'll say the Krauts probably wanted me on their side, and this was an invitation. She never will understand how important I've been to this whole war business. How could you guys ever have gotten by without me stopping in now and then to straighten out the entire First Army supply situation?"

We wished Bernie the best, and a Happy New Year. I walked outside and watched him as he went up to, and over, the bridge. The German Air Force did not show up again that day.

# 22

## *Here We Go Again*

We moved in early January. It was on short notice, and I needed to give the Belgian family something for letting me stay there at night. The cooks had been saving grease in a five-gallon tin, but had no time now to find a place for it. Grease, lard, and such fats had value, because soap could be made from them, and this was a product usually unavailable. I took the tin and ran to the house.

The son was not at home, but his parents were. I soon realized that Dominic had left them with the impression that I would pay for our lodgings. I couldn't. We still waited for three months of back pay to catch up with us. I told them, as best I could, that all the Americans were leaving, and put the tin of grease on the floor. They were unimpressed, and wanted to argue the matter. I had no more time, and left. Dominic the fairy con man had really done a number on all of us.

We loaded up and the trucks rolled, back the way we'd come, to a small town on the outskirts of Verviers. Everything we'd heard indicated that allied forces were attacking, slogging through deep snow, ice, mud, and miserable weather, in an attempt to dislodge the Germans from the ground they'd gained in their Ardennes offensive. Spring was the traditional time to attack or counter-attack, but the Germans had ignored tradition when they'd made their move, and now our generals wanted to do the same. To be in position for the final assault on the German homeland, they apparently felt it was first necessary to take back all that had been lost. Comfort or acceptable living conditions for the front-line troops did not enter into consideration. A heavy price was paid for much of that reclaimed territory, and our services were needed as much as they'd ever been.

Our new location was another empty three-story factory building. This stood alone, apart from any other property, at the end of a hundred-yard driveway. On one side of the driveway were what appeared to have been offices. The other side had a building that was probably used by the maintenance people. Our HQ took the office building, we had the other for supply and my tiny armory. The factory was housing for the replacements and our sergeants who were directly responsible for them. The cooks set up a kitchen in a big garage.

One of the first to stop in was Tom Willis. He'd suffered a minor wound and had spent a couple of weeks in a field hospital at Liège. His First Division had been hastily thrown back into action before they had completely recovered their full strength, as was the Fourth, and any others who thought they'd have a rest for a while. Necessity was the taskmaster served by all.

I had a cousin who was an army nurse. I knew, from correspondence with her, that she was in Belgium, but not specifically where. I did know her hospital's designation. I told Tom her name and hospital number, and asked if she might be serving with that unit in Liège.

"Hey," he said, "Ruth was my nurse there. You should go see her. It's a family thing, so the company commander can issue you a pass for a few hours. Why not try it? I'll give you the directions."

He did, and I asked. All that was allowed was a twelve-hour pass, good from noon until midnight. Liège was ten miles away, and transportation was a sometime thing, nothing dependable. I decided to try it, and borrowed some money from the company clerk.

The company commander's advice was to start immediately, at 10:00 in the morning, although the pass was not active until noon. "Nobody's likely to stop you locally," he said, "but if they do, I never told you to do this. Just try to get back before midnight."

After I'd hiked for a mile or more, a passing jeep stopped and took me within a couple of miles of the city. The driver told me where the hospital was situated, near the top of the highest hill in Liège. I walked until I reached a main road, where electric trolleys were operating. One stopped for me, and I managed to tell the operator where I was going. The courtesy and consideration we'd received from all Belgians was repeated here. The trolley driver refused to accept any payment, and stopped at the foot of a very steep road going up the hill. He nodded at me. This was the place.

It was a long walk, but in time, I arrived at the guard station, where I gave the man there Ruth's name, and told him we were cousins. He went out of his way to be accommodating. He phoned the headquarters. They located Ruth, and she came to the guard station to meet me. The whole hospital staff seemed to think it was something wonderful to have a relative arrive to visit one of their nurses. Ruth took me to dinner in the officers' mess, where I was greeted kindly by one and all. My rifle was a bit out of place, but I leaned it against an outside wall of the building, and put my helmet next to it. The meal was excellent.

We went to a movie after that, strolled around the grounds and talked "family." I noticed the gasoline tank "farm" down the hill from the hospital, and asked how they had fared during the German offensive.

"We gathered together every piece of equipment we could find with wheels and an engine," she said. "We were ready to load all the patients, and ourselves, on these and head out, to any place west of Liège.

"It wasn't so much the German Army we feared. It was those gasoline tanks down there. If they ever went off, from fire, artillery, or bombing, the whole top of this hill would go, taking the hospital with it. That didn't happen, of course, but we were ready."

When I left, Ruth found a jeep and driver to take me down the hill and as far as the main road to Verviers. He could go no farther without express orders from the commanding officer of the hospital. There was no need. I walked, hoping for another truck or jeep to pass. It was almost two hours later when a Belgian civilian truck, a very large one operating on gas in one of those huge bags atop the truck's cab and body, stopped and offered a ride. There were three men in the cab, and I squeezed in beside them. Not one spoke English. I wondered why they were traveling at night, and thought they might be hauling black market goods. That was no business of mine, so I said nothing and shared my cigarettes with them, which I suspected was why they stopped for me in the first place. Perhaps that was unkind, I thought, in view of the treatment I'd enjoyed from all the people in this small country. I smiled as I offered each a smoke, and received smiles in return.

They dropped me off in a strange section of the town, where nothing was familiar. It was dark, there were no lights, and visibility was limited by fog. It was one o'clock in the morning, with no moon, no stars. I could barely see twenty feet ahead. Nothing on the surface of the earth is ever totally black, though. A little light seeps from a house, a truck, a lighted sign, and as long as one stays on pavement, progress can be made. Toward what, we don't always know. I walked in a direction I "felt" was right. Eventually, I came to a large shadowy building I recognized as the railroad station. This had suffered remarkably little damage during the destruction of the rest of Verviers. In fact, the whole town was well on the way to recovering and rebuilding since we'd passed through it during our retreat. A remarkable fact about European communities was the speed with which they could recover from the devastation of war. I could only imagine that generations of familiarity had made them resilient in the extreme. From the railway station, I chose a street I thought was the best, and continued. A half hour later, I walked into my own company's area. The sentry was expecting me, and did not make an issue of the fact that the pass had expired earlier.

It had been a good and a happy meeting with Ruth, but returning was a strange experience. Some of us seem to have a built-in direction finder, something like a homing pigeon possesses. However, I wasn't going to anything that resembled "home." I was going to my unit, my company. It wasn't a place, and I doubt if I'd have found it if that were my only destination. In the darkness of night, without lights, in a strange city in a foreign country, what counted was that I was going to my tribe, my "pack." Guided solely by animal instincts, I walked unerringly in the right direction, made the right turns. A wolf would have done the same, as would a primitive man. Those ancient instincts can surface and be the best guide we have under conditions rarely confronted in a civilized world, but sometimes known in times of danger or unusual stress. For a long time, I marveled at that.

Among others to show up as we got into our routine was one of the group who had stayed behind at Stavelot, in that stone warehouse down by the river. Jack Hanson gave us a rundown on all that had happened since we'd left. "You knew about Father Victor?" he asked.

"No," I replied. "The last I knew about him was that he was looking for a pistol, but he wouldn't say why he wanted it."

"Yeah, he came to us, too, looking for one. And we saw him once after he'd eventually conned someone into giving one to him. Maybe it was a spare that was going to be left behind when everyone bailed out, or maybe Father Victor paid for it. We didn't know, and it didn't matter. You don't know what happened to him, once he had a pistol in his hands?"

"No. We still haven't heard."

"Well, you do know he was shacking up with a local girl?"

"We knew most of the officers were, but not that the list included him."

"It did, and I guess he really enjoyed the experience. The thing was, when push came to shove, he was sincerely ashamed of himself. Repentant, I guess you'd call it. He looked at us, just before things got hot there, and he said, 'I've lived like a man, not the priest I was supposed to be. I can never atone for this. Since I've lived like a man, all I can do is die like a man. Maybe I can be of a little help here that way.' He walked out into the streets, and waited for a Kraut soldier to show himself. One of our guys followed him, at a distance. It didn't take long, especially where he went, down past what little remained of the bridge. The Krauts had got in down there, but not where we were."

"So what happened then?" I asked. "Did Father Victor start blasting away with his .45 pistol?"

"I guess he tried. Maybe he got off one or two shots, but they went high and wild. He had no idea how to handle a weapon, you know. A Kraut killed him with one rifle shot. Guess it was what he wanted."

I nodded. "From what you said, I'd guess that. So you held them off at the stone warehouse. But how many got across the river down below the bridge?"

"Quite a few. And they were juiced up on something. Didn't seem to care what they did. They smashed their way into houses, mad as hell at the people. These were some of the same Krauts who had occupied Stavelot a few months earlier, and they'd told the people that they'd be back, and there'd be a reckoning. I didn't see it myself, but one of our guys said they took a baby, no more than a few weeks old, and nailed it to a wall with a bayonet, then forced the rest of the family to watch while it screamed and died. That's the kind of stuff they were doing."

"Christ almighty," I said. "That's horrible. It's depraved. Are you sure none of them got into the area where you were, where I stayed, halfway up the hill?"

"Guaranteed," he said. "As far as what they did in the other part of town, Zeb Granger did something that partly evened the score. By the way, Zeb is in England now, if you didn't know. He'll go home when he's healed enough."

"He was wounded, then?"

"Yeah. The Krauts got tired of sending one squad after another into the river, then having us take pot shots at them when they reached the middle. They brought up a tank on the other side, and started dismantling the building we were in with their 88. We were all hit by flying rock and shrapnel. Zeb got it the worst. He had a leg blown almost off."

"That's why he's in England now?" I asked.

"Yeah," said Jack. "The Thirtieth Infantry came in about then, on loan from the Third Army. The Krauts pulled back. The medics in the Thirtieth took care of us, and had Zeb sent to England."

It sounded to me as if my kids had survived okay, and I fervently hoped so. "What did Zeb do that evened the score, as you said?" I asked.

Jack was quiet for a little while. "You'd better keep this to yourself," he said. "The high brass may not let him go home if they learn of it. Actually, the Krauts themselves destroyed any evidence with their tank and 88."

"Evidence of what?" I asked, becoming a little uneasy about this.

"Well," Jack continued, "two of the Krauts got across the river from one squad. They surrendered right away, and we kept

them in a room on the same floor where we had our positions."
He paused. "You know how crazy Zeb could be sometimes?"

"Yes," I replied. "There were times he didn't seem to have both
oars in the water. What did he do?"

"He called the Krauts out and offered each a cigarette."

My uneasy feeling was getting worse. "And then what?"

"Well, he even lit their cigarettes for them with his Zippo.
They were dragging on the butts and looking real relaxed by
now. Zeb pulled his trench knife from its sheath, real quick, and
drove it point first into the gut of one of them, then pointed it
up, like we were trained to do, and rammed it in hard to hit the
solar plexus. The Kraut went down like a sack of potatoes. Zeb
wiped his knife on the guy's uniform, stuck the knife back in the
sheath, and grinned at us. 'I always have wanted to do that,' he
said. We all turned away, and one of our guys got kind of sick. It
was right after that the tank pulled up across the river."

I shook my head. How is it possible to sort out your feelings and emotions in a situation like this? Zeb had, beyond any
doubt, saved the lives of a hundred or more Belgians in that section of town. Among them were my young friends, Yvan, Léone,
and Hélène. But had it been really necessary to be so totally
brutal? Maybe not in that particular circumstance, but in the
larger picture, the answer had to be "yes." It was exactly that
kind of brutality that wins any war. I wanted no part of it, and
yet I happily supplied the tools to kill an enemy I didn't even
know. I offered the rifles, the carbines, the ammunition. I was
no conscientious objector, that was a certainty. Yet, I wanted
the war to be fought more cleanly. I wanted to own a piece of
moral high ground, a sense of ethical conduct that would allow
us to win, but never condone what often had to be done. It was
a dream far beyond the reach of the mortals who fought wars,
or supported those who did. I had no justification for any criticism of Zeb, or his methods, or his satisfaction at experiencing
another way to slaughter an unarmed man. Directly or indi-
rectly, we were all guilty of as much, if not far more.

Another side of this internal debate was how to deal with
what the Krauts had done with that baby. By any measure, their
behavior was worse than Zeb's, because it had been directed at
civilians, at a small helpless civilian. If true, revenge was needed.

But wasn't that exactly what kept wars going? An act of obscene brutality or torture must be avenged. It can't be ignored. Then, one act of inhumanity leads to another, and this leads to the sort of hatred that fuels the ability to ignore any and all ethical considerations and get on with the war and the killing. Military and political leaders depend upon righteous indignation and a thirst for vengeance to carry their causes to a conclusion. The best way to arouse such feelings was to publicize the atrocities of the enemy. Invariably, that meant sinking to their level of disregard for decency, to "fight fire with fire." This was the single most insidious characteristic in totalitarian regimes, such as Hitler's. It forced its opponents to imitate its methods, its viciousness, and its depravity.

It was about this time that the news media at home, and our own Stars and Stripes, pulled out all the stops in their plea for retribution. This was founded on what they called "The Malmedy Massacre."

In the confusion following the initial German attack on December 16, men were separated from their units, taken to wrong destinations, and left behind without orders. A group of these unfortunates had gathered at Malmedy, after our sister company had pulled out and joined us in Stavelot. We had no knowledge of what was happening there. German forces were now in control of both Malmedy and the road between Malmedy and Stavelot.

The Malmedy group was composed of a hundred and fifty clerks, cooks, drivers without a vehicle, and miscellaneous others who had little or no combat experience. They were, for the most part, armed with carbines, if they had a weapon at all. When German tanks and trucks arrived, the group surrendered. They were promptly marched into a field, where machine-guns on the tanks and the open rear of a truck raked through them. Some ran for the woods, and a few of them escaped that way. Of the rest, most were dead when the guns stopped firing. A German officer walked through the bodies and used his pistol to finish off any who appeared to be still holding onto life. Four of the Americans in the field, all wounded, faked death and survived to tell the story.

This was touted as an obscene act of ultimate brutality, a total disregard for all the conventions of civilized warfare. At the same time, but drawing far less attention, thousands of casualties were suffered on both sides by "civilized" acts of war. What had happened at Malmedy was unmitigated horror by any standards, but was it really so much worse than what was happening then every hour of every day, in the "normal" course of wartime events?

At St. Vith, no one surrendered. Clerks and bakers, truck drivers and quartermaster supply personnel all found a rifle and a place in the line of defense holding the city against almost overwhelming odds. The media gave front-page coverage to the battle at Bastogne, and it deserved it, but the reason was that it was an airborne division, taken to that city by truck, but nevertheless airborne, and they always made good copy.

St. Vith was far more critical to the Germans. The "patchwork army" that defended it was neither an army nor a cohesive military unit. It was, at first, without a commander. An Air Force general had taken that responsibility in the beginning, because he was the highest ranking officer there, visiting a friend or relative when the attack started. He'd lasted forty-eight hours, then gathered the few majors and captains together, and declared himself "unfit for command." He'd sat, head in his hands, and abandoned any pretense that he knew what to do next. That was left to four officers, none above the rank of major, and the enlisted men in the field. They held St. Vith until relief came from the Third Army.

Jack had one more thing to tell us, and it was something becoming an old refrain in a sorry song. "I suppose you know about the Malmedy Massacre," he said.

"Yes. We all do. Have you got anything special to tell us about it?"

"Not really," said Jack, "but I was there just a short time after it happened. My own wounds were light, and I went along with some of the Thirtieth guys when they chased the Krauts out of the town. We were there when the Air Force was able to fly once more, and wanted to be part of the whole picture."

"You're not going to tell me they bombed the Thirtieth again?" I asked.

"They sure as hell did. Six B-26s, from Ninth Air Force, we were told later, dumped all their bombs on us before we'd had a chance to dig in. There were casualties enough to get the attention of General Hobbs, the division commander."

"I suppose he protested," I said.

"Damn right he did, loud and strong, according to some of the guys who'd been close to his HQ."

"So did the Air Force pay attention?"

Jack shook his head. "Have they ever? Next day, they sent 18 heavies, B-24s, to finish us off. That was just too much. If they'd been paying attention, I think SHAEF could have heard General Hobbs swearing at them from what? Two hundred miles away?"

Little had changed since Normandy. Our ground forces were never able to feel safe when our own planes were overhead.

Our weather turned to all rain, and a lot of it. Even with a roof over us, staying dry was not always possible. Sickness became common, especially dysentery, which spreads as quickly as a bit of questionable gossip. Our "latrine" was a pair of straddle trenches in the hillside next to the supply building. We had a large pyramidal tent covering it, but many rivulets formed on the uphill side, and emptied into the trenches on their way down.

Sick call in the morning became almost the roll call for the entire company. The doctor made a rule. If the fever was under 103, you got some aspirin and went back to work. If it was over 103, but not over 104, you got aspirin and a note excusing you from menial labor for three days. Over 104, and you got a ride to the nearest field hospital. All this kept the situation reasonably under control.

The army sent out some sanitation engineers, who looked at the latrine situation and came up with something they thought was a better plan. A small river ran past our hill and then through the town. They located a pair of utility poles and a crane, and had the poles dropped across the river, about fifteen feet apart. On these they had a platform made, and covered the whole with the tent from our open-air latrine. On the platform they had two rows of seats built, so that our waste material fell into the river rushing below. A wonderful idea, but with a few drawbacks.

First, there were no decent carpenter tools. They amounted to one keyhole saw, very dull, one old crosscut saw with a bent blade, and a hatchet that had known better times, probably in the middle ages. Several "volunteers" were instructed to use these implements to make the holes on which we sat when utilizing the facility. A great variety of shapes was the result.

There was always a line waiting, many anxiously. Dysentery made certain forms of relief most urgent. There was also a sense of humor, since this was about the only way one could look at the marvelous construction our engineers had presented to us.

From inside the tent, and intended for the hearing of those waiting outside, came the calls and comments. "Bombs away" was from those few whose bowels still passed solid matter. Another, as he rose from his seat, was "Next man with a diamond-shaped ass." Others wanted to know if purple hearts were awarded for wounds made by splinters.

That was the "fun" side of it. The rest was dismal. When we had occasion to walk through the town, we noticed that in many places, a street ran right under the river, which at that point would be no more than a foot or two deep. Vehicles forded the river without mishap, and the women of the town used it as an open-air laundry facility, scrubbing clothes at the side of the street and rinsing in the river. Some used flat stones and pounded the clothes clean. Amazingly, this worked well. All talk stopped when an American soldier passed by, though. The looks aimed at us were potentially deadly, and we immediately saw the reason for this antagonism. Floating past the laundresses was a steady stream of turds, brown liquid, and toilet paper. We had turned their laundry facility into an open sewer, and they were not happy about that.

On the other side of the town, the sanitary engineers had another terrific idea. A pumping station was set up. River water was pumped into tanks, chlorinated, pumped again into a large tank mounted on a truck, and brought back to us for drinking water. It made passable coffee, but as long as we could afford it, many of us bought bottled beer from a nearby store. It was excellent beer, locally made, and sold in the old-fashioned bottles with a ceramic top held down by a metal clamp. After we'd bought one bottle and drank it, the vendor refused to sell us added beer if we did not return an empty bottle first.

Whether or not the beer gave birth to longings for stronger drink was not known, but two of our sergeants had an idea that would make them the intellectual equals of army sanitary engineers. They built a still.

# 23

## *A Jeep for the Lieutenant*

Jinks was half of the pair, of course. It seemed perfectly normal that a former regular army, horse cavalryman would know how to build a still. Maybe that had something to do with the fact that he was never paid.

The rest of us were paid, three months accumulated pack pay, which in my case, with the added overseas bonus, minus the war bond bought each month and sent home for me, amounted to almost two hundred dollars. I was rich. So were all of the others, except Jinks, of course. To avoid the possibility of unlikely temptations, most of us sent over half of it home as money orders, available from the company mail clerk.

Jinks and Sammie Weldon, our former anti-aircraft gunners, had remained good friends. Sammie was an okay guy, who just happened to have a fondness for strong drink on occasion. Jinks could always supply the occasion, and a scheme to produce their own nectar for the gods was hatched. It didn't take much. Jinks scrounged around for the necessary tubing, pots, kettles, and whatever they used for such contraptions, Sammie miscounted the kitchen supplies, and discovered that they had some extra sugar, raisins, and a large tin of fruit cocktail.

Canned fruit cocktail was, when we were in a position to enjoy improved rations, the most common finish to the evening meal. It was usually dumped on top of the reconstituted dehydrated potatoes in our mess kits. Now and then, we had canned peaches. Those, too, the kitchen help considered an appropriate topping for potatoes. The potatoes remained tasteless no matter what was dumped on them. It was the fruit cocktail that was in oversupply, though. This wasn't at all unusual. It was execrable stuff, made from the cheapest materials available. It's redeeming features seemed to be that it was easily canned, and if not opened, lasted for several centuries. Few of us cared for it, so there was no outcry when Sammie appropriated some of the surplus for purposes the rest of us did not care to discuss in front of our officers.

The exact location of the still was unknown to any but the pair of miscreants. They said nothing, we asked nothing. Most of us never saw, or tasted, the ultimate results. Apparently, production barely made it to a minimum acceptable quantity. However, other sources of liquid entertainment were available in town, if one knew how to buy it.

Sammie gave us an account of exactly the way Jinks, without money, managed that. They found a small wine peddler on a side street, and entered his establishment with a pair of military boots in hand. Footwear, as in France, was a thing much desired by the natives. The German army, and the German populace, walked on leather stolen from the rest of Europe.

The boots Jinks held in his hands were not exactly stolen. He simply knew how to find them without resorting to outright theft. Often, replacements coming through ordered new shoes whether they needed them or not. When the time came for them to move up and join their division, they were supposed to have two pairs of serviceable shoes or boots. They would examine all three of the pairs in their possession, select the most comfortable two pairs, and leave the other behind. Jinks managed to "find" a new, or nearly new, pair before it was turned in as salvage.

He held one such find aloft for the merchant to see. "Wine?" Jinks asked. His language skills were primitive at best.

"Oui! Vino. Pour sabot," said the proprietor of the shop, and he pointed at the shoes.

"Oui, oui," said Jinks. "To pour." He made a motion as if drinking from a bottle.

The native went into a back room, and emerged with a bottle, from which he carefully brushed the dust of several years. This was one the Germans had been unable to appropriate, probably hidden somewhere in a dark corner beneath dried fruit or potatoes.

Jinks accepted the bottle, looked at it, passed it to Sammie, and handed the Belgian one shoe.

The wine merchant became agitated. "No, no. Vino, shoe," and he made frantic motions indicating that there should have been an exchange of one bottle for one pair of shoes.

"Si, si, monsewer, one bottle, one shoe. That's how it works. Now find another bottle."

Grumbling to himself, and probably cursing all Americans as thieves and brigands, he did find a second bottle, after which Jinks handed him the second shoe. Negotiations were concluded.

The wine was but a stopgap measure, though, while the pair waited impatiently for the slowly dripping produce of the still to accumulate.

Eventually, they had nearly a gallon. It wasn't whiskey. They'd had no grain in the ingredients. It wasn't gin. There were no juniper berries. It hadn't aged enough to be wine, but it was, to a degree that could impair the judgment of most men, alcoholic. That was good enough. Jinks and Sammie decided this was an appropriate time to celebrate. But how do you celebrate in a foreign country, about which you have no more than the sketchiest information? You need transportation, of course, to view the countryside and develop an appreciation for the bounties offered. And where can transportation be found? At the military motor pool, of course.

It took a quarter of their precious fluid to think about that, but once the idea had formed, they knew exactly what to do. The motor pool was just down the street, it was mid-afternoon on one of the rare days of sunshine known to exist in Belgium, and adventure beckoned.

Jinks and Sammie walked into the motor pool, a large, high-ceilinged garage, and found only a couple of mechanics there. The motor pool officer was away. Things were getting better by the minute.

They were two sergeants, and the mechanics were privates, so they played upon the privileges of rank, along with a freshly-concocted story of needing to meet an important general on the other side of town. They needed a Jeep. Of course, they'd sign for it. Of course, it would be returned in immaculate condition soon after they delivered the general to his destination. Why didn't the motor pool lieutenant mention this? Well, maybe it was just too secret, too highly classified to tell him right away.

With two suspicious mechanics watching, they drove out of the garage and headed east. They could now have a little more from the jug at any time, and they did, probably every three minutes, until the cold and partially snow-covered Belgian countryside looked exactly like some half-forgotten vision of summer paradise back home. They stopped just long enough to exchange positions. Jinks now drove, for Sammie had seemed to be having difficulty handling both the steering wheel and the jug at the same time. It takes an ex-cavalryman to do that.

They soon found that MPs had check points, at which all vehicles were supposed to stop and present identification and other nonsense such as passes and authorizations. Rather than embarrass the MPs, they drove right on through the checkpoint.

East is east, and west is west, Rudyard Kipling once wrote, and as far as this couple were concerned, there was really no difference. Except, the soldiers at that second checkpoint were wearing different uniforms, gray instead of olive drab. Who were they, and why had that MP Jeep stopped a little short of the checkpoint, instead of barreling right through, as they had? All too soon, another Jeep-like vehicle had picked up the chase. It was sounding a peculiar sort of siren, and seemed pretty determined to catch them. Time to turn around. In a stretch of road a little wider than the rest, Jinks spun the Jeep to face in the opposite direction. Their pursuers passed just then, and they couldn't help but notice that those strangely-attired soldiers were driving and riding in a vehicle with swastika markings on the side. They had another drink and decided speed would be prudent at this point.

As they tore through the German checkpoint again, the swastika-decorated vehicle slowed, but did not completely stop. It seemed to want the American MPs, with their Jeep, to pick up the chase. They did, and with considerably more skill than Jinks or Sammie could muster at this point. "Abandon ship!" Sammie yelled, and pointed at a large field.

Jinks managed the turn, and he made it across the field, but when they entered woods on the other side, his good judgment failed him, possibly not for the first time that day. They ran headlong into a rather large tree, which refused to move out of the way. Sammie clutched the jug, they "abandoned ship" and bailed out.

The woods were deep and dark, or seemed that way. There were no paths, and their pursuers had apparently given up the game at the edge of the field. The jug was almost empty, so they sat on the ground and made sure it was. After all, you can't leave good drinking stuff lying around loose. Someone might use it and become intoxicated. "Can't let that happfen," Sammie said.

"Nope," Jinks agreed, "can't leaf temptashin in the way of the lower grades. They could get intoshicated."

"Be good for nothing then," Sammie opined.

"Nothin' 'tall."

Eventually, their philosophical ramblings concluded, they stood and, supporting each other, made it back to the company.

They slept soundly for the remainder of the night. In the morning, there was a message from the motor pool lieutenant. He wished to see them immediately.

It was hard for them to concentrate with such monstrous headaches, and the lieutenant was totally unresponsive to suggestions that a little "hair of the dog" might relieve the excruciating pain. He was, in fact, more than a little put out. "You morons!" he shouted. "You good-for-nothing, totally worthless, imbecilic excuses for soldiers. Do you know what you've done?"

"No, lieutenant," Jinks whispered. "Is something wrong?"

"Something wrong? Something wrong? Oh, no, nothing's wrong. It's just that I'll be serving in this army for the rest of my friggin' life to pay for that Jeep. Where is it, by the way?"

"Um, I think, um, maybe it's in some woods," Sammie answered.

"What woods? Where?"

"Well, it's sort of up near the Kraut lines. Maybe they have it now."

Exasperated, the lieutenant pressed for more information. "The Krauts have it. Well, isn't that great. Do you suppose they'd bring it back, it you ask them real nice? Because I think that's what I'll order you two to do, right now."

"Won't work, lieutenant," said Jinks. "It doesn't run so good any more. Radiator's sort of bashed in, wrapped around a big tree, sort of. But don't you worry. Don't you worry at all. Just kind of relax a little, and give us until tomorrow morning, and I think your Jeep will probably show up right here, in this garage. In your motor pool. Yes, I think that will happen. Like I said."

"Tomorrow morning? And I'm supposed to trust you characters to have my Jeep materialize as if by magic, right here?"

Jinks and Sammie both nodded. "Yes, sir," said Sammie. "Just like magic. You go rest somewhere for a while. You seem to be a little nervous today. It's not good for you, you know. High blood pressure and all that stuff."

The lieutenant, with no other options than filing a lost vehicle report, and accepting accountability for the Jeep, sighed and turned away.

That night, Jinks and Sammie kept their word. At about three in the morning, they roused the mechanics at the motor pool, drove in with an operating Jeep, closed the doors and blacked out any opening, then ordered the mechanics to do what they were told. They were sergeants, after all. Paint cans, stencils, a compressor and paint gun, and some fast-drying paint worked a marvelous transformation well before daylight. The lieutenant's Jeep was restored, proper numbers on the hood, all things in order, except, maybe, a minor discrepancy in the papers that were a part of the motor pool records. Jinks and Sammie were not, after all, forgers or counterfeiters.

They were young Americans, in a place they didn't want to be, doing things that had never been a part of their life plans. If they acted a little crazy at times, and took risks never approved by the higher levels of command, so be it. This created memories that would, in the future, produce laughter, a much-needed commodity in many circumstances. Was that so terribly wrong? As long as others were not seriously endangered, couldn't this be called, by some sort of reverse logic, a sign of sanity?

# 24

## *To Have or To Have Not*

Tom Willis stayed with us almost a week this time, waiting for a call from the First Infantry Division to send him forward. The attempt to unite recovering wounded with their original units was falling apart, overwhelmed by the sheer numbers involved. Orders came to simply ship the men wherever they were needed and not to make any attempt to sort it all out.

This caused hard feelings, many directed at us, although we did not make the rules or issue the orders. A soldier in the field has only one real home, and that's his company. No matter how many are lost while he's recuperating, there will always be a few friends left to welcome him back. He'll get that nowhere else, except possibly in a unit like ours, where we'd seen some of them often enough to know them. It still isn't home, though, and no one stayed with us long enough to become much more than a passing acquaintance.

Tom escaped the random assignment of replacements, probably because he was a platoon sergeant, and they were always in high demand—high enough to cause his division to intercede in order to have him back.

Before he left, we had a chance to talk more than we'd ever done before. Cousin Ruth, known to both of us now, was the seed that grew into more topics of conversation.

I'd received a package from home, and this aroused his curiosity. How did someone go about getting one of those? he wanted to know.

"It's easy enough," I told him. "You just need to send a written request to someone—mother, sister, aunt, grandmother, or whoever. Women in the family are generally the ones who do this stuff. They make up the package and take it to the Post

217

Office with the request. The Postmaster has to be satisfied that the material is sent in response to that, so he'll check the letter, or at least that part of it that mentions the package, and stamp it with a post office mark like a cancellation. That's so it can only be used once. The postage is paid, and it's on the way."

Tom had a thoughtful expression. "So that's the way it's done," he said. "I've always wondered."

"You've never had a package from home?" I asked him.

"No. Well, I don't really have a home. I grew up in an institution, an orphan asylum. My parents both died when I was young, and there was no one else."

"Tom," I said, "you don't need to be a member of a family to get a package. All you need is to know someone who would send it to you when asked. Would you like a package? Homemade cookies, probably, maybe a comb, a bar of soap, little things like that?"

He grinned and looked at the ceiling of the supply room. "That would be great, but I don't know anyone outside the orphanage, and no one there has time or money to do that. I can't ask any of them. It would be too much."

"Then let's do it another way. I'll write home, and ask my mother and sister to send you a package. One of them will be willing to do it, maybe both. But my letter will only be letting them know about it. It won't help with mailing it. You'll need to write a request yourself. Do it right now. I've got some writing paper and envelopes. Our letters home go free, and just a short note is all that's needed."

He looked at me as if he were wondering about my sanity. "You sure about this?" he asked.

"I'm sure. Do it, and in a couple of weeks you'll have something personal in the mail, a package addressed just to you."

Shaking his head in doubt, Tom wrote a short note, saying exactly what I told him to. He addressed it, and the next day, I mailed it.

He left before the package came, but it would have been forwarded to him. We just never knew if he received it, because we never heard from, or saw, Tom Willis again. The inescapable conclusion was that his luck had finally run out, and he had fallen victim to the law of averages. It was almost inevitable, but never easy to accept.

Why, I often thought to myself, did this war take the best of us? Why couldn't we lose a few of the worthless creatures in human form, who had never in their lives done a decent thing, and probably never would? Why the best?

Greg Scott, another of our company sergeants, walked in a couple of days later. It was late afternoon, the work load was temporarily light, and he asked if I'd like to join him at a restaurant he'd discovered.

A restaurant? Such a place really existed here?

"Sure," I replied. "Where is it?"

"Less than half mile a from here. The menu is pretty limited. Fried eggs and toast is usually all they have, but it's good. The toast is made with home-baked bread, and they serve as many pieces as you want, with jam. The coffee isn't real, but not too bad."

Except for the coffee, it sounded far better than anything the cooks might have available, and I grabbed my rifle, donned my jacket and helmet, and was ready.

It was, as Greg had said, an easy walk. The "restaurant" turned out to be the cellar of a house, with an outside entrance just off the street. It was clean and neat, with eight tables, each set up to serve four. A middle-aged couple ran the place and did all the cooking, with their daughter, an attractive young woman of nineteen or twenty, acting as waitress. None of them appeared to know much English, but by this time, both Greg and I had mastered a few words of Walloon.

That did not seem to be true of the two Americans who sat at one of the other tables. They were a pair of privates, without any insignia, which meant they were newly arrived, at least in this area, and were likely replacements. They had found this place, possibly by accident, and intended to take advantage of the discovery. One of them was a loud-mouthed know-it-all, who kept up a steady stream of abusive comments aimed at the waitress and her parents.

"I know these people," he proclaimed. "I've been in Europe for five weeks, and I know what they are. You can't trust any of them. They'll take advantage of you at every turn. All you can do is get even with them."

"How?" asked his companion.

"How do you think? Make them wait on us, make them give us anything we want, and don't give them anything. I'll not pay for this stuff they're serving us. Why should I? You're crazy if you do. They don't deserve it."

"I don't even know them," the other man said. "And from what I can see, they're doing a good job with pretty limited resources. I've got no reason to not pay. That would be stealing."

"Stealing? We're Americans. These filthy robbers have been stealing from us for generations. How do you suppose we got into all this trouble over here? It wasn't because any of these worthless scum ever paid us for all the things we gave them."

"Is that true?"

"You bet your ass it's true. I've heard my folks talk about it for years. You watch that broad who's bringing us the food. If she makes one false move, just one tiny mistake in the way she puts our food on the table, she deserves a damned good slap across the face."

Greg and I both turned to stare at him. "I wouldn't do that if I were you," Greg said.

I nodded. "You'd better listen," I added.

"And just what will you two do about it? Oh, a sergeant and a T5. I'm so impressed. What are you going to do, arrest me? Confine me to quarters in that old factory building? Or do you want to mix it up outside the door? A non-com can't strike a private, you know. Or if you didn't know, you'll find out at your court-martial."

The girl came with their eggs and toast. She set them down carefully, and put cups and a pitcher of ersatz coffee within their reach, along with sugar and cream. We watched, Greg with his hands clenched into fists. The loud-mouth made no move. The girl said something to them, and he just shook his head and stared at his meal.

"She asked," I said, "if you wished anything else."

"Then why didn't she say it in English? She's not so stupid as to think we'd understand that garble, is she?"

"I doubt," Greg replied, "that she's stupid at all. Incidentally, do you have a pass to be here?"

"Pass? Who needs a pass in this asshole of the world?"

"You and your friend do. Unless you have passes, I suggest you both get out of here and return to your proper place."

"All right if we eat first, since we're here?"

"Eat and leave."

They were quiet after that, concentrating on filling their mouths with excellent fried eggs and toast. Greg and I had our own order by this time, and relaxed to enjoy it.

The pair finished and walked to the door.

"Hey," Greg yelled, "you didn't pay."

"Screw you, Sergeant," the loudmouth replied, and the two hurried out the door and away.

"Forget it," I told Greg. "They're not worth the trouble it would take to find them."

We paid, and left some extra to help cover at least the aggravation caused by an American whose personal claim on life and liberty could end very soon. Few squad leaders or platoon sergeants would put up with him more than an hour or two.

On the way back, thoughts of Tom Willis kept intruding. I could not help comparing him to the character we'd just seen. Tom was as decent a human being as ever lived, and deserved the respect everyone had for him. He'd been given nothing by a society that believed regimented existence in an institution was all it could reasonably afford for an orphan. He'd accepted that, and when the time came, gave back tenfold what he'd ever received. Now, he was very close to his end, and for what? So that loudmouth in the restaurant could go back to a life of complaining, a life of grabbing everything he could get for himself, and never, even once, give a thought to others? That's the way it was likely to work out, and it produced a sour taste in my mouth, after a meal that was the best we'd known in many weeks. Greg, I thought, was feeling the same.

I had to believe that if there were any justice on earth or beyond, the scales would some day be balanced. In the meantime, I would remember Tom, and forget, as far as possible, that piece of useless trash we'd just encountered in the restaurant.

Things are never quite that simple, though. We don't always control what we remember and what we forget. Further, our judgment of those we meet can be biased by previous experiences. The impression they give may be little more than a façade, a cover-up for their real temperament or nature.

For example, those three seemingly good people, the couple and their daughter, might not be all that they appeared to be. It was evident they were doing their best to bring their lives back to a pre-war basis. That was admirable, and we enjoyed having a facility like their little restaurant-in-a-basement available to us. But how and where did they get enough good bread flour and eggs to do what they were doing, while their neighbors lived on the edge, never knowing if they'd have anything to eat tomorrow?

We'd already witnessed evidence of that at our mess line. Every day, local kids came. Each had a can, often rusty, the size of a one-pound coffee can. A wire had been attached at the open end of the can, to use as a handle. They reminded me of the cans I'd used to pick wild blueberries at home.

These kids were after something other than wild berries. They were keeping their families alive. They patiently waited by the galvanized barrel in which we dumped any remains from our mess kits before we rinsed them in another barrel filled with an antiseptic solution. As soon as we'd dumped our garbage, one or more kids would scoop it up in their cans and head for home.

How they could eat it, and keep a family alive, was more than we could understand. The cooks dumped coffee grounds in the barrel. Grease from the pans went there. Our own mess kit garbage was likely to contain cigarette butts. All of it went in the wire-handled cans and went home with the kids. We imagined they sorted it out on a kitchen table, and then used every bit of it. Coffee grounds can be re-used. Soggy cigarette butts can be dried, stripped, and the tobacco re-wrapped in newsprint, just as we ourselves had done in the Argonne. Nothing was wasted, nothing thrown away.

All of this might be blamed on a choice made by the Belgian government when the German army had arrived at the border, with intentions to use the country as a gateway to northern France. The Belgians opened the border gates and stepped aside. They offered no resistance, with the result that France collapsed, and the British forces on the continent were routed and fell back to Dunkirk, where many of them died and others barely escaped.

The Belgians had remembered World War I, just twenty-five years earlier. In that war, they had resisted. They had fought the German army, alone and outnumbered, while France and England consulted and eventually reached a decision about what they might do next. By then, the cities of Belgium lay in ruins, their farmland stripped of anything edible by foraging foreign troops, their young men dead or wounded. "Never again" was their motto this time.

Had appeasement really done them any good? Now, many of their cities lay partially ruined, the farmland looted first by the Germans, then, to a lesser extent, by the Allied armies. Many of their people had been taken away, the reasons never made clear. In Stavelot, Yvan had tried to tell me about that, but I'd never understood. What and where was "Buchenwald?"

As a national policy, surrender without resistance had little to recommend it, beside consequences of an occupation that might have been less severe than would have been the case following active warfare. Yet, we could hardly blame the Belgians, given their history. What other choice was available to them? To fight again, to die again?

All that said, and added to the fact that we admired the couple who had started the restaurant, how had they managed to do it? If they had the resources, then why were their neighbors starving, or eating garbage that the kids gathered from our mess line? There were serious inequities here.

A partial answer, of course, was the black market. Anything can be bought, if you have the price. It wasn't right, it wasn't fair, and it illustrated the underlying greed of people everywhere—a greed that permits some to prosper while others suffer. In the contest for survival, were the greedy always favored over the altruistic? It seemed that way.

Ed and I had seen an example of that in Verviers, not far from where we were now. Before the center of the city had been destroyed, Woolworth's, an international corporation, had flourished in the middle of war's scarcities and under the eyes of occupation troops. How much had it cost to do that? How much in bribes had been paid to Hitler's minions, or how great an interest in Woolworth's success did the Nazis of Germany have? Finally, how widespread was the protection given to other kinds of multi-national businesses?

# 25

# *Across The Border to Germany*

What part in the whole of this war was played by the multi-national corporations was something about which we could only wonder. The fighting went on as usual. Most of the territory lost in the Ardennes had been recovered, which meant we'd be moving again soon. This would undoubtedly be into Germany itself. The Krauts were in retreat once more, and although there would likely be some determined resistance ahead, the Allied noose was tightening around their heartland.

We began to hear disturbing reports of what had happened in the early days of the Ardennes offensive. General Montgomery, on our northern flank with the English, Canadian, and French divisions, plus some American units, had refused to move. He'd protested to Eisenhower that he should be in command of all Allied forces, not just the northern army. When the attack came, he dismissed it as a feint, not of any real importance. German generals, he proclaimed, were far too intelligent to launch anything like a major attack at this time of the year. He dallied and "tidied his lines" (a favorite expression of his) while thirty thousand Americans became casualties doing their best to hold positions that the Germans never could have taken if those northern divisions had been committed to the battle.

We further heard that General Patton, of the Third Army, became so incensed with Montgomery, he petitioned Eisenhower to turn both First and Third armies northward and dispose of the British once and for all. We'd be better off going it alone, he said. Monty and his English troops only held us back. It was impossible to verify all of that, but it fit with Patton's character, and where there was smoke, there was likely to be some fire.

Patton had, in fact, been forced to abandon his Third Army objectives in order to send relief forces to the aid of First Army. Montgomery was blamed for this, and the subsequent lengthening of the war as a result. Beloved by the British as the hero of El Alamein, Monty had become an irritating thorn in the side of our American commanders. He was a pompous, strutting little peacock, with an irrational view of his own importance and abilities.

At the very end of the Ardennes battle, Montgomery did send in a few of his troops. He then announced to the world that it was he, Bernard Law Montgomery, who had stopped the Germans and reversed the tide of battle.

In a public broadcast, Churchill himself publicly squelched this bit of glory hunting nonsense. He informed the British people and the world that it was the Americans who had done what was necessary, it was the Americans who had bled and died, and it was Americans who had suffered eighty times the casualties of Montgomery's forces.

What was done was done, though, and any effect it all had on our personal lives was quickly relegated to history. Unrelated to any of this, except perhaps the psychological strains all of us endured during these trying times, our mess sergeant suffered a breakdown, and was sent back for rest and psychiatric counseling. Our officers said little about it, and obviously expected him to return shortly. In the meantime, Jinks was asked to become the acting mess sergeant, an assignment he accepted with his typical unconcern for the seriousness of his position, or much of anything else.

That included the Colonel, when he made an inspection call on the company. Colonel Peters was an infantry officer who had served in World War I, when he'd been too young to be given a serious position of command. Now, in our war, he was thought to be too old. He was put in charge of the Third Replacement Depot, which included our company.

Those who served in his headquarters told us a little about him. The military was his career and his life. Yet, circumstances had conspired to rob him of any opportunity to distinguish himself as a leader of fighting men. He was never quite able to hide his disappointment.

The replacement system was viewed as the dregs of the army. We who served in it knew that, and failed to see how Colonel Peters could be unaware of it. We saw him only rarely, and it seemed that each time, he'd become more aged and more stooped with care. Yet, neither he nor we who served under him could allow that view of our role to affect the performance of our duty. We worked harder than almost any other military unit. We absorbed the calumny spread about us by those who knew nothing about what we did. We probably had the highest suicide rate in the military, if only because we were continually denied any crumb of recognition for our services.

Although outsiders and the ignorant might have wondered how in the world a mess sergeant in a reinforcement company could possibly have a breakdown, we knew how. Too many times, he'd been awakened at three in the morning and told two hundred men would be arriving momentarily, and he must find a way to feed them the first nourishing meal they'd have had in two days. No, he could not have been told in advance. No, no one had ordered the foodstuffs he'd need. He had canned goods and dry foods on hand. He should use them. If they were not enough, make do with C or K rations.

Once or twice, or three times, this could be done. In the process, he learned how to hoard a few prime ingredients for the meals. Against regulations, of course, just as ordering extra clothing was against regulations for supply, or keeping spare parts for M1 rifles was against regulations for an armorer. The army survived by the efforts of those who ignored the regulations.

After the mess sergeant had done his thing at two or three or four o'clock, he then started on the breakfast meal for others present. He was not permitted to rest or relax or grab a little sleep. There was an almost daily crisis that needed to be met and defused.

By the time he'd survived this routine thirty or forty times, the demands made upon him had become unbearable, beyond his human capacity to meet. With a man already past exhaustion, demand piled upon demand destroyed his willingness to once more attempt the impossible. Shaken and out of control, he surrendered to the expediency of abandoning his sanity as the only remaining defense against a world gone berserk. He broke down.

Now Jinks had the duty. This might have been a good thing, because our ex-cavalryman was as close to being unflappable as anyone we knew. Yet, there was an unbridgeable gulf between the way a sergeant, especially a carefree, booze-loving, danger-flaunting sergeant, and most officers above company rank, saw the situation.

Colonel Peters came to our supply building and my armory after stopping at the company HQ. In general, he was satisfied, but became agitated when he saw my rack of M1 rifles. "What are these?" he wanted to know.

"They belong to men in the hospital," I told him. "When they had dysentery, and were taken back for treatment, I tagged their rifles and kept them here for them." I showed him the tags on each piece, with the soldier's name, serial number, and date he'd been sent to a hospital.

"They should be shipped to ordnance," he said. "After a reasonable time, they should be sent there, and then reissued, so that men going to the front can have them."

"I do that," I said. "If the men don't return and claim their weapons in thirty days, I'll send them back."

"Very well. But don't keep them any longer than that."

"No, sir."

I didn't mention my earlier problems with ordnance, and that when I sent any of these weapons back, it would likely be without ejectors, extractors, or several other small parts. The colonel was a by-the-book officer, and would not have understood all that.

He did understand Jinks, however, all too well. When he entered the kitchen area, Jinks called all the personnel to attention, which was proper. He then spoke to the Colonel as if they were equals. "We knew you were coming today, Colonel," he said, "and we know you like cake, so there's cake in those pans over there next to the ranges. Why don't you go over and help yourself? I've got a hundred things to do here right now."

Colonel Peters was more than a little surprised. This sergeant showed none of the proper respect for a full colonel of infantry. In fact, his actions bordered on the insubordinate. However, the colonel did take and eat two pieces of cake. He also stopped at our HQ again before he left.

We lost Jinks the next day. He was transferred to a cavalry reconnaissance outfit. It wasn't the horse cavalry by a long shot, but he'd be riding around in a fast armored car, maybe a half track, scouting out enemy strong points and weak spots for the division that would likely be mounting an attack in that area before long. It was a hazardous job, but maybe a little less so for one who had driven a Jeep through enemy lines, survived pursuit by the military police of both sides, and returned little the worse for wear, barring that hangover, of course.

In a few days, we loaded up and moved, this time into Germany, to Aachen, taken in fierce fighting back in October, before the Ardennes. It was the first major city captured in Germany, and it had been badly mauled, much of it pounded into rubble by bombers, then hammered by artillery. After our infantry had secured the city, it became the target of German artillery. Few of its buildings were whole.

Other than some workers trying to repair gas and water lines, there were no civilians. They'd apparently been moved out when the fighting became severe. Our trucks stopped in front of an apartment complex, a three-story structure that was almost an entire city block in length. It had suffered only minor damage, and this would be our home for a while.

The infantry had checked out this building for us, making sure there were no Kraut soldiers or snipers here, or booby traps in the rooms. Utility rooms were in the cellar, with small windows facing the street. To be sure no one was hiding there, a soldier walked past in the street, tossing a hand grenade through each window.

It was not a rear-guard soldier or holdout with a burp gun they caught. One woman, who had refused to leave her home when ordered to do so, had apparently stayed throughout the bombing and shelling. She was in the cellar with her eleven year old daughter, doing some laundry, when the grenade sailed through the window. Their bodies were removed to a cemetery at the edge of the city. No blame was attached to this incident. The woman was not supposed to be there.

The Fourth Infantry was in position just east of the city, and we were here to supply them with replacements. I began to receive many battlefield recoveries, picked up in the local area. Most of them were M1 rifles, with some carbines, and a pair of German Gewehr 43 semi-automatic rifles with the stocks broken and the magazines missing. These were the first examples of a relatively new weapon that I'd seen.

It was interesting that the Germans, who excelled in the design and manufacture of weapons, had been unable to come up with anything to compare with our M1 rifle. Their Gewehr 41 had been a miserable failure.

As with our M1, an operating rod worked the bolt to expel the spent cartridge, after which a return spring loaded the next. Near the muzzle end of the barrel was a small hole connecting the barrel to a cylinder. This used some of the explosive force of the burning gunpowder to drive a piston that operated the rod. The problem with the Gewehr 41 was in the design of the cylinder and piston. They continually fouled with burnt powder particles and then jammed.

This Gewehr 43 now in my hands was supposed to have overcome that problem and be a weapon superior to our M1. It wasn't, and never would be. It was poorly and cheaply made, with stamped metal parts and castings where machined steel should have been used. It was a prime example of how German ingenuity and manufacturing skill had been undermined by the lack of good materials with which to produce their latest weapons.

The German soldiers who had used these two weapons undoubtedly believed that they had the finest pieces in the world. When Fourth Infantry riflemen pinned them down in a shell hole, they returned fire until their ammunition ran out. They then threw their 10-round magazines as far away as they could, smashed the butts of their rifles on the ground to break the stocks, and surrendered. No one, they were determined, would be able to use these wonderful weapons against them. No one wanted to, as long as an M1 was available.

Inspecting, repairing when necessary, and test firing the recovered M1s took much of my time. When I had accumulated eight rifles, all inspected and repaired if necessary, I'd sling four on each shoulder, put a couple of bandoleers of ammo around my neck, and walk to a small gravel pit near the end of our street. Here, I stacked the rifles and, one after another, fired a full clip into the bank. They always worked fine. I returned to my corner of the supply room, cleaned and oiled each piece, and had them ready to issue when they were needed.

Buzz bombs went over frequently, on their way to targets in France or England. We heard from new arrivals who had recently spent time in England that the bombs were taking a serious toll on both property and morale, especially in and around London. The launching bases were not far away now, and became a major objective in every new offensive.

Another kind of bomb flew over, too. These were the V2s, Germany's newest weapon in the last-ditch efforts to keep the war alive. No one ever saw a V2. They flew too high, reaching an apex of 125 miles above the earth. We heard about them, and understood the terror they could inspire in their target areas. The V2 carried a thousand pounds of explosive, and there was no defense against them. Skilled fighter pilots could shoot down buzz bombs. Anti-aircraft could nail one on occasion. The V2 flew high and fast, and no one knew it was there until an entire city block vanished in smoke and flame.

That happened very near us. It was a clear and quiet day. Suddenly a blue flame shot hundreds of feet into the air, we felt a blast that rocked everything within a half mile, and a city block was no more. Many of us were sure it was a V2. Why not? The Germans had been shelling Aachen regularly. They publicly denied it, though, and claimed that never had they targeted one of their own cities with either the V1 buzz bomb, or the V2. But could we believe that? The only other explanation was that a large building had filled with gas from a ruptured pipeline or broken valve, and then had been ignited by an electrical spark. To most of us, this was more of a "reach" than believing it had been a V2.

One day soon after this, Lee Normand came in, returning from three weeks in a field hospital, where he'd recovered from his third wound. We'd seen him twice before, and knew him as well as we could ever know anyone in our situation. Lee was a squad leader in the Fourth, a ruggedly handsome young man, slightly shorter than average but muscular, with blond hair and blue eyes. He had an air of authority about him, but in a way that was easily accepted by all who knew him, even if slightly. He'd never hesitated to pitch in and help out any time he saw a situation in which he could make a difference.

He spoke little now, and moved in line as if he were a robot from whom all spirit and initiative had been removed. When we tried to talk to him, he shook his head and said, "This time I'll die. Just can't do it any more."

Being here meant that he was headed back to his company. This was all wrong. He shouldn't be doing that. We had a small, inexpensive radio, with which we heard the Armed Forces Network when it was broadcasting. A couple of days earlier, President Roosevelt had been on the air, letting us know that every soldier who had been wounded three times had bought himself a ticket home. He would not be placed in jeopardy again, beyond what might happen at a training camp in the States. Such a soldier had more value teaching new recruits than exposing himself to enemy fire. So said the President.

Such a soldier was Lee, and we believed what we'd heard. For a short time, we believed it. More than that, we felt it had to be true, because Lee was in bad shape. His eyes bugged out, his hands shook, and he stumbled when he tried to walk. He was just one loud noise this side of a section eight. He needed to go home, because he'd given all he could give. There was nothing left but raw nerves and poor judgment.

The rifles came, and just as the last time, they were recoveries returning through ordnance. Just as last time, ordnance had done a sloppy job of preparing them. One had a cracked stock, others were missing ejectors, a few had blood stains. I put those aside and replaced them with the rifles I'd personally inspected and test fired and cleaned. I made sure Lee got one of these.

The trucks came and loaded. We watched Lee Normand, sitting on the last seat in a Jimmy, his rifle between his knees and his eyes staring at nothing at all, while the truck moved out, going where the new men and the old would form up into their respective companies and prepare for the next offensive. We felt almost as sorry for those assigned to his squad as we did for Lee. They were in all likelihood facing a death sentence. Leadership in battle requires all the qualities Lee Normand had lost, and no soothing words and false promises from the President were going to matter. The division needed squad leaders, and military necessity demanded that anyone who had once done it would do it again, and the politicians be damned.

Lee lost his squad that night, and we lost him.

Soon after, we left Aachen, riding our trucks and threading our way through burning open-pit soft coal fields. The road was little more than a cart path, with flames and sulfurous smoke rising on both sides. Our bombers had set the pits afire, for what purpose no one seemed to know. Eventually, we left it all behind us, but for a few miles, it was the nearest thing any of us could imagine to Dante's inferno. Or maybe it was real, and the world we thought was ours was entirely mythical. It was through much of this smoky, fuming, choking piece of hellish horror that our Fourth Infantry had just fought its way.

# 26

## *More Work, New Responsibilities*

Bonn was our next stop. A city on the Rhine, it was directly across the river from what was called the "Ruhr Pocket." This was the heart of Germany's heavy industry. Tanks and artillery were made there. It was heavily defended, and had simply been bypassed and surrounded by Allied forces. The Ruhr, it was assumed, would collapse when the rest of Germany did, without the loss of life that would have been required to take it in combat.

We moved down a street parallel to, and not far from, the river, and took over some of the tenements on each side. Parsons, a couple of volunteers, and I set up supply in what had been a pharmacy or, in British terms, a "chemist's shop." We lived in a tenement on the floor above. This was an improvement over Aachen, for Bonn had been less severely damaged. Although electricity and heat were lacking, we had the benefits of running water, and even the means, through a small gas unit, to heat water for hand laundry and a bath. I happily took advantage of this facility.

It was obvious that the apartment had been hastily abandoned by the previous occupants. It was not unusual for the army's advance party to give homeowners, or tenants, no more than an hour to exit the premises, after which the troops moved in. Where the displaced people went was of no concern to us, and entirely up to whatever civilian authority existed in the place.

This apartment, with its absence of battle damage, became a learning experience. On the living room wall was a fairly large crucifix, gold plate on some kind of base metal. These people had been devout Christians, probably Catholic. This perception was reinforced by other small religious objects around the place. Once more, it gave the lie to what we'd been told at home about all of Germany being an atheist nation. There was a buffet in the dining area, on which was an attractive glass container, shaped like a barrel on two supports, with a spigot that poured wine when opened. It held a little more than a quart, probably a liter. Other items bore testimony to a life style above what we might have expected in a city tenement, no matter how well-kept. Germany was the cleanest country in Europe, and this was evident no matter where we looked, inside or outdoors.

Most interesting to me, however, was a model automotive engine, about a foot long, made entirely of clear plastic, which would have operated at the touch of a button if the battery had not been dead. I could turn it by hand, and when I did, gears rotated, pistons went up and down in order, valves opened and closed, and if the battery had been active, small red lights would have shown the spark plugs firing in proper sequence. The details in this model were fantastic, and I could have spent hours turning it and observing, just to see how all the parts worked. The company logo was prominent on the front of the engine. This engine was a Ford V8.

How and why? I wanted to know. What German teenager, interested in automotive engineering, had used this as a study guide, and why was it a Ford V8? I asked around, and the answer surprised me. Ford Motor Company operated in Germany, supplying engines for German army vehicles, throughout the hostilities. What I'd never realized was that it was a multi-national corporation, and it made no difference where its factories were located, it would go about doing business in as normal a manner as possible, just as Woolworth's had in Verviers, and probably elsewhere.

The Woolworth's Ed and I had known was now in ruins, probably from German rocket artillery, but had it been protected before that? Had it been exempt from bombing by the U.S. Air Force? What about Ford? Did orders exist that defined its plants as "do not target" sites? How many other large corporations were playing both ends against the middle in this struggle? How many, with the help and connivance of the politicians they owned, were going to profit from this war, no matter who won or lost? Was this what so many died for—more profitable business deals for the already wealthy? The evidence certainly suggested that.

Just thinking about this gave rise to a new and more intense level of cynicism. Was modern man so devoted to material gain, he was now abandoning any consideration for the ethics of the past or the spiritual values of generations to come? It seemed so, and I was at a loss to either explain it or accommodate what remained of my beliefs to it.

I'd learned to question everything concerning the morality of politicians. I also doubted the value of every religion with which I was the least bit familiar. Each was devoted, first and foremost, to self-interest, to the furtherance of their own particular articles of faith, regardless of the cost to those whose ideas were slightly different. It was peculiarly evident in all of it that the closer two systems were in their proclaimed mission, the more antagonistic they would likely be to each other. Catholics versus Episcopalians was a good example. The hatred they had for each other knew no bounds, but I failed to recognize more that the smallest, most petty differences when I'd attended their services.

Yet, I could recognize a need in every one of us. At bottom, we were spiritual animals, desperately seeking something beyond the physical senses to sustain us in our journey through this life. The musty old platitudes of yesterday were not enough for anyone who desired something that could satisfy both the hunger of our inner being and the needs of mankind. As far as an afterlife, the suppositions proposed by our backward-thinking clergy may or may not have meaning. The kid who has just been shot and knows he's dying could find comfort in the idea, but beyond such a situation, I could see little practical value for it. All we were ever sure of was what was happening to us in the here and now. I could accept the possibility of an afterlife, I supposed, but if true, it was the one place in this cosmic immensity which I refused to share with those who had instigated and encouraged this insane killing spree that was World War II, or any other war. The politicians and the generals on both sides could go to hell.

One personal concern was that no room was allowed in any current belief system of which I was aware for compassion. The military frowned on it. The clergy shied away from it. Every day, while we cleaned out the pharmacy and set up shelves and places for the supplies soon to arrive, an elderly man came and stood outside in the street, staring at the building in which we labored. It soon became fairly obvious that this had been his pharmacy, and he probably wanted to get inside to fill some prescriptions for those who needed the kind of help he'd always provided—sick people, crippled people, people in pain.

There was a small room at the rear, with several shelves, each stocked with an enormous variety of bottled and packaged pharmaceuticals. Surprisingly, most were natural remedies, made or concocted from the medicinal plants found everywhere in Europe. German medicine, so advanced in some areas, relied much more heavily on these ancient curatives than I would have imagined. Of course, this might have represented wartime shortages.

We needed the shelf space, and I began to pack these drugs in cartons.

Parsons walked in and flew into a rage. "What are you doing?" he screamed. "It's going to take you hours to do that, and I don't want it done that way, anyway. Let me show you how you're going to get these shelves ready."

He used his arm to sweep along the length of a shelf, dumping all the contents on the floor.

"There. Now do that to the rest of the shelves, then sweep up all that junk and start putting stuff where we can see it." He walked out muttering and shaking his head.

A man's life work had just been turned into trash. I did not know the man, and he was technically an enemy, although a civilian, but he'd never done me any personal harm. Beyond that, I could see the fear and hurt in his eyes when I looked at him every day. I felt only sympathy, an emotion not encouraged now that we were in Germany.

A funny thing about this was that the army actually practiced an extremely ambivalent attitude when it came to our relations with the Germans. A non-fraternization order was in effect, meaning that we were not allowed to even speak to a civilian, outside any militarily necessary communications. The first time this rule was violated brought a fine of a month's pay. A second offense meant five years in prison. It was thought by many to be virtually unenforceable, but a serious effort was made, and many young men found themselves on the way to calling Leavenworth their new home, just because they had said "Hello" to a German.

At the same time, orders came down from SHAEF stating that looting would absolutely not be tolerated. These orders were clear and specific. We were told to shoot on sight anyone seen taking something that did not belong to him, and shoot to kill. Lengthy trials were not wanted. Dead looters were deemed to be sufficient. So American soldiers could be seen walking past store fronts in which the huge display windows had been smashed by bombs or shellfire. On a stand might be cameras, fine binoculars, or jewelry. Everyone walked past with little more than a glance, and that would be not at the display in the window, but at any other soldiers within rifle range. There was little looting in Germany, although back in Belgium and France, no such prohibition was enforced.

There may have been a reason for this—a reason rarely mentioned and unsuspected by many, although it was fairly common knowledge Almost half (45 percent, by some estimates) of the United States Army was at least partially of German descent. Their families had comprised the largest single ethnic group of early immigrants to America. Eisenhower was unmistakably German, although the name had been slightly anglicized in the spelling. There was an Eisenhauer family near us in Bonn. There was even a current joke about this—"every German POW has a cousin in Milwaukee."

Yet, Germans had fought and killed those cousins, as our soldiers had killed them. In a sense, not too far from reality, this was a civil war, cousins killing cousins, nephews killing uncles, German in-laws dying from American bombs, bullets, and artillery shells. Like so many other things, this knowledge changed nothing.

A bridge had crossed the Rhine just a short distance away. It had been blown up by the Germans in their retreat to the Ruhr Valley, and the entire center span now lay in deep water. On our side, about eighty feet of the approach to the bridge remained intact. A group from our company, mostly replacements led by one of our sergeants, decided to walk out on this stub of a bridge for a little sightseeing.

They returned shortly, with some well-chosen epithets for the German soldiers who occupied the other side of the Rhine. In a move that had seemed hardly sporting, the Krauts had fired a couple of long bursts from a machinegun at our sightseers. These had beat a hasty retreat as bullets whined, spanged, and ricocheted through the remaining bridge superstructure. No one was hurt, though.

No one was hurt, either, when our own artillery decided to entertain us with a little night music. It was a battery of 155mm "long toms," firing from twelve miles to the rear at targets across the river. For some unknown reason, they decided three o'clock in the morning was an appropriate time to drop some of their heavy stuff on the German positions.

The first time I heard a 155 shell with a loose rotating band going over, I thought it must have been a fast-moving freight train, on some invisible railroad track in the sky. It sounded like nothing else. All we could do when one of those slamming, banging, rattling things went over our heads was to burrow into whatever blankets or bed covering we had, put hands over our ears, and wait it out. A couple of artillerymen with us at the time explained why they made the noises, although that did nothing to alleviate the irritation and loss of sleep.

Those big artillery shells were in many ways just a huge version of an armor piercing rifle bullet. It's possible to fire a steel projectile from a steel barrel, but the rifling in the barrel would not last long doing that. Without rifling, all accuracy would be lost. So a bullet is enclosed in a jacket of copper, a softer metal that will follow the rifling in the gun's barrel, rotating as it passes through, and do no great harm to the accuracy of the weapon. It's not practical to make copper-jacketed artillery, though, so bands of copper or brass are placed in at least two places on the projectile. These take the rifling with ease, rotating as they travel the length of the barrel. But sometimes a band will become loose. It then makes one godawful racket when it travels through the air to its target zone. It wakes up all the sleeping soldiers below it, especially if it's been fired from a distance and is dropping downward on its way to the target.

Those shells whose rotating bands were not loose made a thunderous "swishing" noise going over, still enough to awaken the dead and near dead, but not quite the noise that made us jump three feet straight up from our sleeping position. Night after night, they did this, sometimes continuously for a half hour, sometimes with quiet intervals, during which we thought they'd finished, but soon learned that was a false assumption. For us, this was a supreme aggravation. For the Krauts who were in the target area, it was likely much more.

The worst of it was that it awakened, every night, the German crews of their artillery. They woke in less than the best of moods, and wanting revenge. The range of their 88s was far too short to reach the long toms for a meaningful exchange of fire, so they shot at us, or where they thought we might be. We were lucky, though. Some tenements were hit, but we suffered no loss of life. That was not the fault of our 155 battery.

Good news, of a sort, arrived shortly. A new development in army procedures was inaugurated. The political idea of sending home all men who had been three times wounded had not worked out. It was simply ignored by military commanders, who had too many other things to think about. A decision was made to send home, instead, all who had been overseas the longest. Two years was the minimum time needed. The only present member of our company who qualified was sergeant Parsons. His overseas duty had begun before Pearl Harbor, when he'd been sent to Iceland. The powers-that-be would not have recognized all of that, but did count the time from Pearl Harbor onward. He was called to company HQ and issued orders that would take him home for a 45-day furlough, after which he was supposed to return to duty with the same assignment as before. They called the plan "rotation." It worked, although not as had been originally conceived, and not for very long. It worked long enough to relieve Parsons and leave us without a duly authorized supply sergeant.

Both lieutenant Markinson and our commanding officer asked if I would be willing to accept the responsibilities of supply sergeant, since I was by far the most familiar with the work involved. I could not have a promotion until the 45 days had passed, though, because it was possible another staff sergeant with experience in supply would be sent to replace Parsons. I'd do the work, but not have the rank or the pay. The work had to be done, obviously, and equally obvious was the fact that no one else in our company knew how to do it. I accepted the assignment, with the understanding that I was still company armorer, and would happily return to that when it became possible. I quickly realized that I was expected to do both jobs until other arrangements had been made concerning supply.

With the help of some of the previously wounded now going through the system, things went smoothly enough. Bill Holman, a signal corpsman, and I became good friends. He was also a T5. We worked well together, often long, exhausting hours, but we managed. Sometimes we had sergeants, staff sergeants, and technical sergeants who willingly took orders from us. In nearly every case, they were infantrymen, wounded once or twice or three or four times, going back to their companies to do it all over again.

Parsons never wrote, so we did not have any idea if, or when, he arrived safely at home. Whatever our differences might have been, I came to realize what a fine supply sergeant he'd been. His were not easy shoes to fill.

# 27

# *The Survival of Liège*

With a sense of loss for the comforts we were putting behind us, we loaded our trucks and left Bonn. The road led along the west bank of the Rhine to a point south of the Ruhr, where we crossed a pontoon bridge. After traveling east about forty more miles, we arrived in a community with a school that had already been selected for our use. Schools were generally a preferred location, because offices, such as the principal's, served well for company HQ, and a double classroom was ideal for supply. Other classrooms could accommodate large numbers of replacements, sleeping on the floors. Most schools also had an area that easily adapted to the kitchen and mess, often something that had been used for a school lunchroom. The final advantage was that the schools in most of Europe had been closed until the worst of the fighting ended. School-age kids, like my young friends in Stavelot, looked forward with happy anticipation to the time their schools were once again allowed to offer an education. They missed the books and the studying.

In my supply room, changes came rapidly. For a time, I felt that this job was beyond my capabilities, if only because I was asked to do the impossible. No previously wounded and returning sergeants appeared to help out. I was alone and forgotten.

Part of the problem was that we had a new lieutenant assigned to us. He was something we'd never had in the company—an officer with a battlefield commission. We were reminded of deBourbon, who also held this distinction, but not during his association with us. Stan Kendrick, although a decent sort of guy, was far removed from the aura of natural leadership that belonged to our former representative of French nobility. Stan had earned his commission in a similar way, though. As a PFC (private first class), he'd taken command of the few survivors of his company after all the officers and non-coms had been killed or seriously wounded. With a wisdom and maturity beyond his age, his rank, or experience, he'd saved what was left and held the company's position until reinforcements arrived.

The standard procedure for the award of a battlefield commission was to send the appointee to Paris for a ninety-day course in the elements of command and responsibilities of an officer. He'd been through all that, and now wore his lieutenant's bars on his brand-new uniform.

Stan was easy to get along with, eager to please, and never reluctant to step forward when asked to volunteer. From my perspective, his one failing—and it was a big one—was that he knew absolutely nothing about supply. He had no conception of the amount of work involved. He had no idea what his part in it all should have been. He signed everything that I prepared—all the reports and requisitions—without ever giving any of them as much as a glance.

The double classroom assigned to me had windows facing a courtyard in front of the school. When his signature was needed, I opened a window and called out his name. He was usually out there, somewhere within hearing distance, and trotted into the building and to the supply room, where he signed any and all papers I thrust at him. That was the extent of his involvement. A couple of times, I mentioned that I needed help, but it just didn't register. I mentioned it to our company clerk, and to lieutenant Cicciloni, and was rewarded with one infantry rifleman who reported for duty. His name was Martin Blank, and like most returning wounded, he had his own story to tell, something that I heard with interest a few days later.

I was grateful for this one helper, but we faced a task that needed a minimum of five men. Within a few days, six hundred replacements and returning wounded arrived, most in need of something. The manner in which we learned how much of each item was needed was a system that I had designed, and sergeant Parsons had used. Our own sergeants handled the mechanics of the process, gathering the men into groups. Each man was handed a mimeographed sheet of paper, on which he entered his name, rank, and serial number. Articles of clothing were grouped according to general type, such as underwear, outer-wear, jackets, shoes, and miscellaneous. Beside the name of each was a space to check, if that item were needed, and a line on which the soldier entered his size when that applied. The sergeant called out, in order, each item on the list, and instructed the men to check, or not, and put in their sizes where needed on those items checked.

All the papers were returned to supply, where we made a written total of each item and each size needed in that item. With experience, we could estimate the number of popular sizes to requisition. For example, in trousers, size 32/33 (32 waist, 33 inseam) would fit about twenty percent of the men. If fifty men needed trousers, we knew that at least ten of that size should be ordered. In shoes, size 9D was far and away the most used. But we had to know how many of the other items and sizes, and we needed to confirm our estimate of those popular items. It was not a quick job, and usually took several men at least a full day.

Martin and I did it all. We worked from six in the morning until two the following morning, every day. A couple of hours of sleep, a couple of cups of coffee from the cooks, and we'd start again. That was only the beginning. When the requisition was filled at battalion and shipped to us, usually within forty-eight hours, we had to unload all of it, make shelves from the cartons, and organize it to issue the items to the soldiers coming through in a steady line. At the beginning of the line, those mimeographed sheets were returned to each soldier. He held it in his hand going through, a member of our crew looked at it, and handed him the appropriate item as he passed. It took six or eight men handling the line to move it quickly. There were two of us.

Nothing ever came out right, but not because we were so short-handed. The numbers just never worked. At the end, there were always surpluses and shortages. If the shortage were in a critical item, such as shoes, I'd need to send a special requisition for more, and hope I'd get them before the individual's shipping orders came. Sometimes I did, sometimes not. To be certain that no man was held back for missing shoes, socks, or other uniform parts, I added an extra ten percent to the quantities we thought we'd need. There were still shortages. In some cases, there might be a surplus of the next larger size, and this could be substituted.

The accuracy of our tally for the requisition was almost beyond dispute. We checked everything six ways from Sunday. Part of the reason for shortages was easy to imagine. A man with his piece of paper in hand might look at what he'd written on it, and decide the size was wrong. He'd correct that while going through the line, and in so doing create a shortage in one size and a surplus in another. He might decide his field jacket was not as new as he'd like, although he'd not checked that item, and now add it his "need" list. Someone else would then be short. It was an imperfect system, but with the extras ordered, was as good as we could do in the limited time we had.

Another suspicion, never fully confirmed as fact, was that truck drivers might accidentally "lose" some items while on the road to our company. A pair of "lost" new shoes could metamorphose into a bottle or two of wine along the way.

Often, we'd find many of the missing items after the replacements had shipped out. They left things behind. For men like our sergeant Jinks, who was never paid, this was always a treasure trove of trade goods, convertible into wine, liquor, beer, women (possibly) and civilian food. What he did not appropriate was sent to the rear as salvage material.

The fact that army was getting sticky about salvage led to the establishment, in the next classroom to ours, of a salvage center. One of our sergeants, Jacob Goldman, managed this, and relieved me of a totally impossible added duty. He used German POWs to do the sorting and bagging, the first time we'd done that, and the first time most of us had ever been in close physical contact with any of our former enemies. They were regular army men, Wehrmacht, not SS troops or any other such fanatics. They wanted only an end to the war and to go home, and had no objection to doing a little work to pass the time. Sergeant Goldman was Jewish, and spoke some German. To my surprise, I learned that Yiddish was a form of German, so the transition was an easy one for Goldman. The prisoners didn't seem to mind at all that their overseer was a Jew.

One day, when there were a few minutes free, I stopped in to see how this sorting and salvage work was coming along. Sergeant Goldman was in conversation with a pair of the prisoners, and I knew enough German to pick up the gist of the conversation. They were men who had served in Russia, and had miraculously survived the long retreat from Moscow.

The greatest danger, they said, was the "Jabos." That was pronounced "Yah-bohs," the name given to the fighter-bombers. The Soviet Air Force had a lot of them, and they had decimated the troops walking the long winter roads out of Russia. In many cases, barely ten percent had survived. There were few doctors or medics, and wounded men usually froze to death.

All old, used clothing was supposed to be turned in by the individuals at the time the new items were picked up. The old pieces were simply thrown in a heap in the supply room, and this was added to whatever the POWs were sorting out and bagging. All of it was sent back through supply to wherever the salvage companies had set up.

After midnight at the end of another exhausting day, Martin sat with me while we each smoked a cigarette, and said, "I want you to know I'm staying with you as long as I'm needed, or until my orders arrive. I also want you to know that I never imagined how hard you and a few of the others in this company have to work. I didn't realize anyone in the army had a job this tough. How do you keep doing it, day after day?"

I smiled at him. "It's not always this bad, Martin, and I really appreciate your help. As a whole, this system probably has one of the highest suicide rates in the armed forces. A lot of the guys assigned to it buckle under. I won't do that, because I don't let it get to me that much. But if there weren't guys like you around, I'd chuck it. It's simply not worth the hassle. I'd try to find a job as an armorer, which is what I know and like, a lot more than this."

"Boy," he said, "I'd get out of this if there were any way at all. Where were you during the Ardennes?"

"In Stavelot. How about you?"

"Liège. I was one of eight guys left there when my outfit pulled out to join others trying to stop the Krauts from getting any farther. Every one of us was given a musette bag and told to wait. Know what was in that bag?"

"No. I can't imagine."

"Grenades. Incendiary grenades. They could burn a hole through a quarter inch of plate steel. We dispersed around the perimeter of that gasoline tank farm. You know where that was?"

"Yes, Martin. I was there a little later, after the danger had passed. You were going to destroy those tanks?"

"That was our assignment. We were told that at the first sight of a German uniform, we were to run through the tank farm, tossing grenades at the base of as many tanks as we could. Man, that would have been some fire. It probably would have taken most of Liége with it. There was no way any of us could have made it out alive, but we all knew that. It was what we could have done to stop the Krauts from going all the way to Antwerp, and it's what we were ready to do, no question."

"Well," I said, "I'm sure glad it wasn't necessary. My cousin is a nurse in that field hospital on top of the hill there. They'd been warned, and would have tried to get out, but who knows if they'd have made it?"

"They wouldn't have," Martin said. "By the time they'd loaded the hospital on trucks, that hill would have been surrounded by flaming gasoline about four feet deep. Nothing would have got out."

Martin's orders came two days later. I wished him the best, and resigned myself to doing what I could to handle supply as a one-man operation. It would be far from best, but maybe I could make it work. Maybe.

I went through the motions with the next group, but could do nothing but guess at the numbers needed on my requisition form. I did guess, and it all worked out a lot closer than I'd have thought possible. Perhaps this was because I bumped my "margin" to twenty percent instead of ten. A couple of our own sergeants helped at the last minute, issuing what was needed from the stocks that I'd guessed were enough.

We moved again soon after that. A huge truck, a semi-trailer, backed in, and with a little help, everything in supply went into it. Even Lieutenant Kendricks pitched in with the loading. He still had no idea what he was doing.

I'd never learned the name of the town, which wasn't too surprising. I'd never been able to leave the supply room any longer than it took to grab a cup of coffee from the cooks. I longed to return to being just a company armorer, but realized that would probably never happen again. I had no tools, no weapons, no reserve ammunition, no way to perform the simplest parts of that duty. I could still defuse one of our own grenades, but we rarely found one these days.

# 28

## *Keeping It Clean*

Marburg was, in itself, a small sign of sanity in an age of mass madness and delusional nightmares. A university town, it was without any industry even remotely war-related. As a consequence, bomb damage was minimal and schools were numerous. The streets were tree-lined and well maintained. Civilian life here appeared quiet and unhurried, with elderly people and children much in evidence on the sidewalks. Young men were notable only by their absence.

It was hilly country, and our first quarters were in a school halfway up a fairly large hill. The town itself occupied a valley below us, with a river to cross, should we ever have occasion to visit there. The bridge was intact. Up on the crest of the hill behind us was a larger institution of learning, possibly a college or university. We did not know its name. It, like all other schools we had not occupied, was closed and locked for the duration of the hostilities. Beyond was woodland, an old-growth forest in which we might become lost if we should wander too far into its confines.

At first, my supply room was small, a former office of some kind, but I had the use of a more adequate space in a garage near the school on the hilltop, if that should become necessary. The front entrance of the school we now occupied was next to my room, and the other side of the entrance was a similar room used as company HQ. We were comfortable enough, and out of the weather, a condition to which we were rapidly becoming accustomed.

Lieutenant Kendricks, the one with the battlefield commission, had been transferred out. The war went on, and experienced line officers were, as always, needed. This left us without a supply officer. My own promotion to sergeant came about, but it was understood that nothing beyond that was possible until we knew whether or not sergeant Parsons would return. I could do his work, but could not have his rank, and even my sergeant's rank was only a company assignment, and might be revoked at any time. It was a small thing, and had no bearing on my duties. I sewed my new sergeant's stripes on my uniform, but that changed nothing that I could notice.

A newly arrived officer was appointed to supply, but some difficulty arose almost immediately. One of our own sergeants, Roberts, apparently had approached lieutenant Zender before he'd even appeared in the supply room. They hatched some kind of scheme to take over company supply. I had several loyal friends in the company, and knew about this almost as soon as it had happened. They could have supply, as far as I was concerned, but not in this way. It was too obvious what they had in mind. A small city was nearby, fairly wealthy and with much to offer. On our side, there was access to almost unlimited quantities of scarce clothing and footwear. The projected takeover stank of black market plans and possibilities.

Another new officer had arrived, and this was our first experience with a West Pointer. Captain Harcourt gave the impression that he would be exacting in his demands that every member of this company act in accordance with the highest standards, militarily and morally. He was generally welcomed, as was his insistence on proper decorum in all things. There was never any doubt about where we stood with this West Pointer, and in many ways this was a blessed relief.

Our mail clerk was another who had left and been replaced, by an older man who was highly capable, if not always the epitome of military spit and polish. Sid was a former insurance agent. Paper work was natural for him. He not only shared my supply room, but pitched in to help with requisition forms and other countless pieces of written information necessary to an army when not too close to the line. I came to like him. He suggested I speak to Captain Harcourt about the situation with Zender and Roberts.

I did that, when the Captain stopped in the next day. I made no direct accusations, but simply said, "I don't care if lieutenant

Zender and sergeant Roberts want to run supply. Let them do it, and send me some place where I can use my armorer's training. But first, let them get in here and learn something about the work. I don't think either of them is capable of coming in "cold" and doing it. I spent over a year working with sergeant Parsons, and still have much to learn."

The Captain returned the next day, and informed me there would be no more talk of those two taking over supply. I would remain as the supply sergeant, and when it became possible, would receive the next promotion in rank to make that official, and irrevocable as far as the company was concerned. He thanked me for bringing the situation to his attention. I felt he had immediately made some discrete inquiries of his own after I'd talked to him. Sergeant Roberts was transferred out in three days, Lieutenant Zender in a week. I was stuck with supply, but it would continue to be honest, with no black market dealings.

Sid's mail clerk duties became steadily more involved, and he needed space he didn't have. The best solution was to move supply to that empty garage, which we did. At one corner, beside the entrance, was an enclosed office. I moved into that as my personal quarters, and had the large truck garage for the supply room.

Soon, another reinforcement company arrived. They were the one that had been in Malmedy at the start of the Ardennes offensive, dubbed the "Battle of The Bulge" by the news media. They were still kidding sergeant Schmidt about his wound, and subsequent purple heart, during the evacuation of Malmedy. He'd run across the street to retrieve some of the papers that should not have been left behind. The Germans were shelling the town at the time. An 88 went off nearby, and a small piece of shrapnel went through Schmidt's nose as he ran. His companions said it was the one body part that was surely going to be hit, because it was the biggest piece of him that was unprotected and vulnerable. He took the joking in good humor.

Battalion supply also came in, and we learned that our two companies and battalion were expected to operate as a single unit. Technical Sergeant Daniels was still running battalion supply, but the lieutenant-colonel who had wanted the pearl-handled revolvers like General Patton's was long gone. He'd been a replacement, and he became someone else's problem, although I doubted it would have been for very long if he'd taken his attitude with him to a line infantry unit. The third company in this battalion, the one that had been near St. Vith in the Ardennes, was still elsewhere, and would remain on its own. I'd have liked to speak to them about that MG with the rusted barrel, but would not have the opportunity, it seemed.

We set up as battalion in another large building, about fifty yards from my garage. It appeared to have been a gymnasium of some sort, with a high roof, but no basketball hoops. Daniels and the other company supply sergeant, Richards, had their offices there. The first replacements arrived two days later, and we began the education of Sergeant Daniels in the finer points of company supply. He was willing enough, and he listened attentively, but he was also shocked and amazed at what we needed to teach him.

Getting the tally of how much and what sizes of each item was done in the same way I'd been doing it. Daniels worked with us to add up the totals. It was at that point, about two the next morning, that he was shocked. "Why," he asked, "do you want to order twenty-five pairs of size nine D shoes, when our figures show we only need twenty-three?"

"Because," I replied, "I always add ten percent to cover losses and shortages."

"Ten percent?" Sergeant Richards added, "I always go twenty percent, and sometimes there are still shortages."

"I don't understand that," Daniels said. "How can it happen? I know that when your orders left battalion, the count was always accurate. I'll vouch for that. Why do you need more?"

We could almost hear the thoughts running through Daniels' head. He was wondering if it were possible that we were both involved in some sort of shady operation—black market, maybe?

"All I can say," I told him, "is to wait and see. Go through this whole process with us, and you'll understand. As to why it happens, there are several explanations, none of which help us very much. But when we're done, a few guys will be short an item or two, always, and there will be a few surpluses in other items. It never comes out exactly right. If you can see a solution to this, please let us know. We'll both be grateful."

"I'll second that," said Richards.

One more duty assignment became mine, although it was a gesture only. Since I was the only person in the battalion who had been trained in small arms repair, I was made battalion armorer. All it meant in this place was that I was the person to whom others brought found materials such as ammunition or weapons. I did accumulate some items, such as a large cloth bag filled with loose .45 caliber ammunition, and an older model M1911 pistol. When I had a little free time, I walked into the woods and did some target shooting, just for the fun of it.

Salvage was still something with which army appeared to be obsessed. New rules were made regarding what the replacements might carry with them when they left us. It would be only the prescribed list of clothing items, plus equipment such as cartridge belts and backpacks, canteen and blanket, etc. Nothing extra, nothing not part of a standard uniform issue, would be permitted, and all such items would be put in a barracks bag and tagged with the owner's name and serial number.

A lot of personal items were in those barracks bags, with the owners assuming that they'd retrieve them when it was time to ship out. That didn't happen, and I don't think it was army's intention that it would happen. The army wanted its fighting men to be lean and unconcerned with anything not related to their duty on the line. The result was that my big garage was partly filled with bags of mixed salvage material. There was no time, nor was there the manpower, to do anything with it. We had no German POWs here.

The general feeling was that this war was winding down, getting close to its end. The war in the Pacific was not, but we were not immediately concerned with that. Replacements arrived, they came through our supply line, and sergeant Daniels became aware of all that we'd tried to tell him.

In anticipation of the war's end, officers were offered a sergeant's rank if they signed up now for two years of post-war duty. Otherwise, they'd be discharged as reserve officers without any active rank, although their presence at reserve training sessions would go on for an indeterminate length of time. Officers of any kind were never completely released from the military. That was a condition of their wartime job, a "string" attached to their service that some, but not all of them, realized when they accepted their appointment to Officer Candidate School. My refusal of such an appointment at Aberdeen was now a decision for which I was grateful.

At the Elbe River in Germany, our forward elements had met the Russians. This line was agreed upon as the limit to both our advance and that of the Soviets. Soon after that, our soldiers were joining them in Berlin, as partners in occupation duty. General Eisenhower and his field commanders had decided that for us to take Berlin would cost us 100,000 casualties. We stopped and let the Russians do it. The only value to that city was political, and it was obvious that the Soviets were perfectly willing to spend twice that many men to gain an advantage in any post-war negotiations about who would control what in Europe.

This joint occupation, after the Soviets had eliminated all resistance, created some problems that had been unforeseen. The black market flourished in Berlin just as it had, and probably still did, in Paris. Cigarettes were twenty dollars a pack, a candy bar five dollars, a bar of soap ten, etc. American troops were becoming rich. Many sent money home each month far in excess of their military pay. Gambling became widespread, with thousands of dollars involved in simple poker games. I witnessed one in which no one was allowed to play until he first put twenty thousand dollars in front of him, and showed a willingness to risk it all. Those returning from Berlin frequently carried their money in a musette bag.

This was a situation intensely disagreeable to army, possibly because American privates were, in many cases, making fifty times the money paid to our generals. A law was created that soldiers could send home only the amount of their pay plus a ten percent allowance for gambling winnings. The joke making the rounds was that in Berlin, everyone gambled and no one lost.

There was an explanation for this situation. We were paid in occupation marks, the currency of Germany at this time. Our rate of exchange was ten cents per mark. The Soviet army, contrary to the beliefs of many, was actually better paid than we were, and gave its soldiers another huge advantage. They valued a mark at just two cents American. This made the pay of a Soviet enlisted man at least six times ours.

The Soviets loved American goods. They especially liked our watches, their first choice being the Mickey Mouse watch on which the arms rotated around to tell the time. One of these, sold in drug stores at home for $2.98, was worth two hundred dollars or more to a Russian in Berlin. An enterprising American, with people in the States who could find Mickey Mouse watches and mail them to him, could quickly accumulate huge wealth. Getting it home was the only problem. For those with enough money, and many had that, there was a way around this limitation. It was to locate an officer who wanted very much to share in the current wealth. All letters home were censored, by any officer available. They would sign the outside of the envelope, and this was enough to satisfy the postal system. Money orders, in all denominations, could be bought on a limited black market operated within the military. Some mail clerks became wealthy, along with the few officers who signed their name on the envelopes that contained money orders far in excess of the sender's pay. It worked out that a soldier with fifty thousand dollars might pay almost half of that to get it home. Still, what remained was a tidy sum with which to start civilian life once more. As far as I knew, Sid, our mail clerk, never became part of it. He knew about it, I was certain, but refused to participate.

I liked him even more for this. Sometimes it seemed that basic honesty was becoming a trait far too rare, but that was a misconception. Most of us valued our honesty, and deplored not only the actions of the few who did not, but could never quite understand the thought processes that drove them to their criminal behavior. Any value system that succumbs so totally to personal greed becomes, in the end, of no value to anyone, and breeds nothing but contempt for those who practice it. I held to that belief, as did those whose friendship I treasured.

On May eighth, 1945, the war in Europe ended, the hostilities reduced to a few isolated areas where fanatics held out in suicidal attempts to fight on. We may have had a drink or two with those close to us, but it was not a huge celebration. It was, in fact, accepted as the natural consequence of all that had happened here, but beyond it and beneath the expressions of joy was the sad knowledge that this was only half of it. We still had the Pacific to face, and we'd surely be going there.

We moved again soon enough, and this time to a destination far to the south, to an ancient city originally constructed by the Romans over two thousand years ago. The secrecy that had surrounded our every move in the past was no longer necessary, but force of habit, if nothing else, barred us from sharing some information. When we arrived, we learned that we would spend some time in Trier (pronounced tree-air, with the accent on the second syllable), on the Mosel River and bordering Luxembourg.

# 29

# *Consequences of Being Human*

Trier occupied both sides of the Mosel River, and what we'd heard about the city having its beginnings in Roman times was true. The bridge that connected the two sides was a prime example. Its foundations and buttresses were of Roman construction, built around the year 1 or a little earlier. They were still in use today, still strong enough to support a bridge that handled the pounding of tanks, and the wear and tear of endless truck traffic. Those ancient Roman civil engineers had known what they were doing.

The Mosel valley, along the banks of the river, had many vineyards, most of them small. This was wine country. The river itself had its source across the border in France, where it was called the Moselle, and where it also nurtured vineyards and produced good wine.

The city of Trier had been damaged, badly in places, but not as badly as other German cities we'd seen or passed through. There was a story, published in The Stars and Stripes, about how General George "Blood and Guts" Patton had taken Trier. Eisenhower and SHAEF had chastised Patton for plowing ahead too much on his own, without notifying headquarters what he was doing. When he'd approached Trier, they had advised him to bypass it, because it was too heavily defended. It would need aerial bombardment, heavy artillery, an armored division, and another division of infantry to successfully take it, and none of those were currently available. Patton replied, "Have taken Trier with one division of infantry. Shall we give it back?"

257

Not far from the bridge over the river was our next home—another school. This one was three stories high, with a street on one side, separated from the school only by a sidewalk, and on the opposite side a small field, probably used for outdoor calisthenics and games that did not require a lot of space. A tent was erected on the field, and two straddle trenches dug inside, making it our latrine. There were facilities in the school's basement, but apparently an adequate water supply was questionable with two to three hundred men living here. The cooks did set up their kitchen in the basement.

My supply room was an oversized classroom on the first floor, with windows facing the field. A new helper arrived, a young man named Wesley North. He was an excellent worker, and always willing to take on any job I thought he could handle. The paperwork was not a strong point with him, but with anything else, I could rely on him totally. We began to build the sort of relationship Parsons had had with me, except I tried to be very careful not to overuse my authority.

Some time soon, lieutenant Cicciloni told me, I'd receive a promotion to the rank that went with my job. The company had received word that Parsons would not be returning. If he were sent overseas at all, it would be to the Pacific, as would all the others who had gone home for forty-five days. Three of the earliest who'd been sent back did return, and came to our company to wait for a permanent assignment. They all had the same story to tell. Rotation had failed, and plans for any more had been cancelled. Altogether too many who had gone home seemed to vanish as their forty-five days reached their end. The army was too busy building up for the Pacific campaign to assign a lot of manpower to tracking them down. So a few thousand had deserted, but that word was not used, ever. They were AWOL, a less serious infraction, or they were charged with some sort of civilian crime, such as disorderly conduct, and held in civilian prisons if they could be caught.

At one end of our building, on the second floor and separated from the classrooms, lived a civilian family. The man was Herr Lehrer (meaning Mr. Teacher) Helden. He was the caretaker appointed by the city, and the one who dealt with us on any matters of mutual concern or interest. He had been a mathematics teacher at this same school. His family consisted of his wife, three sons, and two daughters. It was illegal for us to speak to any but Herr Lehrer, and only on official business with him. The non-fraternization law was in full effect, and enforced as much as possible.

Beyond the Helden apartment, in a small el of the building, was another room that was assigned to me. This would be the armory, and I'd received a dozen rifles to keep there. I also had a key and kept it locked when my presence was needed elsewhere, as it usually was. There were no armorer's tools, and no ammunition, unless our officers had some they kept in the headquarters room.

We went through the routine of checking for worn out or missing clothing and equipment, but without the urgency with which we'd been accustomed to doing it when it was replacements we prepared for duty on the line. Everything now was a bit relaxed, and the cooks had extra help in the persons of a dozen Italian POWs.

These men, although not yet released to go home, were in no great hurry to do that, and agreed to stay on as semi-permanent KP help for a time. I believed they were given a small, regular pay for this, and it was probably the reason they were staying here. Italy was economically distressed, with few jobs available for their returning servicemen.

Germany was no better, and one of the teacher's sons, Helmut, was former Wehrmacht (regular German army), with a future that was bleak or non-existent at this time. He'd recently arrived home after some time as a POW. He had served in Normandy, where his unit had surrendered after numerous casualties. I learned of this when I had an opportunity to talk to him briefly a couple of times, in a semi-official capacity, and likely bent the rules a bit in doing it. He spoke better English than I did German, a testament to the education received in their public schools. Conversation, in a mixture of the two languages, was relatively easy. From our short talks, and his attitude, I learned to like Helmut. I could not say the same for his younger brother, Franz. A former Hitler Youth member, Franz had been fanatical in his loyalty to "Der Führer," and could not yet accept the reality of Germany's defeat. He was now a psychological basket case, and I never fully trusted him.

It was soon apparent that the Italians were not the willing workers they had at first appeared to be. They dawdled, they talked among themselves, they totally ignored the one of their number who spoke English, and had been put in charge of the group for that reason. Lieutenant Cicciloni, who had grown up in a home where Italian was used as much as English, spoke to these men in an attempt to determine the cause of their reluctance to cooperate. He quickly learned what it was all about. There were twelve of them. Eleven had been sergeant-majors in the Italian army. That was the highest rank obtainable for enlisted men. The twelfth man had been a private, and just happened to be the only one who knew English, and therefore was attempting to give orders to his superiors. They could not allow that, and would not. Cicciloni solved the problem by making the English-speaking man an interpreter only, passing on to the senior sergeant-major any and all orders from the cooks. The others went to work with a will after that, and even tried to do enough extra work to compensate for their earlier recalcitrance.

We were transferred to the Seventh Army, since we were now beyond the boundary of First Army territory. The Seventh had come up through southern France, from the Mediterranean shore. Not one of us liked this change, and with great reluctance we cut off our beloved First Army insignia and replaced it with the colorful triangle of the Seventh.

Nothing else changed. If anything, the army grew more particular, becoming ever more absorbed in the new rules and regulations, their implementation and the punishment of any who disobeyed. The non-fraternization law was one that received the focused attention of many officers who had too little to do. Fines were imposed, as were prison sentences for repeat offenders. Then, in what could only be seen as a curious double standard, pro stations, which offered all the paraphernalia and medications designed to prevent venereal disease, were staffed to operate twenty-four hours a day. The army did not want any man out of action for a preventable disease, but didn't seem to mind if we were exposed to it and took precautions, as long as no conversation was held with the women who provided the service. We could only shake our heads in disbelief. The pro stations kept busy, talk with any civilian became very guarded.

This situation could not, and did not, last too long. Someone in headquarters finally decided a small amount of common sense might be applied, to the relief of all.

In the area of human relations, other matters were also treated with unusual severity. Rape was always something that occupied the minds of the military legal geniuses. The penalty was, as we already had been told countless times, execution. It was not long until some of us realized this was the result of an irrational fear on the part of our highest headquarters staff. Germany had surrendered, but was not quite the supine and toothless lion they might have wished her to be. If sufficiently provoked, something similar to Nazi extremism could be rekindled. In no way did they want to alienate the German population, and were apparently dedicated to its protection. Once again, there was that simmering suspicion that at its bottom, this had something to do with international commerce.

We heard from new men arriving that some young German women had found a way to take advantage of the army's paranoid attitude. They would walk into a company area, ask to speak to the commander, and when that was granted, immediately break into tears. They'd claim to have been raped by one of the soldiers here. A physical examination would show that she'd had recent sexual contact, but nothing more. The girl would insist, the company commander would call for an assembly, the girl would walk past the ranks of men until she stopped in front of one. This man, she would say, was the rapist.

He was arrested on the spot, and if we believed the stories going around, court-martialed within a day or two, and executed the next day. Not until this had happened several times did anyone investigate the girl, and learn that she, like others doing the same thing, was a professional prostitute who had found an effective way to continue fighting the war.

History repeats itself, as has so often been noted. The literature of war contains many examples of this method of doing battle with an enemy. As also noted, those who ignore history are condemned to repeat it. SHAEF seemed to have the attitude that incidents of this kind served a worthwhile purpose. It really didn't matter if three or four, or fifteen or twenty American servicemen were wrongfully accused and then executed. What mattered was that an example had been set that would serve to prevent others from wandering too far from the established standards of behavior.

This applied equally as well to other deviant actions. The army had early learned the value of propaganda, and made it effective in many ways. For example, the classification of some acts as deadly crimes made execution a necessity, but in contrast to the popularizing of the rape punishment, the army wanted neither its troops nor the civilian population at home to be overly concerned with this. So an announcement was made, and often repeated, that no American soldier in this war had been executed for desertion. There had been thousands of deserters, but this was never acknowledged, and it was true that none had been put to death for it. This was because none had been accused of, or tried for, desertion. Other crimes were named, such as rape, murder, insubordination, or cowardice, all of which were reason enough to bring in the hangman or the firing squad. We had no deserters in Europe, only about seven thousand men who were unaccounted for at the war's end, and a hundred and twenty-nine bodies that the army admitted had been executed and quietly buried.

Army kept the pressure on in any way it could. There was a fear, many of us believed, that any relaxation of laws would lead to the worst that officers at all levels could imagine. This would be open rebellion, or mutiny. No one talked about it, but it was there, hovering beneath every desperate measure to suppress even the remote possibility that it might happen. Whether this was a real threat on the part of enlisted men, or only perceived as such by the officers, the Army continued to employ draconian measures to eliminate the possibility.

When it became common knowledge that rotation was no longer a possibility, we were told that we had been included on the list of units soon to be shipped to the CBI (China-Burma-India theater). We would not go through the United States, but ship from a French port, probably Marseilles, through the Mediterranean and the Red Sea, directly to our destination. No leaves, no furloughs, no passes would be permitted at any time or in any place.

Our mood became generally one of angry despair. We were further informed that in the assault on the Japanese home islands, which would quickly follow our control of the CBI, casualties would be extremely high. We should expect that half of us would die on the beaches.

This drove many of us to an uncaring attitude concerning every aspect of our current lives. In wholesale numbers, we ignored the non-fraternization law. So what if we were caught? Better a fine or even a couple of years at Leavenworth than almost certain death on the beaches of Japan. There was a growing bitterness evident in all things, often expressed as the darkest of black humor.

One afternoon, we heard an explosion, somewhere on the street that led away, up a slight hill, from the school. There was a group of tenements there, built in the form of a hollow square or rectangle, three stories high. Access to the area surrounded by the building was a large opening in the short side. Three others and I ran there, and entered the courtyard.

It had been an explosion, beyond any doubt. There was a gaping crater in the courtyard. The ground was still smoking, and the explanation had to be a UXB (unexploded bomb).

Families lived in these tenements, and the kids used the courtyard as a play area. One kid would do that no longer. Next to the bomb crater, we found a small girl's shoe, black patent leather with one of those wide single straps that buckled to keep it on the foot. The shoe, like the ground, was still warm. Of the child, the only signs were red blotches and bits of clothing sticking to the wall of the building.

One of our guys looked, and said, "Hey, what do you expect? These kids play around a UXB, and then that's them all over." We laughed.

# 30

## *The Incident at Trier*

Danny Randall was our assistant company clerk. He was a T5, which meant he wore a corporal's stripes with a "T" beneath them to indicate "technician," the same rank I'd had as the company armorer. There was so much paperwork involved with the replacement system, no one man could handle it properly. Sergeant Furman was a near genius with personnel records, shipping orders, and all the numerous papers involved in moving men from one place to another, but he needed someone else to take care of the more routine clerical work. This became Danny Randall's job.

Danny dealt with the civilians here in Trier, particularly matters that involved Herr Lehrer Helden and our use of the school. There was an idea around that the United States would eventually compensate the local German government for this, although Danny would never comment on it. Maybe he just didn't know. All in all, he must have handled his job well, because there never seemed to be any friction between this one German family and our company.

Late one Friday afternoon, Danny came to supply and asked if I'd like to accompany him to the home of Herr Lehrer Helden on the following evening. There were some papers that needed his signature.

"Sure," I said, "but will it be legal for me to go there? The nonfraternization law is still in effect. You'll be on official business, but what would be my excuse?"

"I'll put you down as my assistant," Danny replied. "Don't worry about it. You want to go?"

"Yes. I'd like that."

On Saturday morning, the PX (Post Exchange) truck arrived, and it had a reasonably good assortment of tobacco products, soap, candy, and the various sundries wanted or needed by soldiers in the field. I thought of Herr Helden, and remembered that Helmut had said something about his father once enjoying cigars, but had not smoked one in four years. In all likelihood, this was a not-too-subtle hint that, as an American, I might be able to do something for the old man that no one in Germany could do. So instead of my ration of seven packs of cigarettes, I substituted two boxes of five cigars each, of a popular brand. I picked up the usual ration of candy and gum, and a couple of other items, such as razor blades and shaving soap.

As was probably inevitable, the kids in the neighborhood had found a way to make their presence known. The two school doors on the street side of the building somehow seemed to be unlocked much of the time, and small kids, averaging ten years of age, showed up in the hallways and in my supply room. They were no trouble at all, and as friendly as any kids we'd met in Europe. Candy and chewing gum were irresistible magnets, and compelling reasons to get along with the American invaders. They did more than that. They brought little things to us, small gifts that they felt would be equal in value to what we gave them. Gertrude, a beautiful little girl of about ten, with blonde hair and blue eyes, regularly supplied me with wine. It was not, I learned, the finest wine of the region, but good enough, and I developed an appreciation for this major product of the Mosel Valley. Once, she brought a bottle of champagne, from which I learned the morning-after effect of this beverage. Get pleasantly sloshed in the evening, sleep it off, and wake up with mouth and throat as dry as the Sahara desert on a midsummer day. One drink of water, and the experience of the previous night repeated, if at a somewhat lower level.

Gertrude and her friend visited and talked almost every day, and because I did understand some German, they became "my" kids, although we never developed the bond I'd had with Claude and René in France, or Yvan, Léone, and Hèléne in Belgium.

No matter the nation, the language, or the culture from which they derived, kids were much the same. They all had the same desires, the same attitudes toward life, and the same loyalty to those who treated them fairly. Children do not have enemies, unless the adults teach them that.

The day ended, and Danny and I went to the apartment of the Heldens. We were cordially received and invited to sit in the living room with them. I presented my small gift to Herr Helden, and watched him smile in appreciation while he thanked me. He opened one of the boxes of cigars immediately and lit one, which brought more smiles.

Present with us was Frau Helden, Helmut, whom I already knew, and his sister, Hildegard, next in age after Helmut. Hilda was born the same year that I was, a few months earlier. She was dark-haired, brown-eyed, slim, with a good figure, and the most attractive young woman I'd met in continental Europe. We were immediately comfortable with each other, but only as friends who might, under different circumstances, develop a stronger attraction. I smoked a pipe as often as cigarettes, and had it with me. After Herr Helden lit his cigar, it seemed permissible to smoke. Hilda gently took the pipe from me, filled it with tobacco, and lit it after I'd put it in my mouth. A little later, she played the piano at one side of the room. She played expertly. During the music, Herr Helden excused himself for a few minutes. When he returned, he had glasses and an open bottle of wine. This was local Mosel wine, but of a superior quality than what Gertrude and her friends had been bringing to the supply room, or what some of our company had found locally and bought with cash or trade goods.

The few hours Danny and I spent with these people were a wonderful experience. We left just before it became dark, and when we exited the outer door to the small field, lieutenant Markinson was there, waiting for me.

"Sergeant," he said, "I think you should spend some time in the armory, putting things there in order—right now, Sergeant."

"Yes, sir," I said, and went to the armory room, no more than forty feet from where I was. There was nothing there that needed "putting in order." I understood what the lieutenant was doing. He was letting me know that I'd just broken a law by spending time with the civilians. He was telling me that he was aware of this, and although he was reluctant to press formal charges, I'd better not do it again.

It had never been my intention to become any closer to the Heldens than I just had. In spite of Hilda's attractiveness, all thoughts of anything beyond a casual acquaintance were pushed from my mind. Kay was waiting for me in England, and I was certain we'd be talking about wedding plans when next I saw her.

The times we'd spent together, in town or walking along the Belfast Lough shore road, had become a prelude to serious thoughts of life after the war. We'd postponed making any commitments, because we could not, given the uncertainties of the times. We had shared our passes as often as we could get them. We'd also shared, in defiance of all rationality, the idea that we would become serious as soon as that became possible. That would be if I survived, if she survived, if Britain survived.

Her military unit, a motor maintenance company caring for light trucks and other vehicles, had moved to England a few months after I'd gone there. It was now fourteen months since we'd seen each other, but we'd maintained a steady correspondence. I felt, all through that time, that I had something special, something too valuable to diminish or cheapen by a relationship with any other woman.

In a general softening of the harsher terms of existence imposed by the army in recent times, it was announced that one-week furloughs would be granted for any who qualified. This included me. There were three places we could visit. These were Paris, Switzerland, or Britain. If Britain were the choice, as it would be for me, the army provided transportation to a port in England; from there I'd be on my own. I applied for one of these furloughs and waited for approval.

In the meantime, I noticed some things to which I'd not given much attention before. One was the manner in which Hilda had become the mainstay of her family. She did whatever was necessary to keep them together and healthy in the midst of shortages, a shattered economy, joblessness, and all the sorry consequences of a war that had destroyed almost everything they'd ever known of any value. Other parts of Germany, we learned, were far worse off than Trier, but it was bad enough here.

In the basement of the school, I'd see her doing laundry, and it was not her family's clothes she washed. It was American uniforms. I did not know who the soldiers were who had taken advantage of this situation. If it were our officers, it might be excused. They were entitled to a little extra service, if only by reason of their rank. Not since England had they enjoyed the attentions of a "striker." But if Hilda washed clothes for an enlisted man, I felt a deep resentment. We weren't paid enough to have laundry service, unless engaged in some illicit activity, such as the black market. Yet, I made no inquiry into this matter. She did what she felt she had to do, to survive. Criticism of her activities was not something I had any right to express.

Changes were in the wind, though, and not happy changes. Into Trier one day marched a regiment of special troops, of a kind we'd never seen before, although a few of our replacements and returning wounded knew about them. They were French Moroccans. They marched with unbelievable precision, turning into what had been a small German army post. They raised the flag of France on the flagpole, and with bugle calls and the presentation of arms, made the place a part of France.

This was not literal, we soon learned, but Trier and the Mosel valley, by agreement of the ruling powers and victors in this recent war, were to be henceforth a French occupation zone. We'd be leaving.

This wasn't such bad news, until we learned from the few who knew about them exactly who these soldiers were. We quickly observed that their field uniforms and equipment were American. From a distance, they appeared to be American soldiers. That impression vanished at close quarters. This was an elite regiment. They were all over six feet tall, in perfect physical condition. With the exception of their French officers, they were all black. This was not the various shades of brown we called black in the case of our African-Americans, nor were they any shade of gray. They were black as the deepest pit of an anthracite coal mine, pure and hard.

If their everyday uniforms were the same as ours, their dress clothing was decidedly not. They wore perfectly tailored powder-blue trousers and tunics, with a red fez atop their heads, making them seven feet tall in a parade. Their arms were American, with one exception. Each one of them carried a special knife, which was his preferred weapon if he could close with an enemy.

Hastily written orders came down from army, and were read to all of us. From this point onward, we were never to leave our company area for anything but official duties. If we were required to go to some other part of the city, we would march in formation and armed, with never less than four in our group. We would not be on the streets at any time after dark.

These French Moroccans, our informants told us, belonged to a religion that believed heaven was composed of endless looting, rape, and killing. To them, war was a taste of heaven on earth, and they loved it. We should not underestimate their willingness to kill any one of us for whatever change we might have in our pockets. A dollar or a hundred, it didn't matter too much. The money was not, in itself, as important as the sheer joy they'd know in cutting the throats of a few Americans. If we met any of them on the street, we would step aside, but have our weapons loaded and ready, and never turn our eyes away from them as long as they were visible.

Yet, they were a beautiful sight in a full-dress formal parade. It was obvious they had been drilled to perfection, and enjoyed letting the troops of other nations know how good they were in this, as in the bloodier duties they performed.

French Moroccans had been used in Italy, in a special way. When Allied forces had captured a small town in the mountains, and were following, as quickly as they could, the retreating Germans, information was always needed. In what direction had the Germans gone? What towns north of here might they go to next? How many were in the company, or battalion, or regiment? What heavy weapons did they have?

Local authorities were frequently obstinate about revealing any of this. Until the past few weeks, or even days, they had been allies of the Germans, and many still honored that relationship. They refused to talk to our officers. Time was often critical. Bringing in a company of French Moroccans and turning them loose on the town solved this problem. Two days and nights of screaming victims, of laughing, yelling, knife-wielding rapists and torturers, were usually enough. The town was in shambles, there were few, if any, survivors, beyond the reluctant authorities, kept separately from all the mayhem. At this point they talked, and did so volubly. The Germans were pursued, and another Italian town was no more. The war went on. The next dress parade of the Moroccans was a thing of marvelous beauty.

Our army had been slowly moving toward full integration. At this time, we had a young black American with us, a professional boxer with hopes to make it into the big time. He was friendly, laughed a lot, and good to have around. Our Sergeant Goldman became a close friend of his, at least in our present position and circumstances.

Goldman had regularly visited a nearby wine cellar of immense proportions. It must have contained ten thousand bottles or more, all on racks. The door had been smashed enough to prevent locking it, and every few days, he and Stanley, the black boxer, visited and brought back a few bottles. They kept themselves in a semi-euphoric state that didn't seem to bother anyone else very much.

The next day, however, was the Fourth of July, and they, plus several others, agreed that something special should be done to commemorate the day. They located a very large wooden box, big enough to hold two hundred or more bottles of wine, and carried it to the wine cellar.

There, they stopped, not because they wanted to, but because a pair of Moroccans sat in front of the door with a machinegun, ready to discourage visitors. It was most likely that this had been ordered by their officers to prevent their own troops from raiding the place, with possibly disastrous consequences to both the city of Trier and their own discipline.

But Goldman and Stanley, and the others, were not Moroccans, and felt they had a right to appropriate enough of the wine to make their Fourth of July celebration a memorable one. The Moroccans would not move, and made it evident the machinegun was loaded and ready to fire. It was a standoff of sorts. When all the talking had been done, and it was leave or die, Stanley solved the problem. He walked up to the machinegun crew, took a hand grenade from his pocket, and pulled the pin. He held it in front of him, at arm's length. No one had any doubt about what would happen if the machinegun were fired. Stanley would die, of course, but the grenade, released from his grip on its handle, would explode, certainly killing the Moroccans. They picked up the gun and their ammo and walked away.

Stanley tossed the grenade into the wine cellar, destroying a few hundred bottles, but there were thousands more. The group filled the box and, with four of them struggling to carry it, returned to the school and their quarters. Thus began an incident that might have killed many of us, had there not been a few cool heads around.

They started that evening, continued all night, and carried on the next day, the Fourth. It was at first little more than an orgy of immoderate drinking, until a few brought up the subject of the CBI, and our imminent departure for that far place. The anger of many gave birth to words that added fuel to the fires of potential revolt. It grew, and it became nasty, until "mutiny" was the only word that could describe it. Over a hundred men were ready to desert, and in the process take this city apart. A few probably considered the presence of the Moroccans, and realized that they would be used in such an event. Once the Moroccans became a part of it, the whole thing could easily escalate into a confrontation between French and American forces.

I was of little help in the effort to bring the situation under control. I had no idea how serious it had become, because I was on the roof of the school, stretched out and asleep on the floor of an air raid warden's lookout shelter. I had locked the supply room door, and only a few of the others in the company knew where I'd likely be found.

One of them did locate me, and said that I was needed immediately in company HQ. I climbed down the ladder to the third floor, down the stairs to the first. It was unnaturally quiet, an indication that something was not right.

In the company HQ room, I found Danny with his head down on his arms at a desk. He was weeping. Lieutenant Larson, at another desk, was also weeping. Neither would explain what it was all about, but I could guess, from what I'd known earlier. While I slept, there must have been a near-riot here. At the very least, some words had been used that showed disrespect for authority and a willingness to indulge in outright rebellion. Danny and lieutenant Larson, doing what they could to pull the teeth from a growing disaster, had either been overwhelmed or ignored, or both.

Lieutenant Cicciloni came in. "We could have used you here a while ago," he said to me. "Where were you?"

"Up in the lookout shelter, on the roof," I replied. "I'm sorry. I was tired, and nothing was happening in supply."

"You hadn't been drinking?"

"No, I hadn't. I knew some were doing that, but I never joined them."

"Okay, Sergeant. It's quiet now, but you could have helped if you'd been aware of it. For a short time, we were outnumbered."

"What's going to happen to the men involved?" I asked.

"There were just a half dozen who were mostly responsible. They'd stirred up the rest, whose main crime was just drinking more than was good for them."

"Lieutenant Markinson and Sergeant Furman—where were they?"

"They went for help, in case we needed it."

"Not the Moroccans?" I asked.

"No, not the Moroccans. The Seventh Army has a Corps headquarters just five miles away. They took the company truck and went there. But Markinson called when they arrived, and the worst seemed to be over, so they returned."

"They're here now?"

"Yes," said the lieutenant. "They're talking to Sergeant Goldman, and trying to decide what action should be taken. Goldman and his crate of wine were central to the whole incident, although it appears that it quickly grew beyond his control."

"Then we're okay now? Nothing else needs to be done?" I asked.

"No. You might have made things easier for us all, but you weren't here when we needed you, and it's over now. Go back to your supply room."

I did that, while I thought about how dangerously close this company had come to the kind of trouble that could have killed a number of us. I also thought that this just wasn't the sort of thing that happened with American soldiers. Some of us had been talking insurrection. This wasn't anything so very new. Americans had always been willing to fight for their independence, when enough of them felt aggrieved or oppressed. It had happened back in 1776, when our nation was born. Of course, the American Civil War could also be viewed that way, but at the end the country was still united. Armed rebellion did not happen today, in our modern world, in the United States of America or by the military forces that represented it. It was an action more typical of some Central American banana republic, where the peasants might revolt against the repressive regime of a dictator.

Yet, if Sergeant Goldman's crate of wine had been guilty of a misdemeanor, it was the army's insistence that we go to the CBI to die, without any opportunity to see our families and friends back home, that had made it into a felony. I could blame the wine, and I could blame Goldman's foolishness in getting so much of it, but I could not really fault those who, with their inhibitions dissolved in alcohol, protested too loudly and with too much vigor. They were only being human, and in a way typically American.

# 31

## *To Paris, to London, and to Kay*

The day passed and calm returned. I was called to company HQ again, and wondered if perhaps some of the blame for yesterday's incident might yet be placed on me.

It was something entirely different. My application for a furlough had been approved, and all the documents, travel vouchers, etc. were ready. A truck would be here tomorrow to pick up two others and me, and take us to Paris. I was going to see Kay again.

Wesley was still with us, and I asked to have him put in charge while I was away. That was approved, and for the rest of the day, I instructed him in procedures and the inevitable paperwork. He was nervous about it all, but willing.

I packed my personal items, the things I'd need on the trip and in England. Money was a necessity, and I had little. There was a solution to this, and although it went against everything I believed, I decided to use it. I had at least ten cartons of cigarettes, because I smoked very little, and had for some time bought and saved my weekly rations. At least half of these were about to become the cash I needed. I'd go through Paris, and from all reports, a black market buyer worked every street on which an American with a barracks bag might walk. The transactions were quickly done. I'd be lighter by a few cartons of cigarettes, but with a thicker wallet. The only down side was that it was illegal, from the army's point of view, although barely so on the streets of Paris. Even the police participated, by assigning territories to individual black marketeers, and then protecting them from the infringement of others, all for a cut of the profits,

274

I supposed. Even policemen needed to eat, and many had families.

In the morning, I made a quick stop to say goodbye to Hilda. She came downstairs, eliminating the need for me to go any farther than the door. We held each other tightly, and kissed, fiercely. It was the first, last, and only time we kissed, and we both understood that it was more an expression of a desperate longing for something like normalcy in our lives, rather than the kiss of two potential lovers.

Yet, there was a little something there, something that defied the old adage that "absence makes the heart grow fonder." As we separated, a pair of tears escaped from her eyes. My own eyes threatened to behave in a like manner. Yes, I thought, this beautiful girl could easily be the one with whom I'd happily share all that the rest that life had to offer. It would never happen, though. First, there was Kay. She was a known quantity, the rock-solid foundation on which my hopes for the future were built. For well over a year, we had been faithful to each other, and would remain that way. Nothing, I believed, would ever shake that foundation of our love.

In thoughts and in letters, we'd held grimly to the idea that we had a future together. All we'd needed to do was survive until the day we'd be free. If the army and our governments had not approved of our relationship, they had at least tolerated it, and would not keep us confined in the military forever. With peace now looking possible, we could make plans.

That was not the case with Hilda. Even if Kay had not existed, Hilda and I were an impossibility, and we both knew it. There could be no communication of any kind, no letters, no telephone calls, no personal visits. Any chance of seeing each other would be forbidden, probably for years to come. If the non-fraternization law had not worked perfectly, the post-war quarantine of Germany would be an iron-hard barrier impossible for people like us to negotiate. Only the military and government officials would be allowed to have contact with Germans. I had no intention of remaining a part of the military.

We were aware of all this. All we could have was a simple hug and a farewell kiss, even those illegal. There was no point in trying to discuss possibilities that could never be realized. We held hands a brief moment, and I turned around.

There were those who, if they knew of this situation, would have told me I was only acting like a teenage boy—overly emotional and filled with the uncertainties of approaching manhood. My reply to that would be that I was the same teenage boy, now barely past that age, who had accepted the responsibilities of the jobs I'd held and performed them with all the dedication and skill of a thirty-year-old, or a man of forty or fifty or sixty. I could not see that age had anything to do with it. I'd done my part in sending twenty thousand young men and boys forward to a combat assignment, where the majority had surely died. However, I'd helped send them knowing I'd done all that was possible to ensure that their weapons were functioning properly and that they had their ammunition, that they were clothed and outfitted properly, that they were as prepared as I, either as an armorer or supply sergeant, could make them.

No one could have done any more, at least in those areas. Much more could have been done in the matter of preparing them psychologically, but that was army's responsibility, not mine. The army had failed. I had not.

I ran to the truck and jumped aboard. Lieutenant Markinson stood by the tailgate, and told us that we'd not be returning to Trier. Within a day or two, the company would be going back to Marburg, and that was where we'd rejoin it on our return. Our papers already showed that.

Trier would be turned over to the Moroccans, as part of the French occupation zone. I shuddered when I thought of what could happen to Hilda and her family. They were good people, even if Helmut had been my enemy for a while. With the war ended, they should not become potential victims of an occupation force that relished blood-letting and may not be always under the control of its officers. Just as I had when leaving Stavelot, I felt totally helpless to do anything about it.

There were just the three of us now leaving, but others would be added as we went along. First, we'd all go to Paris. Some planned to stay there, a few would go to Switzerland, and I'd go to England.

I'd written to Kay earlier and told her there was a likelihood I'd have a furlough, and wanted to spend it there. She had made arrangements for me to stay with an English family that lived not far from her camp, in the town of Castleford. They had a son in the British navy, and I was welcome to use his small bedroom and bed. Mrs. Taylor also wrote to me and made the invitation official, for whenever I could manage to get there. They thought highly of Kay, and would do what they could to make my visit a pleasant one.

My travel orders covered transportation both ways, in continental Europe and the ferry ride from Etretat, on the French coast, to an English port. From there, I was on my own. I'd take a train to London, then change to another for the ride to Leeds, in the English Midlands, a bus from there to Castleford.

In the beginning, our truck took us through a totally devastated Germany. Many cities and towns had not a single resident, nor a single building without severe damage. As we'd done at St. Lo in Normandy, and Verviers in Belgium, we slammed and jounced over makeshift roads made by tanks with bulldozer blades. Thankfully, we were not sitting on ammo boxes this time. Eventually, we arrived in Paris.

This was a city alive. If not vibrant with music, great restaurants and wonderful entertainment, it was at least a busy place. The reports had been true about the black market activity. I'd not been in Paris more than twenty minutes when I was approached and asked if I had cigarettes to sell. Compared to a few months earlier, the price was depressed, but I supposed that was to be expected. I accepted what was offered and sold six cartons. The city was glutted with American cigarettes, American booze, Coca Cola, and a fair amount of clothing. Food was still scarce.

We had been advised to check in with an army "casual" facility, where a cot for the night and toilet facilities would be provided free of charge. We did that, and then each went our separate ways. The "Rainbow Club" was open and doing enough business to satisfy the most avaricious night club owner back home. It offered any and all kinds of drink, a small stage on which a singer tried, unsuccessfully as far as I was concerned, to compete with the intense racket of a thousand or more bar patrons all clamoring for service. I had one drink, paid, and walked out.

This wasn't for me. A stroll around part of the city would be far more enjoyable. The Eiffel Tower was closed, as were the major museums, but I walked along, sensing the ambience of the "City of Light" while prostitutes offered themselves and street vendors sidled up to buy or sell almost anything. Sidewalk urinals, nothing but metal troughs with a shoulder-high canvas screen around them, added their odor to the summer heat. It was at first a unique experience to relieve ones' self in public while watching traffic and pedestrians pass. Signs on the buildings along side streets told us not to urinate there. Other signs prohibited smoking on any form of public transportation.

Meals were not a part of my travel package, although the everlasting S on S was offered free near the casual quarters. I passed on that, and investigated a civilian stall with what looked like small, filled hamburger rolls for sale. The vendor looked askance at me, but sold me one of his products with no comment. It was not too bad, an unknown meat between two pieces of good bread. Shortly after that, an American soldier who was resident in Paris told me the meat was probably cat. Back in the Argonne, Bernie and I had watched Bobby put his mess kit on the ground when he thought he might be eating cat. Now, I'd just eaten it myself, and although I seemed to be suffering no ill effects physically, I had to wonder if this were some sort of weird psychic retribution for our inconsiderate action with a kid gone over the edge psychologically.

Parisians had been unable to buy meat for years, and every animal in the city had eventually become a candidate for consumption between pieces of bread. There were no dogs, cats, or pet birds left in Paris. There were no pets of any kind. They'd all been eaten. This, in a way, had aggravated the food shortage, because the lack of cats and dogs had presented an unrivaled opportunity for the proliferation of rats. These rodents had managed to destroy much of the stored grain supplies, along with any other foodstuffs not kept in metal containers or concrete vaults. Once the city was freed of German occupation forces, letters had gone to our government in Washington, begging the American people to send cats to Paris. They needed fifty thousand to restore the city's balance between predators and prey. I guessed I hadn't helped that situation much by eating part of a needed predator.

With time on my hands, I explored the Paris subway system, the "Metro," and found that it was excellent. Signs made it very clear where each train would stop. The terminals were well organized, access made simple, and the rides were smooth. A little familiarity made it simple to travel from any point to the Gar du Nord, the railway station I would use the next day for my train to Etretat.

The time passed uneventfully, and on the following morning, I boarded a continental European passenger train for the first time. Inside, it was similar to English trains, one of which I'd used traveling from Liverpool to Crewe after first arriving in Britain. An aisle ran the length of the car down one side. Small compartments, each with room for eight passengers, were off the aisle. In the compartments, we sat on one of the two benches facing each other. It was an arrangement that was conducive to easy conversation with our traveling companions.

The greatest deficiency in the railway system was the method used for coupling the cars. If the ride was smooth after it started, the start itself was nothing to make us believe that would be possible. On each end of a car was a huge hook, probably ten inches or so in height. A chain of three large links was dropped on the hooks, one link on each car, with the center link hanging between. The start of a train was a noisy affair, because the chains were snapped taut one at a time, as the engine moved forward. We could hear the banging and clanking approach us down the line of cars. In a sense, this was good, because we had some warning and could brace ourselves for the time our car would jump into motion. A pair of large, spring-loaded round bumpers on the end of each car prevented serious damage, but also added to the noise of getting a French train under way.

Once moving, we could relax, make friends, and enjoy the ride. In my compartment was an Australian soldier, also taking his leave in England. We enjoyed each other's company, and he told me about his Anzac division, and his experiences in Holland. At one point, they had captured a German airfield intact. The Krauts had all fled, but there were hundreds of new aircraft on the field, ready to fly and unable to do so. He said there was not a single drop of fuel anywhere. Just as in the Ardennes, the Germans were again defeated by the inability to run their engines long enough to make tanks or aircraft usable.

We arrived at Etretat and were told we'd spend a night here and take the ferry tomorrow. Folding cots in a large hall were our sleeping accommodations.

In the remaining daylight, we were allowed to roam around the village, but were warned not to approach the beach. Mines frequently washed ashore here. This was an old community, probably in existence since the time of William the Conqueror, in 1066. In normal times, it was a fishing village, and pleasantly picturesque. Now it was a base for mine sweepers clearing the coast and the English channel of the explosive devices left by both sides during the war.

After we crossed to England, we used another train to reach London. The Aussie and I parted company there. He had a different destination and would be taking a different train. I asked a station attendant where I should go and what time the next train left for Leeds. He took the time to give me very explicit directions.

"Ye'll not be staying in Leeds, would ye?" he asked.

"No," I replied. "I'm to find a bus there to take me to Castleford. Does that sound right?"

"Aye. It sounds right, and the best thing to do, just as soon as ye may. Leeds itself is off limits to all but home troops, ye see. Best ye not stay there long, although they'll not bother ye for just passing through, and mayhap not at all. You Yanks had little to do with the dustup that closed the city."

"Is the bus station near the railway?" I asked.

"Aye. Just a short walk down a street ye'll see when ye leave the train."

"Why," I asked, "is Leeds off limits? Can you tell me?"

"Aye," he replied, "'Tis no great secret. Bit of a rumpus between Canadians, home troops, and Aussies. Should have been over in a night, but they'd not let it alone. Kept going back for another go at the other fellows, you see. The local Bobbies couldn't handle it. So they closed the city, then reopened to home troops only. No Americans were involved. Some of us wonder which side you might have been on, if that had been the case."

"But you say they'd not object if I walked from the railroad station to the bus?"

"No, not likely. There's been no trouble in recent days, and you're not planning to stay in Leeds in any event. If stopped, just show your orders to the Bobby and explain to him your reason for passing through Leeds. He'll let you move on, I'm sure. And good luck to you, Sergeant. May you enjoy your stay here."

"Thanks," I said. "By the way, your accent is not native to London, is it?"

He chuckled. "Not a bit of it. I'm from near Leeds myself, but we railroad workers move about a bit. Ye'll hear a lot of folk speak as I do when you reach the Midlands."

I thanked the man again for his help and boarded my train a few minutes later. The ticket to Leeds was inexpensive, a matter of less than three dollars American.

The transfer to the bus was easily made, and the trip to Castleford marred only by my failure to get off at the right stop. "Cutsyke" was the name of the area in Castleford to which I was going. I hadn't told the driver that, and of course did not know until it was too late that we had passed the road to Cutsyke. He was accommodating, and told me to stay on the bus, that he'd be returning within minutes, and would drop me off at the right place then. He did that.

It was almost a mile walk from there to the street on which the Taylors lived. A middle-aged couple passed me on the way, going in the opposite direction. They soon turned around, called out and asked if I were Russell. I stopped and met the Taylors. We continued together.

Their house was the last in a row of tenements, a pleasant place, with the advantage of a side yard, which the other homes did not have. Here, they kept a few chickens, providing them with fresh eggs that did not count against their monthly rations.

I'd been given a book of civilian ration coupons, and been told to present these to the lady of the house if I were staying with a family. I did that, and learned a little about how this nation, dependent on foreign imports for so much of what they used, had managed to survive through all the difficulties of the war. Each person was allowed one fresh egg per month. A few spoonfuls of sugar was a month's ration. Fats, such as margarine, were limited to what an American might put on two or three pieces of bread, for a whole month. Meat was something like a half pound per person per month. On it went, the government allowances of almost everything we thought was essential. They "made do" and survived. The Taylors' eight chickens probably kept them and their young son healthier than many, but the list of rationed items seemed endless. Mrs. Taylor took my coupons and added them to her own.

That evening, they phoned Kay and told her I had arrived. She came out on a bus and we were together again for the first time in fourteen months.

# 32

## *Searching for Colin*

A few kisses and a lot of hugging on the sidewalk in front of the Taylor house, and we were ready to pick up where we'd left off over fourteen months earlier. A neighbor watched us from a window in the next apartment, and later told Mrs. Taylor it was a "beautiful reunion." Of course it was.

I held Kay by her upper arms and pushed her back to thoroughly look at her. Again, I realized how much I'd missed this beautiful young Irish woman. Her blonde hair, cut to meet military regulations, framed a face that was softly rounded and reflected a joy she seemed to find in the smallest aspects of life. It was a face that, in advanced old age, would be much loved by grandchildren. Her figure was full without any fat, and those beautiful green eyes were ever ready for a smile. Knowing her, and realizing, for the hundredth time, how constant she'd been with her expressions of devotion in letters, made me a most fortunate young man.

It had been Kay, with those letters, who had often provided me with the only sign of sanity during those long and often despair-filled months. Of course, there were letters from home. Family and friends all wrote, and each letter was appreciated. But Kay was here, in Europe. She was far closer to where it all happened, far more involved in the same trials, disappointments, and total submission to the demands of the military. She was able to express much of that in her letters, if always with appropriate regard for the censors who read our mail before we were allowed to send it out. She wrote to the heart of our mutual longings and frustrations, and she wrote good poetry, something I hoped to do some day. Her sister Maureen was also ATS, still in Northern Ireland. Her brother Colin was in the British army and now somewhere in England. Without knowing them personally, I was certain that they, Kay, and I had a different perspective on the war than anyone back home could possibly have had.

For example, our government strove mightily to instill in the people a sense of being a part of it all, but never fully succeeded. The letters from home invariably carried a distorted view of what was actually happening overseas. Food rationing was almost a joke, for in spite of frequent shortages, the amounts normally allowed an American family appeared, to their English counterparts, to be an inducement to uncontrolled gluttony. All the little things, such as saving metal toothpaste tubes and the tinfoil from various packaging materials, were not much more than another attempt to make the people feel they contributed to the war effort. Most of those carefully cleaned substances were eventually tossed in a landfill, I was sure. Propaganda and psychological conditioning were at the heart of it all.

That was none of my concern at this time, though. Kay was here. I was here. We had a few days to express our feelings for each other and make decisions about the future, to whatever extent we were able. But not this day. She had to return to her camp before taps, or whatever the British equivalent was. We walked down the street for a short time, arm in arm, then returned to the Taylor's. I'd stay here for the night, Kay would take the last bus back, and in the morning I'd go to her camp and we'd find out what we might be able to arrange as time off for her.

The Taylors, with their younger son, a ten year old they called Robbie, were wonderful. They tried to make me feel as if I were a part of their family, and succeeded. We had a pleasant chat for the rest of the evening, after which I retired to my bedroom and dumped the contents of my barracks bag on the bed.

There were still five cartons of cigarettes. Kay would use some, and I could give some to Jesse Taylor, and still have enough left, with a carton or two to sell in Paris on the way back if necessary.

After a sound sleep and a wonderful breakfast of fresh eggs, fried in a dollop of precious lard, followed by tea and scones, I was ready to tackle whatever difficulties might follow in arranging time off for Kay to spend with me.

The bus took me to the gate of Kay's camp, where the sentry expected me. He called on the phone to let Kay know I was here, and she appeared ten minutes later.

"We're going to see Captain Adams, the camp commandant," she said.

"Okay," I replied. "What will we ask him for?"

"For as many days as possible of leave time for me. We're busy right now, so he may be reluctant to allow much, but we'll ask anyway."

We entered the commandant's office when the clerk in the outer room told us he was ready to see us. Captain Adams was seated at a desk, and stood to welcome me. He was a rather short man, middle-aged, with gray hair, but lean, as all the English were at this time. There was a kindness about him, but also the sense that he could be a stern disciplinarian when necessary.

I was ill at ease, and realized I'd been living under field conditions so long, I'd forgotten all the military protocol for conduct indoors. I couldn't even remember if I should remove my cap or leave it on my head. I turned to Kay, and followed her lead, taking the cap off and holding it in my hand. I saluted after her, clumsily, I was sure. But Captain Adams seemed not to notice.

"How much leave time do you have, Sergeant?" he asked.

"A week, sir," I said, "of which I've already used a day."

"You'll be returning to your company then?"

"Yes, sir. In Germany."

"Let's hope the rest of this war will be concluded before any further deployment is necessary."

"I certainly hope so, sir, but guess none of us can be sure about anything until it's really over."

He smiled briefly, and looked at Kay. "You know as well as I that we're extremely busy, and short of help at the same time."

"Yes, sir," she said, and looked at the ceiling, as if in prayer.

"So I regret," the Captain continued, "that I feel unable to allow as much leave time as I'm sure you would like. Two days is the best we can do." He looked at me. "Private Bradley is an important part of our motorcycle maintenance team. They'll perform slowly without her."

He stood and offered his hand to me, which I took. "I wish you the best, Sergeant." To Kay, he said, "Your papers are ready with the clerk. Go, and enjoy the time you have. Dismissed."

She and I saluted, did an about-face, and left.

The pass was dated from noon this day until noon the day after tomorrow. The clerk, a frail-looking young woman wearing glasses, smiled at us and said we could leave any time, but why not show the sergeant a little of the motor pool and work area while we waited for the next bus?

Kay did that. A male sergeant was in charge, a pleasant man who seemed to have a small joke for every occasion. There were three other ATS girls on the maintenance team. They and the sergeant were apparently pleased to show me around.

Kay went to her barracks for a short time to collect a few personal items and articles of clothing, then returned.

"Where to now, my love?" I asked her.

"Back to the Taylors, and then maybe you'd not mind doing something that would be most dear to my heart."

"And what would that be?"

"I'd like to have you meet my brother Colin."

"Wonderful," I replied. "I'd like that. Then you know where he is?"

"Yes. I had his post address, of course, and Lucy, in Captain Adams' office, tracked down his company's location for me. It will be a journey of more than two hours by rail from Leeds, but it's the one thing I'd really like to do with this time, if you're willing."

How could I not be willing? We'd be together, and traveling on a British train would give us much time for semi-private conversation.

We told Mrs. Taylor our plan, and I asked her to hold more than half of my money for me, to insure that I'd have it when we returned.

I had a small canvas overnight bag with me, and packed a change of underwear, socks, soap, toothbrush, razor, and the everlasting cigarettes. Kay's few necessities also fit easily.

We arrived in the railway station at Leeds a little after noon, and learned our train would leave at two. This gave us time for a light lunch of tea, scones, and jam. Every British railway station, large or small, had a lunch counter where passengers could obtain such fare at a reasonable price.

We purchased our tickets, strolled the station for a while, and boarded the train. It was not crowded. We shared our compartment with an elderly couple who talked very little.

I held Kay's hand and confided in her how uncertain and nervous I was about every part of this adventure. These feelings had nothing to do with her, or us, but everything to do with our present semi-immersion into civilian life. I wasn't sure I knew how to behave. I was convinced that my sense of values had undergone extreme modification, and drifted far from the norm as any civilian would see it. Yet, I was a civilian, too. I was certainly not a soldier, despite outward appearances. My problem was an inability to any longer relate to the concerns of good people like the Taylors, the old couple riding with us, the train conductor, or even the black marketeers of Paris. Theirs was a different world now, filled with petty concerns unrelated to the realities of life. Those realities were, from my viewpoint, composed primarily of military expediencies, at the core of which was personal survival. Life was about living and dying, and everything else was trivial by comparison.

I told all this to Kay while the train carried us ever closer to a meeting I both anticipated and feared. Her family was an unknown quantity to me, and yet it was evident that she desperately wanted their approval of our relationship, or the possibilities inherent in it. She seemed to feel that if we could win Colin's approval, the rest would fall into line. I was not at all sure of that, but we had to make an effort, at least.

Our train took us in a generally southern direction, or a bit west of south, to the city of Shrewsbury, near the Welsh border. This was an ancient settlement, its beginnings going back to before Roman times. Some effort had apparently been made to preserve the best of that, but everywhere were the signs that the modern world had inundated the lesser vestiges of that distant past. Row houses and tenements were built on foundations meant for Roman castles. Winding village streets had been straightened and paved. There was a gray sameness to it all that was depressing.

Yet, our search for Colin began here. We asked a Bobby for directions as Kay showed him the address she had for Colin's company.

He shook his head. "I'm a bit new to this city," he said. "I could only guess where your friend's unit is located."

"My brother's," said Kay. "Colin Bradley is my brother, and I truly need to find him."

"With the Yank?" The Bobby nodded at me.

"Yes, with the Yank."

Again, the Bobby shook his head. "I'm afraid I'm of no help to ye. There's a company of Irish at the southern end of the city, but I've no idea what sort of unit it is, or how ye'll find your brother. There's a pub in that direction, too." He looked at his watch. "I'd suggest ye stop there, have a bite to eat and a spot of tea, beer if ye'd prefer, and ask about."

It was the best advice we had. It was the only advice we had, and we followed it.

Being half lost in ancient European cities was becoming an old story with me, but this time all instincts failed. From the pub, we walked up one street and down another, all of it pointless wandering. The day wore on and darkness came. We joined a group of people headed for homes in the suburbs after the pubs had closed at eleven. Those we spoke to were sympathetic, but had no solid information to offer.

"We'd best find a Toc H," Kay said at last. The Toc H was roughly equivalent to our YMCA, a place where weary travelers could find sanitary facilities, a place to wash or shave, or brush teeth, and a cot for the night.

Some of the people, when asked, pointed us in the right direction. One couple offered to let us sleep on the floor in their living room, but had no extra blankets. "Ye'll need to keep each other warm," they said, with a smile and a knowing nod. Kay thanked them, but declined the offer.

Nearly exhausted, we found the Toc H. The women's part of it was in another building a hundred yards or so up the street. We separated, and Kay promised to be back early in the morning.

There were plenty of empty cots. Most were in tiers, four high, attached to pipe frames. Two blankets and a pillow were on each. I washed and chose a cot on the second level, removed my shoes and tied them to the upright next to my cot by the laces. I had nothing else worth stealing, and doubted if even the shoes were in danger. Toc H places were generally safe from thievery or vandalism.

# 33

## *Making It Official*

At a counter in the dining room, the Toc H offered something similar to a continental breakfast. It was served cafeteria style. When Kay arrived, we each took a tray, and from the limited choices picked up tea, scones and jam, and a sweet roll. The cost was slight, and included a second cup of tea if we wished. We carried our trays to a tiny round table-for-two, next to a window that gave a view of a brick wall across the street. I looked for no particular symbolism in this, but it matched our depression over the failure of this mission.

"Should we spend more time looking for Colin?" I asked.

Kay shook her head. "No. I've decided I have an error of some sort in his address. We can do nothing but return. I'll learn later, when I write to him, where we went wrong, but I see little point in pursuing it any further here and now. I'm sorry to have put you through all this."

"Don't be. It was something we needed to try, and maybe we'll have another chance, some time in the future."

She stared at me, and from her eyes, I knew she'd been crying earlier. "What are we going to do, Russ? I mean, what sort of future could we possibly plan in this horrid world of ours?"

I shrugged. "Not so horrid at all times," I said. I reached across the table and took her hands in mine. "Suppose we just pretend that the war is over, and our lives are ours to live. For just this day, let's pretend that much." I stopped and thought carefully about what I was going to say next. "If it becomes possible to make our wishes a reality sometime soon, would you then marry me, Kay?"

Tears ran down her cheeks, but she smiled through them. "You know I would. Yes, of course."

"Then let's use what's left of this day to find you a ring to wear—an engagement ring. There must be jewelry stores in Leeds that would have something appropriate. First, we'll go back to Castleford. I'll need the money Mrs. Taylor is holding for me. Then to Leeds, and a ring for you."

We managed to catch an early train, half filled with workers on their way to jobs in other cities and towns. Our compartment was filled, but at every stop one or two left the train, usually replaced by fewer new passengers. By the time we reached Leeds, there were just four of us. Kay had fallen asleep, leaning against me, and I found that to be a source of pleasure.

Mrs. Taylor seemed surprised to see us so early, but understood when Kay explained. She smiled when I told her why I needed the money she was holding. "It will be expensive," she said. "There's a wartime tax of a hundred percent on all jewelry, so you'll pay twice what it's worth, but there's no help for that. Just choose wisely, and I'm sure you'll find what suits you both."

With that, we returned to Leeds, and ignoring the prohibition against all but home troops, found a jewelry store with a fair selection of rings. The elderly clerk was carefully neutral about it all, and if he disapproved, kept that to himself. Not all of the locals wanted their young women to marry an American. Of course, Kay was Irish, so may have been exempt from such censure.

The ring we agreed upon was a pretty little thing of pale gold, with a diamond not much larger than those used in industry, but it was within our budget. Kay loved it, and couldn't stop smiling for the rest of that day.

While we waited for the bus to Castleford, I noticed fresh fruit and vegetable stalls in a nearby building. We walked in. It was a small farmer's marketplace, and although fruits were noticeably lacking, a variety of vegetables were offered for sale. I saw some fresh beets, one of my favorites, and something I'd missed for well over two years now. "Could we buy some of those?" I asked Kay.

"Of course," she replied. "Why would you question it?"

"Because I have no ration coupons with me. Mrs. Taylor has all of them, or all she's not yet used."

"But," Kay said, almost laughing, "ration coupons are not needed for a small farmer's market produce. You may buy anything here without affecting your ration allowances."

I eagerly picked out some good-looking beets and asked the farmer if he could put them in a bag for me. He did, although he needed to charge a few pennies extra for the bag. The beets were remarkably cheap.

Kay had an engagement ring, already on her finger, I had a bag of beets, and we arrived at Castleford and the Taylor's in a happy mood, far different from that in which we'd started this day.

"We have the rest of today and tomorrow morning," I said to her. "How should we use the time?"

"Remember how much we enjoyed the cinema when we were in Ireland?" she asked.

"Of course. Is that what you'd like to do now?"

Mrs. Taylor broke in. "If I may suggest it, what you two need most is a little time together, without others about. You've had no opportunity for such, and I strongly urge you to take it now. Use the heath across the street and lose yourselves in the heather there."

I looked at Kay and grinned. "Could we?"

She smiled. "And why not?"

The field was a large one, probably twenty or more acres, almost entirely covered with heather, much of it in flower now. The whole expanse appeared to be painted a soft, pastel bluish purple. We had no idea what specific kind of heather this was, and didn't think that really mattered much. There were thousands of varieties known in Britain. The only thing they had in common was that they grew in soil generally too poor for anything else. The heather here was of a taller type, waist to almost shoulder high, with a few scattered stands of small trees added as accents to the scene, and patches of colorful wildflowers here and there.

We found that trails went through it in all directions. When we followed some, we discovered little half-hidden alcoves of matted and flattened plants, where others had stopped to talk, smoke, or possibly make love. We saw one in which the heather had already recovered to a great extent, and stopped there to sit in silence for a few minutes. Mrs. Taylor had been right. We needed this time alone.

We hugged, kissed, and just held each other close for a few minutes. When we released our embrace, I lit a cigarette for each of us, and stole sidelong glances at her while we smoked.

"Are you as aroused as I am?" I asked.

She grinned. "Probably more so. But we're not going to do anything about it, you know."

"Kay," I said, "I have a condom. The army provides them, free, and encourages us to always have one on hand."

"Why? Did you think I was diseased?"

"Of course not. But they're also effective for preventing a pregnancy."

"Which will not happen anyway, if we control ourselves. No, I can't do that. For one thing, my church forbids the use of such things."

"They'd rather have you pregnant?"

"That was unworthy of you. You know I'm Catholic, and you should know that the church wants us first properly married before we indulge ourselves in what we so desperately want.

"I know you're not Catholic, and this has bothered me some, but it's not an insurmountable problem. We could work around it. What we could not work around would be a bastard child, with both of us in the service and you likely somewhere on the other side of the world when the baby arrives. We simply can't risk it. If you think about it, I'm sure you'll agree."

I did think about it, and did agree, but it was damnably hard to accept. I lifted her hand, the one with the ring, and kissed it. "Then this," I said, nodding at the ring, "is all we have to bind us to each other. It's this ring, and a year and a half of accumulating love and desire. Until when? Will there ever be a day when we can live as normal people, as a normal couple?"

She smiled, but sadly. "We don't know the answer to that. Perhaps no one does. When the world slips into this sort of situation, where armed conflict seems the only way to settle issues, we all pay a price. Before it's finally over, it will make little difference whether we're English, American, Irish, German or Italian. We'll all be beaten down to a common level of near hopelessness. But we can't give in to that, dearest. We must, as long as we're able, hold to our dreams and continue to believe in their possibilities. It's our dreams that keep us human."

"You're right, of course," I said. "Let's walk around a bit, just to ease the tension in those parts of us that are not permitted to know each other yet."

We spent the next hour strolling, hand in hand, down the heather trails. Twice, we met others, with whom we exchanged pleasant greetings in passing. It was a warm, lazy day in July. Birds flew overhead. Insects provided a faint background sound with their muted clicks and chirps. The dusty blue/purple of heather was as easy on the eyes as the sea might be from a lonely beach in the first soft light of dawn. We had no reason to hurry to or from anywhere.

I'd overlooked something, though, and when we at last returned to the Taylor's, I asked if Kay might be able to spend the night here. Returning to camp, then taking the morning bus back here, seemed a foolish waste of the last few hours of her leave time.

"Of course," said Mrs. Taylor. "She's stayed the night before, with one of her ATS chums, when we all stayed out late at the pub."

"Is it also possible," I asked, "that we could all go out to a pub for dinner tonight? To celebrate our engagement, of course. I think it's my place to do this, and I've enough money left to take care of it for all of us. How about a place that has good fish and chips? I'd really like that."

"Oh, yes," she replied. "There's a great fish and chip place just down the road a piece. It's a pub, too. If it's not too much, it would be lovely to have a neighbor couple join us. They know Kay, and will be almost as thrilled as Jess and I about this engagement."

"And Bobby?" I asked. "Will he be able to come along?"

"Oh, I'm afraid not on a school night. We'll likely stay out too late for that. We'll have a nice young lady from nearby stay with him until we return. Bobby likes her, and won't mind too much."

She phoned Jesse's work place and left word for him not to "dawdle" on his way home, for we had news to share with him and we'd all be eating out. "I'll cook your beetroot for tomorrow's dinner," she said to me.

It was a happy group that walked the mile or so from the Taylor's to the pub, and we became happier yet as the evening progressed. The fish and chips, which everyone decided to have, were nicely complemented by endless refills of beer.

English money could be a source of confusion or amusement, depending in part upon how much one had imbibed. Most of it was coins, and I wondered sometimes why English men did not acquire a permanent "list" from the weight of the money in one of their pockets.

It began with the farthing, a copper coin rarely seen and of little value except to make change. It was worth a quarter of a penny. Next there was the half penny (haypenny bit), followed by the penny, a large copper coin about three times the size and weight of our American cent. Then was the three penny (thrupence), followed in turn by the sixpence. Twelve pence made a shilling. Simple enough, and shillings were common, but the next step could confuse the best of us. The silver florin was equal to two shillings, the half crown equal to two and a half shillings. Both coins were common, but the crown did not exist in modern coinage, so we went to paper currency next, with the ten shilling, or half pound, note. The pound was the standard in paper, with the five pound note a rarity, and by tradition signed, by any who used and passed it, on one of the margins.

Prices, if over a pound, were always quoted in three units—pounds, shillings, and pence. I was used to this, because it was the same money we used in Northern Ireland. But before we became too complacent, the price of any large item was often given in guineas. There were no guineas, had been none for a couple of centuries, when it existed as a gold coin equal to a pound plus a shilling, or twenty-one shillings. The guinea had value only as a conversation piece. Yet, when we were told the price of Kay's ring, it was twenty-two guineas. I had to mentally convert that to twenty-two pounds plus twenty-two shillings, or twenty-three pounds and two shillings. We were paid at the rate of $4.03 American to a pound, so the ring cost about $93.00.

Of course, half of that was tax, so this was not an expensive ring. Kay still loved it, and that was what really counted. I never tried to estimate what the cost would be in the States, but it would have been even less, because the army penalized us in the exchange rate. In the open money market, a pound was worth about two and a half dollars, but we paid the 4.03 rate. This was intended, we were once told, to make our pay a little more equitable with British military pay.

After the second beer at the pub, and to the accompaniment of laughter from our English friends, I emptied my pocket and dumped all the coins in the center of the table, then asked the waitress to simply take whatever was needed to pay for each order we placed. This detracted not in the least from the joyousness of the occasion, and saved me a possible headache.

It was a leisurely walk back to the Taylor's. Kay and I strolled hand in hand, with an escort of some of the nicest people I could imagine. I fully understood why she'd wanted me to stay with the Taylors. It wasn't just because they were convenient to the bus line from her camp, but because not once, in the time spent with them, did I hear a word of criticism directed at any person of different background or ethnicity.

These were the people who had saved England, who had defended it with their lives, then endured the privations of a nation besieged and lacking nearly all of the resources to survive against impossible odds. They had survived, though. I fervently hoped that their son, now serving in the Pacific, would return to them alive and whole. That was the very least they deserved.

Kay insisted that she sleep on the sofa downstairs in the living room. I went to my bed in the little room upstairs, next to Bobby's, and worried about the chance that Kay and I might never share a bed and a life. In spite of her low opinion of the world at large, she still had more faith in our future than I did. What could I offer, once this war was over? I'd not finished my printer's apprenticeship, although I was certain I could find a job where the knowledge I did have would be useful. It just wouldn't pay very much. The military had nothing to offer but low pay and uncertainties. I wanted, for Kay and for us, far more than I could see as reasonable possibilities. Finally I slept, sensing her presence so near, and yet so temporary.

# 34

## *The Last Night and Farewell*

After breakfast, Jess Taylor offered to give me a short tour of the bottle factory where he worked. Kay had already done this, a few months ago, and urged me to go while she and Mrs. Taylor took time for some "woman talk."

Jess was a mold-maker, member of a four-man department that was apparently considered a sort of elite among the glass workers. They were the experts who created the means by which thousands of identical bottles could be produced on the machines in the main part of this large building.

His co-workers thanked me for the cigarettes I'd been sending them. I'd given a pack to Jess every morning before he left for work. He, in turn, had shared them with the others. Jess was a generous man, something I fully realized now.

The tour was interesting. Although I understood the basics of glassmaking, I'd never before seen how it was done in such volume, and the almost infinite variety of sizes and shapes that could be made with the molds. However, I was anxious to spend a little more time with Kay before she left, so bid the mold makers goodbye and returned to the house, a little more than a mile away.

We had an hour before the bus arrived, so we walked the heather field once more, but slowly and not very far.

"Will you be back this evening?" I asked her.

"Oh, yes. We'll soon be counting our remaining time together in minutes, and I want every last one of them. And you'll be leaving in the morning?"

"Yes," I replied. "My orders are to be in London before two in the afternoon, and make the connection then for the ferry port."

I stopped and held her close. "I love you, Kay, and always will. Someday this world will not be turned upside down. Someday, we'll replace those dreams that you said keep us human with a thing much better—a life of our own, to do with what we will."

She wept, but softly. "If there's a just God anywhere, that will happen. I believe it. Our love cannot be limited forever."

The bus came and Kay left. I told Mrs. Taylor not to plan lunch for me. I'd walk around a bit, and find something when I became hungry enough.

She nodded. "We'll be having your beetroot for dinner. You'll be back for that?"

"Oh, yes, probably long before. I need to examine my own feelings, and think a little of what can or cannot be done in the future, if there is one." I half smiled. "The choices are pretty limited, aren't they?"

She nodded, with an expression of deep sadness.

Jess had taken me to a different pub one evening after dinner. It was only a quarter mile away, in the opposite direction from the place we'd had the party, fish and chips. This one was strictly a barroom, in the American style. People came here to drink, not to eat or celebrate, except in limited ways. It was owned and operated by an American expatriate from Chicago, a Salvatore Vitrini, who had come to England a few years earlier and stayed.

I went there now, and arrived just as it opened, at noon. There were no other customers. I sat at the bar and ordered a whiskey.

"Blended, scotch, or Irish?" Sal asked.

"To tell the truth, I hardly know one from another," I said. "I'm pretty much just a beer drinker."

"Then I'll give you something not too harsh, and you can follow it with a beer."

That worked fine for me. About halfway through the beer, I experienced a slight mellowness that was exactly what I'd wanted. I relaxed and looked at Sal Vitrini from Chicago. He was middle-aged, with gray hair not far from becoming white, a powerfully built man who might have been a middleweight boxer in another time and another place. An Italian or Sicilian, by the name, from Al Capone's town. I couldn't help but make that association, with all that it implied. But it was none of my business. Sal had apparently made a place for himself in this English community, and probably planned to live out his life here. I wanted to know more about how he'd managed that.

"When did you come to England?" I asked. It seemed an innocent enough question.

He hesitated and looked sharply at me. I could guess what he was thinking: here's a young American soldier with a New England accent, wondering if I'm remotely connected with the Chicago mobs of the thirties. "In 1938," he answered. "Don't tax your brain by imagining things that may not be true. And, don't ask questions about things that are, or could be the truth. Keep your conversation to generalities and local affairs, and we'll get on just fine."

"Okay," I said. "Local affairs. That could include the way a man from Chicago, or elsewhere, fit into the local scene and made a life for himself here. Without in any way getting personal, can you tell me how that might be done? I don't want particulars, just generalities. For one thing, about how much money would be needed?"

Again, Sal waited before he replied. Finally, "Probably a great deal more than you might think. This place was a bargain at thirty thousand dollars, and I paid cash for it. It gives me a home upstairs and a living, but not enough more to pay back the purchase price, if I'd needed to borrow that much. My best advice to you is to forget about it. If you're wealthy enough to go this route, there are other options that would be much better."

"It's just an idea I'm exploring," I said.

"Yes, I understand that, but the cost of what you're thinking extends far beyond mere dollars. You'd need to write off your family, your friends, and any connections you have at home. You'd need to become another person, even adopt an alias. And there's never any guarantee that someone will not guess who you are and why you're here. Your fingerprints alone would give you away, if the local police ever had occasion to check them. Unless you'd spent a year or more carefully planning this sort of move, someone would find you and it would all end. Your house of cards would come crashing down around you, and you'd walk away with nothing, if you were even allowed to do that much. It would depend, of course, on who wanted you and how badly."

I ordered another beer. "I don't suppose you'd have anything I could buy for lunch?"

"I could make you a sandwich. Cheese or fish?"

"Cheese." I put my head in my hands and my elbows on the bar. It was only a wild idea, and Sal seemed to have put it all beyond the realm of possibilities.

When he returned with the sandwich, I asked him one more question, something I thought was a critical part of this whole idea I was considering. "Did you become a citizen of England?"

"Yes. It was the only way to insure that I could stay here indefinitely. That's one other thing you'd need to give up—your citizenship. I can't imagine why you'd consider it, unless you'll be facing a court-martial when you return to your company. When will that be?"

"Tomorrow. At least, I'll be on my way then. And I've committed no crime, unless you call selling some cigarettes on the Paris black market a criminal activity."

"Not if they were your personal rations. Why, exactly, are you thinking along these lines?"

"A woman. A young woman I love more than life."

"I should have known. You need to realize that she would be one of the first things you'd lose."

He was making sense, and I'd been on the point of surrendering to nothing but ill-considered and emotion-driven foolishness.

"Thanks, Sal. You've helped me see things a bit more clearly. I guess there's no way to come out ahead in this situation, beyond giving it a lot more time and hoping I'll still be alive when it becomes possible to do something sensible."

"That's enough to hang onto for the present. You're not the first, nor will you be the last, to face a situation like this."

Two men entered the barroom and took seats a few feet away. Sal took their orders and put another glass of beer in front of me. "My farewell gift," he said. "Take your time with it. It'll not be busy here for another couple of hours."

One of the customers looked at me and spoke. "Farewell? Are you leaving, sergeant?"

"Yes. Tomorrow."

"For any special place?"

"Germany right now. Maybe China/Burma/India a little later. They said half of us will die there, or on the beaches of the Japanese home islands."

He and his friend both lifted their glasses. "Then here's to you, sergeant, and may the Lord preserve you and all the others who may soon join you there."

"Thanks," I said, "and I think I'd better leave now. I've had about my limit, and although it's not far, I do want to walk in the house upright, rather than crawling." I handed Sal one of my remaining pound notes, and accepted the change, from which I left a florin on the bar.

I turned at the door and waved to Sal. "Thanks. You've been helpful."

"You walk the line and watch your back," he said. "Give my regards to Jess and his Mrs. They're good people."

"I know that," I said, and left.

Mrs. Taylor looked sharply at me when I walked in the house. "You've been down to Sal's," she said.

I nodded.

"Maybe that was a good thing. He could talk to you in ways few English barkeeps would be able. But you need to rest a bit now, before Kay arrives. Go upstairs and stretch out on the bed. I'll call you when it's time."

I did, and she did.

I walked outside to meet the bus, and Kay stepped off it smiling.

"Something good has happened?" I asked, after we'd kissed.

"In a way. It's a small thing, but that's all we have these days, isn't it? Do you remember Sergeant Lawton? You met him that first day. He's in charge of maintenance at the motor pool."

"Yes. The tall, lean man who always had a joke."

"The same," said Kay. "He's my immediate superior, of course, and after I'd told him a bit about us, and showed him the ring, he hatched a plan to give us a little more time together before you leave. He's really a dear man."

"What does this plan involve?" I asked.

"Only that you leave the Taylor's tonight and return with me on the bus. There's a place less than a mile from my camp, where you might stay the night. It's not a Toc H, but is a lot like one. There are cots and facilities for washing, shaving, and so forth. The major difference between this and a Toc H is that there's a bar here."

"Not a problem," I said. "And you'll be able to stay with me until the last few minutes tonight? Then what about the morning?"

"That's where Sergeant Lawton comes in. He's discovered that he will need some parts he normally purchases in Castleford, and he'll have the use of a lorry to go pick them up. He will also need an assistant on this errand, and that will be me. We pass right by the place you'll be staying, and by a rare stroke of good fortune, we'll also be stopping next to the bus terminal at Castleford, just in time for your transportation to Leeds."

I laughed. "This sergeant of yours does plan things well, doesn't he? That's great, dear. The only drawback is that I'll need to say goodbye to the Taylors tonight. That will be difficult."

"I know, but they'll understand."

They did understand, of course. I handed Jess one of the remaining cartons of cigarettes, and gave Mrs. Taylor half of my remaining money, which was very little for all they'd done for me, but she hugged me and even wept a little when it came time to leave. Jess shook hands for a minute or more, and even Bobby, aroused from bed and half asleep, put his arms around my neck and wished me the best.

We left the bus outside the camp, but did not go in. With my barracks bag slung over my shoulder by the cord, we walked slowly toward the place where I'd spend the night. It was a large, gray building, rather dismal looking, on a piece of ground that was more coarse gravel than anything else. We walked past it and checked my watch, to be sure Kay could return to the camp gate in time.

"There's a bar inside?" I asked her.

"Yes. It's in the entrance area, with the sleeping quarters off to the left. Some of the girls and I have stopped in here a few times for a beer. It's not much, but it's close to camp."

We waited until the last possible minute, when Kay went inside with me. "We'll be by in the morning about eight," she said after we kissed.

I went to the bar, dropped my barracks bag on the floor at my feet, and sat on a stool. There were no other customers.

A tall, rawboned woman approached. "A small beer, please," I said.

She drew the beer and put it in front of me. She possessed a mouth she could twist into a look of strong disapproval, and this she did. "I suppose you got what you wanted from the Irish slut," she said.

I'd been looking at the beer, and now looked up at her quite suddenly. "What? What did you say?"

"You heard me, Yank."

I sat up straight. "Why did you call her that?"

"Humph! She's Irish, isn't she?"

I took some coins from my pocket, put the price of the beer on the counter, and stood. "I ordered a beer, and I'll pay for that beer. But no power on earth can make me drink in the company of someone like you."

I picked up the barracks bag and headed for the sleeping quarters.

"Suit yourself, Yank. That doesn't bother me in the least," she called after me. "You'll be gone soon, and it's good riddance, I say. The whole lot of you will be gone—Americans, Irish, Canadians, Anzacs, and others. Decent people will then have our country back, to live decent lives without your presence."

I stopped and turned around. "You're wrong about one thing, woman. The 'whole lot of us,' as you put it, will not be leaving soon. A half million will stay in the graveyards of France. They were the best of us, and they'll never be leaving now. Part of the reason they died was to insure that you and your 'decent people' would have the freedom to drip that venom from your poisonous mouth without fear of lethal retribution. Think about that once in a while, as you live out your decent lives in the decent little holes you've burrowed for yourselves through the darkness of your souls."

I stalked off, into the room with the cots.

They were, as Kay had indicated, nearly identical to those at a Toc H. I woke early, washed and shaved, and looked around for someone I could pay for the use of the cot.

An elderly man was checking through the room, replacing blankets on any cot that had been used. "Can I pay you for my cot?" I asked him.

"You didn't pay last night?"

"No. I was late getting in, and there was only that woman at the bar. I didn't think to ask her if she could accept payment."

"I heard about that little dustup you had with her. She's a nasty old bitch, but dangerous if she controls anything you need badly, such as food, water, or sleeping accommodations. Guess you shook her up a bit, and she forgot to collect for the cot. You can just give me the shilling, and I'll pass it on."

I thanked him, and gave him the coin.

Whether it was planned or not, I couldn't tell, but there was none of the usual tea and scones available. I waited, outside in the early light of another day, for Kay, Sergeant Lawton, and the lorry. Lorry? I smiled at myself. Getting to think and talk like a Brit, calling a truck a lorry.

They were on time, and after we'd arrived near the bus station in Castleford, we all went to a nearby canteen, where Sergeant Lawton insisted on acting the host and paying for our breakfast.

It was tea and scones, of course. I wondered if anyone in Britain ever imagined anything like a coffee and doughnut for breakfast. Maybe, in another year or two, when normalcy returned to this war-battered island.

The bus arrived. Kay and I held each other as long as we dared. I wiped a tear from her cheek and climbed aboard, where I watched through a window until all I could see was a tear-blurred, fading image of someone I was sure represented all that was left of anything worthwhile in my life or in Europe.

# 35

## *The Camps*

The return trip to my company was made without incident or interest on my part. I cared for nothing, was unimpressed by London, Paris, or points between or beyond. I felt exactly as Kay had described the condition of humanity after a war that had lasted too long—beaten down to a universal level of hopelessness.

The one thing that I could find at all remarkable was the marvelous efficiency with which our military had coordinated the truck, rail, sea, and bus transportation to take me to my destination and bring me back, without confusion or unreasonable delays. Someone, somewhere, knew what he was doing.

The company I'd left at a schoolhouse in Trier was now in tents, in a large field several miles from Marburg, Germany. I reported in at company HQ, then walked to the supply tent.

Wesley was there, laboring over some requisition forms spread out on a makeshift desk of packing cartons. A tall, handsome black man stood at the counter, patiently waiting.

Wes turned around and saw me. He looked like something from a bad dream. His eyes were red-rimmed, his whole body sagged with exhaustion. "Man, am I glad to see you!" he exclaimed. "I can't make head or tail of these req forms, and this fellow..." he indicated the black soldier, "has been here three times today, and I still can't understand a word he says."

I dropped my barracks bag and stepped behind the counter. "Can I help you?" I asked the black soldier.

"Surely hope so, Sarge. All's I wansa pockashiff."

I checked under the counter, found the pile of handkerchiefs, peeled off two, and handed them to him.

He thanked me and left, rolling his eyes upward.

Wesley had watched. "How'd you know what he wanted?" he asked me.

I chuckled. "You learn, after a while, to guess a little and interpret a lot. He said 'All's I want.' That meant it was a small item, not a pair of shoes or field jacket, but maybe an undershirt, a pair of socks, or a handkerchief. 'Pockashiff' was more likely handkerchief than anything else. End of problem. It all comes with the job.

"Wes, you look like hell. Give me a quick rundown on where you stand with the requisition, and I'll take over. You crawl into a corner somewhere and get some rest."

He gratefully complied.

It took a little over an hour to complete the requisition form, during which the mail clerk brought me a handful of letters. Someone in HQ apparently had told him I was back. There were some from home, and one from Claude, the French kid in the Argonne. That was a pleasant surprise. He'd asked for my military address, and I'd given it, but had not counted heavily on receiving mail from him. The letter was written in French, but I could get the gist of it, and found someone with a better grasp of the language to fill in what I missed.

In a matter of another hour or two, I was back into the routine, probably a good thing. It dulled the sense of loss I still felt from the inability of Kay and I to arrive at any definite plans for the future. The CBI still hung over all of us here, with its promise of wholesale death in the jungles or on the beaches.

Although no mass movement of complete units to Marseilles and shipment through the Mediterranean and Red Sea had begun, many individuals had left. It was house-cleaning time, and every company with problem personnel was using them to fill shipping quotas. Lon Truhall had left, his loss of control during the drunken Fourth of July affair reason enough to put him on the list.

Lon was not going to the CBI, though. Someone who rode the train to Marseilles, assigned as a guard, returned and let us know that Lon had managed to find a bottle during the trip, had become drunk, and punched a second lieutenant in the nose. Lon was sent to Leavenworth for a number of years to think about that.

Other companies were losing similar potential troublemakers. The petty thieves, the lazy, the ignorant, the insubordinate, all were leaving for a new assignment, where the odds of survival were going to be poor.

Some came to us who were not immediately shipped out. One was a staff sergeant from Services of Supply. His rank precluded a summary assignment to the next train for Marseilles. Punishment, for a first three grader, must result from a formal court-martial or board of inquiry. He'd had neither, so he waited until someone with enough authority could convene the necessary officers. In the meantime, he made himself as disagreeable as humanly possible. He was overbearing, arrogant, demanding, and he owned a motorcycle, which he used for a trip to Marburg every day. This was a German civilian machine, which meant he could not use our gasoline. It would quickly burn out the engine. He needed the less refined, almost kerosene fuel used in most German vehicles. He apparently had plenty of money, and was well able to buy this, or anything else he wanted, on the black market. He refused any duty assignment, and ignored all orders.

This character was not quite as bright as he thought, though. He irritated too many people wherever he went, and this included most of the truck drivers who drove the road to Marburg and back, hauling supplies from the train depot. They became tired of his antics in cutting them off on the winding road that went over the hills, or speeding past them on the straight-aways. On one fateful day, two truck drivers, one going toward Marburg, the other returning, decided to put an end to this bothersome nuisance. Just as he passed one of the trucks, the other speeded up enough so that the motorcycle was between them. They eased together. What was left of the staff sergeant was scraped off the road and wrapped in a rubber sheet for transport to the nearest graveyard. There was no sorrow at his loss. No one even asked his name.

The hostilities here in Europe had officially ended over two months ago, but individual Germans and small groups fought on, unwilling to surrender. Some pockets of resistance in the Bavarian mountains had to be dug out and exterminated one at a time, an action that, done correctly, involved few casualties on our part, but took time.

In the north of Germany, the remaining troublemakers were as often as not teenage boys who had been part of the Hitler Youth movement. They developed a nasty tactic of stringing fine piano wire across a road, anchored to trees on each side. It was pulled taut at just the right height to catch a Jeep driver in the neck as he drove past with his windshield folded down. The result was decapitation, the man's head rolling off the side of the road while a headless body, blood fountaining from its neck, continued with the Jeep as long as the road ran straight, or until the body slumped against the steering wheel.

Very soon, every Jeep was equipped with an upright piece of angle iron, welded to the center of the front bumper and braced on each side. This snapped the piano wire and left the driver with his head still attached.

The whole situation demonstrated a failure on our part to adequately connect with Germany's youth. There should have been a few well-trained psychologists assigned to this segment of the population, but that never happened. Soldiers of the regular army, like Helmut in Trier, had been no problem. They searched for ways by which they could survive until their country was whole again, but harbored only minor resentment, and little lasting bitterness, over their losses. They had fought, well or poorly, and had been beaten. So be it. Life, for the survivors, went on, and they made the most of whatever remained of their former opportunities or possessions.

It was the teenage kids who were unable to accept defeat. Imbued by their politicians with an irrational view of their position in the world, and an almost insane desire for revenge against all who had disrupted the grandiose plans of their Führer, they fought on, in the dark of the nights and in the cellars of the ruins that had once been their homes. Reason had no place in it. Continuing dedication to a lost cause ruled their lives. Only by an equal dedication to reversing the effects of all they'd been taught could they be saved. A few returned German soldiers, such as Helmut, might make a difference, and I hoped he was doing something along that line, at the very least with his brother Franz.

Day after day, there was greater evidence and more confirmation of a horror we'd never suspected during all the fighting. Just a few weeks ago, we'd learned what Buchenwald, and Dachau, and Auschwitz, and others were all about. It was what Yvan had tried to tell me, but his limited English and his sense of sick revulsion had not allowed him to get through and make it clear. Now those American forces that had overrun the camps and entered their world of twisted nightmares had their stories to tell. Six million Jews, Gypsies, Poles, and political dissidents had been killed, most of them cremated and the ashes sifted for the gold that had melted out of their teeth.

Those who saw it all firsthand were too stunned at first to accept the reality of it. Army HQ had clamped an immediate quarantine on the camps. Those who entered wore gloves and masks. The sick and the starving lay in huge masses, most unable to walk through the open gates, many still dying each day. Medics came as quickly as they could, to decontaminate the places and inoculate the survivors against a multitude of diseases prevalent in these humanity-filled cesspools.

The media called their release a "liberation," but that word implied far more than most were capable of achieving, at least in the beginning. They were not allowed to leave the camps until they were reasonably clean and obviously recovering from their afflictions. Although necessary, this compounded the horror of what had been done to them.

All of us, without exception in my view, so abhorred what we were compelled to believe, we could only wonder how this could have happened. What drove men and women to inflict such torture on their fellow beings? How, in the name of all religions that recognized the existence of a supreme being, could it have happened? Beneath all the horror and attempts to explain it was the ever-present acknowledgment that this was deliberate "ethnic cleansing" of a nation and the lands it controlled by right of conquest. Beneath that again, and less obvious, was that Christianity itself, as the dominant belief system, had a part in it all. Ancient hatreds had been played upon, old jealousies and fears enhanced until the personnel needed to operate the camps were ready and willing.

It takes only a few to bring about a thing such as this. When the Communists took over Russia, only one person in 2500 belonged to the party. When the Socialists of Germany, as Nazis, elected to go down this road of ethnic extermination, book burning, and the suppression of all dissent, they had not been present in great numbers, either.

It didn't take great numbers. It didn't need a majority. It needed only the willingness of most people to look the other way and the refusal to publicly condemn the actions of the ruling few, until it was too late.

Could this happen at home? Those of us who raised such questions were forced to admit that it could, and rather easily. The same prejudices in our politicians, with the same pattern of excuses, would certainly make possible another modern horror equal to what the Jews called the "holocaust." When this war finally ended, those of us who survived and went home had to prevent that. We were the ones who could do it, just as the ex-soldiers of Germany were the ones who could keep things in check here.

If the world owed us a debt for putting an end to Hitler's wild dreams of a German super race, we in turn owed it to the world to stop that same thing from happening elsewhere. Political activism, at all levels, was an obligation we dared not shun. The war had matured us, and we could demonstrate that, and force the recognition and acceptance of responsibility and sanity in government, by our involvement in the political affairs of our nation.

As these ideas developed, my first letter from Kay since we'd been together in England arrived. In it, she asked me to consider remaining in Europe after the war, and particularly in Ireland. It was too early to think about that. I'd already considered it, but not seriously. It was too early for anything but to finish this war and then examine plans for the future.

What she asked was one such plan, but one I was almost afraid to think about. I remembered what Sal had told me back in Castleford. He'd followed such a course, but he'd had a sizable amount of ready cash to do it. That was something I did not have. He'd planned well ahead, and knew exactly where, and when, he should make his move. I'd not yet had an opportunity to do anything remotely like that. I'd never been allowed to visit Eire, the part of Ireland that was Kay's home. I tried to reply, in a letter, but knew it sounded as if I were making poor excuses to her expressions of a fond dream. I could not yet consider that sort of action.

# 36

# *The End of Salvage*

All of the small arms issued to our company members were collected by a team of strangers and taken away, to a storage facility, we assumed. This eliminated any possibility that I'd be needed as an armorer in the foreseeable future. It also eliminated most of the threats of armed mutiny that undoubtedly worried SHAEF from time to time.

There were a lot of German handguns circulating about, however. They were bought, maybe fired a few times in some nearby woods, and sold, sometimes at a profit, more often at a loss. For a short time I owned a beautiful Walther 6.5mm pistol, in a holster, with an extra magazine and some ammo. It was an officer's sidearm, a piece of quality workmanship, but why did I need it? I'd bought it for twenty dollars, fired it a few times, and finally found a buyer willing to pay the same. I happily turned it over to its new owner, and instructed him in the use of the safety and the proper way to hold and fire the little weapon.

Possibly to calm our fears and soothe our misgivings over loss of our issued weaponry, plus our uncertain future, a non-com liquor ration was instituted. With some units, this had been in effect a long time. We were one of the last to be recognized as entitled to it. Once a month, we received one bottle of good whiskey and one bottle of gin, vodka, or some less popular intoxicant. We paid for these, but the cost was minimal because there were no taxes on any of it. Good whiskey was extraordinarily cheap to make, and those who gained the most by its sale were the government agencies that imposed and collected those taxes. For two or three days after our rations arrived, we had a somewhat drunken company. Sobriety returned as the whiskey ran out, and no great harm seemed to result.

It may have been the intention of the army to have many of us a little off balance when, on August 6, a weapon far more destructive than anything we could have imagined was introduced to the world at Hiroshima, Japan. Those who had radios heard about it first. Later in the day, a special edition of The Stars and Stripes was rushed to the rest of us.

We had difficulty believing it. One bomb, dropped from one airplane, had killed nearly a hundred thousand people? How was that possible? What unknown, primal power of the universe had been harnessed and then released in all its churning fury on this hapless world of ours? Who had conceived such a monstrous bomb, and why?

A few tried to point out that the earlier fire bombing of Tokyo had produced more casualties, but that was many bombs from many aircraft. It was the idea that this was a single, gigantic explosion that was so difficult to accept.

Three days later, Nagasaki was destroyed by another single bomb. Loss of life was less only because there were fewer people in the target area. What was happening on the other side of the world? How many of these bombs did we have? Was the plan to eliminate one Japanese city after another until all that was left were some rice paddies?

As the media elaborated on this newest addition to the arsenal of governments committed to warfare, we learned that immediate death accounted for only a part of the casualties. Many more suffered from a hitherto unknown ailment, at least among the mass of people. This was radiation sickness. It would kill or cripple as many more, but over a period of a year or two, and it was not an easy way to die.

From our viewpoint, all was not completely evil in this introduction to atomic war. There was another side to it, at least in our present circumstances. The next day, August 10, Japanese leaders publicly announced their willingness to surrender.

This, more than the surrender of Germany on May 8, was cause for celebration. Those of us who still had some whiskey used it. I shared mine with Wesley, and we talked a little of home and life in a civilian world. We were off the hook as far as the CBI was concerned. There would be no need for us to go there, or to die on the beaches of the Japanese home islands.

A point system was set up to give a measure of priority to those who should go home first. One point was allowed for each month of service. Another was allotted for each month overseas. To reunite family men with their dependents a little sooner, twelve points were given for each minor child, up to a limit of three, or thirty-six points. Five points were awarded for each combat award. The system was relatively simple, and as fair as anything the army had ever devised. Dates for passage home and discharge were geared to this point system, but it soon became evident that the timetable could not be closely followed. There were too many of us with 80, 90, or 100 points, all qualified for discharge in September. The army had set impossible goals for itself.

Yet, they tried, and it worked better than many of us would have thought possible. We were reminded that we'd known, from the first day of our induction into the armed forces, that we'd be expected to serve for "the duration plus six," the duration of the war plus six months. If we accepted the surrender of Japan as the end, it might be some time in February, 1946, before we could expect to be released. We did better than that.

My personal desires were not the same as most of the others. I desperately wanted more time to spend with Kay, planning our future life together. I asked my company commander if it might be possible to obtain a transfer to the United Kingdom for six months.

"How would I apply for something like that?" I asked.

"There's a standard form. We have a copy here. You fill it out, I countersign it, and we forward it to headquarters, in this case Depot. The army gives nothing away without some benefit to itself, so you must state how they would gain from such a transfer."

"Added service from me," I said. "I'd be happy to agree to an extra six months of service, beyond the time I'd normally be released, if I could spend that in the U.K."

"It's just barely possible they'd buy that. But for the most part, troops are leaving the U.K., not arriving there. What could you do that might interest them?"

"I'm familiar with aircraft machineguns. With just a little added training, I could service them. The entire Air Force isn't going to just disappear, or be put in mothballs, is it? They must be going to keep a few units active."

"That's likely. So is the likelihood that they already have such service personnel who will stay on for six months or a year, or whatever. But make the request and we'll send it in. Just don't get your hopes up."

There were other matters that needed my attention, for some of the same reasons. One was the religious difference between Kay and me. It was a stumbling block for Kay, I thought, mostly because of her family. If I could eliminate the differences, it surely would help. I called the battalion chaplain's office and made an appointment.

He was not exactly overjoyed to see me. "What do you want?" he asked, in a gruff, unpleasant voice.

"I want to learn about Catholicism," I replied. "What's involved in joining the church? What does it stand for philosophically? How is it different from the little Congregational church I attended while I grew up?"

"A lot of questions," he said. "First, learn to limit them. Few of the Catholic clergy enjoy questions, and I'm not one of them. Here. Read this pamphlet. Memorize the prayers on it, and call me again in a week."

He handed me a cheaply produced folder with the "Our Father" and "Hail Mary" prayers. I knew these, maybe not the exact words used by Catholicism, but the differences were small.

He waved me away when I tried to speak again. "Another week."

I wished for Father Victor. He would have been far easier to approach, and may even have helped me reach a decision. But Father Victor had died in Stavelot, pointing a .45 pistol at some spot ten feet above the head of the German soldier who had killed him.

Next, I did what I thought might be of some value in helping Kay with her part in all this. I wrote to her brother Colin, to her sister Maureen, and to her folks in Eire (Ireland). I told them all how much Kay and I loved each other, and how much we wished to do the right thing. I tried to make it clear that I felt our best chance for a reasonably satisfying life together was not in Ireland, but in America.

This was not, I pointed out, about money, although I would not deny that was a part of it. I had no skills that would be of any value in the working world of Eire or Ulster. I did have the beginning of some skills in printing, which I was certain was a trade that would grow substantially in the near future at home, and have opportunities for any who became a part of that field in the next few years. For me, this was all about making the best possible life for Kay. I could not, in good conscious, do any less.

Not one of those to whom I'd sent a letter responded. Something was decidedly wrong, and I was at a loss to know exactly what it was.

I received more letters from the French and Belgian kids. Little René sent one letter after another, about ten days apart. Claude wrote again, and I heard from Yvan, Léone, and Hèléne. They all asked me to visit them soon.

In the meantime, the supply work went on, if anything at a greater volume than ever. The flow of men had simply reversed, with the majority headed for home and only a few moving to units still in the field.

Salvage operations became something on which our immediate superiors now concentrated with ever increasing vigor. Everything from shoes to helmets must be sorted, tagged, and sent to quartermaster units assigned specifically to this duty. German POWs from a nearby camp came to do much of this sorting, bagging, and tagging, and they worked steadily. Now and then, one might ask if he could exchange a worn out shirt or sweater for one that was going into a salvage bag. I permitted this, and received even more dedication to the work from them. I gave each man a cigarette at the end of the day, a cost of just pennies for me, but something they might be unable to buy without paying inflated, black market prices.

Ernie, our company truck driver, stopped in one day while the salvage work was in progress. "Hey," he said, "I'd like to show you something if you have time to take a little ride with me."

"These POWs will be through for the day in a few minutes. Can you wait that long?" I asked.

"Sure. You're going to be surprised, I can guarantee. I won't say any more now. You've got to see it to appreciate it."

See it we did, a little over a half hour later. It was about five miles out from the center of Marburg, a huge gravel pit thirty to fifty feet below the road grade level. It must have been two miles across. Dirt roads went down into it and all through it. Two and a half ton Jimmies drove down in a steady stream. Empty trucks made another stream, exiting onto the main road. Twenty to thirty fires burned throughout the pit, some fiercely, and the trucks continually dumped more material on each. Columns of smoke rose high into the air.

Ernie stopped at the side of the main road, with a good view of everything happening in the pit.

"What is it?" I asked.

"It's your salvage material, all that stuff you've always so carefully sorted and tagged. The bags are brought here and burned.

"But why?" I asked. "I always thought a lot of it could be saved, just by washing or cleaning it. Where are the quartermaster units that were going to take care of that?"

Ernie chuckled. "Same place so many other pieces of army information and special units are—in the imaginations of those who made up that bit of fiction. Everything is burned, and always has been. Even helmets go into the fires, and are later raked out of the ashes as bits of steel slag. This place can be dangerous at times. Some of those bags have weapons and ammo in them. It goes off in the heat, so at the first 'pop,' everyone moves back a hundred yards or so."

"This doesn't make sense," I said. "All these months, we've been sorting and tagging stuff, only to have it burned?"

"Yep. But it does make a kind of sense. We've not had the huge epidemics that killed so many during World War I. This is one of the reasons. Those bags have stuff in them like old sweaty and unwashed underwear or socks. They stink, and they probably contain thriving colonies of bacteria that could be contagious. Burning it all without even opening the bags is a proper procedure for eliminating the chance of uncontrolled epidemics."

"Okay," I said, "I'll admit it probably works, but what about the guys who spent days sorting, bagging, and tagging the stuff?"

"Let's hope they washed well at the end of each day."

Ernie started the truck, found a spot where he could turn around, and we headed back.

I shook my head. "All that wasted time," I said. "Didn't anyone anywhere consider that part of it? There was no need to do all that work. We could have just thrown the bags on trucks and sent them to the fires."

"Of course you could," Ernie said, "but that's not the army way. If we don't waste a good part of our available manpower hours, we're not doing things right. Waste is a part of it all, probably always has been. I can imagine Caesar keeping his legions busy by having them put new wooden shafts on all their spears, and using the perfectly sound old ones to cook the next meal. How else would you occupy the troops and maintain discipline when they're not actively fighting an enemy?"

"Then so much of what we do is nothing but make-work projects?" I asked.

Ernie pointed at a stain in the road. "That's where the wiseass with the motorcycle bought it. That was a bit more than make-work. It was carefully planned."

I shuddered at the thought of how that staff sergeant had been eliminated.

"I wonder," I said, "how much more it has cost us to burn all that material, as opposed to operating a real salvage system."

"Well," said Ernie, "there's another side to the whole thing. The uniforms, shoes, jackets, helmets and liners, even cartridge belts and first aid pouches, all had to be disposed of one way or another. They could have been buried in a series of deep pits, but a few smart civilians, wearing their four year old rags and desperate for better clothing, might have dug it all up. It was far safer to burn it."

"Then," I said, "it was never really going to be salvaged?"

"Of course not. It had to be destroyed so new uniforms and all the rest of it could be ordered from the manufacturers with government contracts, and the politicians involved could get their rewards, and the labor union leaders could become wealthy manipulating wage contracts. It takes eleven men behind the lines to keep one combat soldier supplied. That's just the military part of it. The combat soldier probably creates additional jobs for at least a dozen civilians. It's all part of the whole picture. If we don't use enough material legitimately, then we need to destroy enough to support all those people. Ending things too efficiently or too cheaply would invite a collapse of the system. Economic disaster would be all we'd go home to when it was over. When there are no shortages, we need to create them. Then everyone is happy, with the possible exception of the kid who gets his head blown off trying to move on to the next battlefield objective."

"Have you always been such a cynic?" I asked Ernie.

"Driving a truck gets you around to a lot of places where you see things others might not."

"Like the burning pit."

"Sure. You get so you can find justification for almost anything."

"Except common sense," I added.

"Well, if you want that, you'd better find another world. It's a pretty scarce commodity on this one, especially with a war going on."

When we arrived at my supply tent, a message was waiting. I was to report to company HQ at my earliest convenience. Maybe, I thought, that transfer to the U.K. had been approved. That was a bit of wishful thinking, but it could have really happened. Maybe a lot of things could happen. Maybe this war now ending had possessed some examples of rationality.

# 37

## *Going Home*

In our company HQ tent, Lieutenant Cicciloni first apologized. The company officers had forgotten that I'd been existing in a sort of limbo, unable to receive the promotion in rank authorized by our T of O. Somewhere in the States, or possibly in the Pacific theater, Sergeant Parsons wore the stripes and rocker that were mine by reason of the service I performed, but not mine by reason of an outdated army regulation. The forty-five days I was supposed to have waited had expired long ago, as had the reason for it.

"The next orders that come down from Depot," the lieutenant said, "will have your staff rating on it. Every officer in this company has agreed to this, and we're sorry it was overlooked. You've done an excellent job with supply."

No mention was made of a transfer to the UK, so I assumed that was a dead issue.

The deactivation of our company was not too far in the future, so this promotion had no great meaning. I did sew on the stripes, though. If even for a few weeks, I had at long last joined the ranks of first-three-graders. I was a member of the fraternity that ran the army. Only a court-martial could reduce this rank, and I had no intention of conducting myself in a way that could make that even a remote possibility. Accountability still belonged to the officers, but responsibility for nearly everything the company did or did not do was at least partially mine, just as it was with the top three grades in every other company of the U.S. Army.

That responsibility, I learned quickly enough, was going to involve interminable paperwork. No replacement company could disband and prepare for the journey home until all materiel was accounted for and all accounts balanced. I needed to fill out a form, in triplicate, to explain why we no longer had our original tents, our .50 caliber machinegun, our reserve ammunition, or even our grenade launchers for the old Springfield rifles.

Most of this was routine, if time-consuming, for it had to be done in addition to all the supply work that never stopped as long as soldiers were moving through on their way to a still-active division or on their way home.

All of the first batch of papers were returned. New regulations required five copies, not three, and there was a flaw in the address of the office to which they should be sent. Someone farther along in the paperwork line might have corrected that, but it was not his responsibility. It was mine. The nit-picking was becoming severe.

Eventually, I was able to satisfy the powers-that-be on all items except one. Our cooks were still using the second-hand field ranges that had been found for them when we were in Landers, following our retreat from Stavelot and the Ardennes. Headquarters wanted to know what had happened to the original ranges.

I'd been part of a four-man team that had gone to Stavelot from Landers to assess the damages to those ranges and any other equipment we'd left behind. I'd not gone into the town, but remained, with another of the group, a couple of miles in the rear, on direct orders from the lieutenant in charge. He insisted that someone should be able to take word back to our company, if he and the driver encountered enemy action, or a mine, or any other kind of obstacle. They returned unharmed, with a full report that they shared with us. The garage that the cooks had used as a kitchen had taken several direct hits from German artillery. Every one of the ranges had been destroyed.

When I questioned him about the school where I'd stayed, he said that the corner of the building in which we'd had our supply, and which housed my personal quarters, had also been hit by artillery. There was nothing there now but a gaping hole. If I'd not left when I had, I'd not be alive now.

We'd returned to Landers, where the lieutenant left a report with our HQ. This report, plus my knowledge, from what I'd been told at or near the scene, was the basis for my five-copy explanation of what had happened to our original field ranges. I simply stated that they had been lost to enemy action, something that was true.

The papers bounced back. "You cannot claim a combat loss," said an attached note. "You were not a combat unit, therefore could not have lost the ranges to enemy action. Explain what happened to the ranges."

How was I to do that? Granted, we were not a combat unit, but those were not freshly baked cupcakes the Krauts had been throwing at our former kitchen, either. Those people in headquarters needed some sort of reality check.

Lieutenant Trent was our new supply officer, recently arrived. He had signed the forms I'd sent back, as part of his duty. Now, he began to worry about that "accountability" part of the job. The ranges probably cost several thousand dollars. Would he be charged with that? And would he need to accept those charges to let the rest of the company go home? Were we all stuck here if he did not accept the charges?

"Don't worry about that yet, lieutenant," I told him. "We're not through with the possibilities open to us."

I sent a note to HQ, with one copy of the rejected explanation for our losses. In the note, I suggested sending a truck and some men to Stavelot to pick up the remains of those ranges, just so there would be something tangible to verify my claim of combat losses.

This was quickly rejected. "Explain how the ranges were lost." was scrawled across my note. Talk about a one-track mind!

We stewed about that, the lieutenant and I. None of the other officers had a clue about how to proceed, but did remark that the whole company could be assigned as "keepers of the field" at this place outside Marburg. We could grow old here, waiting for some clerk in a distant headquarters to locate his brain.

I asked about our sister company, the one that we'd worked with part of the time, and had escaped from Malmedy just before we'd left Stavelot. They were here, in this same field, and no more than a quarter mile away. "Maybe it would be a good idea to go talk to their supply officer and find out how they handled this," I told lieutenant Trent.

He did, and returned shortly. "They're all in the clear," he said. "By tomorrow morning, they'll be deactivated. They'll be headed for Antwerp within hours after that. A different clerk must have handled their loss report. The wording was no different than ours."

"Then here's what we're going to do," I said to him. "I'm going to make up a shipping memo right now, sending all of our missing equipment to them. We'll give them three copies, if they want any, and have two more for our own. You go over there and have their supply officer sign everything, showing they received all of it. Bring back our copies. I'll put one with a new loss report and send it in to HQ. We can't lose what we don't have, and by tonight, we'll no longer have those ranges they're so concerned about."

"Yes, but neither will they," lieutenant Trent objected.

"And who cares? They'll be deactivated before anyone can do a follow-up. All that really matters is that everything balances. We're not dealing with real, solid material here, just numbers on pieces of paper. If we can show that ten subtracted from ten leaves nothing, we're all going home."

Lieutenant Trent, still with some misgivings, did as I'd asked, and it worked. HQ didn't care where we'd sent the ranges, as long as we did not try to claim that German artillery had demolished them, as it had. We were not a combat unit, so that couldn't happen. Army HQ staff, at many levels, had some strange people assigned to it.

German prisoners continued to sort, bag, and tag salvage. I made no effort to stop it, even if some of them raised an eyebrow when I told them to put a half bag of undershirts with a half bag of pants, and label it socks. A cigarette for each helped reduce the number of questions, and calm the suspicion that this supply sergeant had definitely gone around the bend.

The level of ridiculous orders sent down from army HQ grew almost daily. A lot of clerks were apparently having serious difficulties adjusting to the absence of war. Peace can be hell.

The latest obsession was with the "statement of charges." I had a few of these forms, but had never used one, even when I knew that I should have. It would have created more work than it was worth. A statement of charges is a form on which a soldier admits, by signing it, that he is at fault for the absence of an article of equipment or clothing.

This was a long-standing regulation, and in a prolonged period of peace, might have discouraged a drunken soldier from offering his shirt, his shoes, or even his rifle for a little more to drink. In the here and now following a great war, it served no real purpose, beyond creating more work for supply, for company HQ, and for Army Finance, who were obliged to deduct the value of the missing item from the soldier's next pay.

It angered those who were told they must sign the form, and this was understandable. My advice to each of them was to wait a few days, until a group of men passing through had left, then to examine the area in which they had stayed. There were bound to be numbers of articles left behind, probably just what was needed to avoid a statement of charges. Sizes didn't matter, because the item was not going to be worn by the man who needed it. Any size would do. It was only an exchange, something old for something new. If he required a new pair of pants size 32/33, and turned in an older pair that was size 38/30, no one cared.

At the end of a month, the furor over statements of charges had subsided. I had on hand two that had been signed. I tore them up and threw them away. So much for that.

It was in November that our company was notified that most of us were due for shipment home. On no more than two hours notice, I gathered my effects into a duffle bag, said goodbye to a few who were still in the area, left the supply tent to whatever fate awaited it, and reported to another part of this huge field.

A full colonel greeted us. He was in charge of the officers, and nominally in command of us all. There were eighty-four of us, together only because we were headed for the same separation facility in the States. Another man and I were the senior noncoms. The colonel asked that one of us take command of the enlisted men, and thereby a set of our shipping orders, equal to the set he had. It came down to the date on which we'd each received our rank, the earlier being the senior. It was the other staff sergeant, by a couple of days, but he asked if I'd take the assignment, with him as assistant. He did not want the responsibility. I accepted. Not much bothered me any longer, after getting through the hassle of closing out the company and my supply "room."

Trucks arrived, and we were taken to the rail depot in Marburg, where we boarded a French train. Interestingly, the French rail system served most of Europe, including Germany, even during the hostilities. The frequent target of our bombers and fighter-bombers, it had suffered many casualties, in human terms, in its rolling stock, and in its rails.

The cars were something out of the past. Square, boxy, and lacking any kind of interior comforts, each had, in peeling paint on its exterior, the words: 40 Homines; 8 Chevaux. These were the famous "Forty and Eights" of World War I. A car could accommodate either forty men or eight horses. The coupling system was the two large hooks and the heavy, three-link sections of chain. A pair of spring-loaded, round bumpers prevented excessive damage to the contents of the cars when starting and stopping. The French passenger train on which I'd gone from Paris to Etretat was the same. It was quite likely that both freight and passenger cars were designed with the same coupling system, so that they could be used on the same train, pulled by the same locomotive.

Our destination was Antwerp, Belgium, now the primary port of embarkation for troops leaving Europe. A group of cooks accompanied us, and twice a day unloaded field ranges onto the ground next to the rails, where they prepared food on the spot. Toilet facilities were any place a few feet away from the rails, in the nearby grass or shrubs. We loaded thirty-five men to a car, a concession to the fact that modern soldiers were larger than those of an earlier generation. There were no horses on this run.

The engineer climbed to his position in the cab, and two others went with him, with what appeared to be a large assortment of tools, including welding equipment. After much creaking, squeaking, and spinning of locomotive wheels, we started to move. Antwerp was two hundred and fifty miles away, not so very far.

On our first run, we covered nearly five miles, then stopped while the two repairmen went out to the engine and did their thing with the welding torch. An hour later, we started again.

I think the best run we had was eighteen miles, before further repairs to the boiler were needed. A walk along the train when it was stopped disclosed the reasons for all this stop-and-go. There were countless bullet holes in the boiler tubes. Almost as soon as there was enough pressure to move the engine, one or more would begin to leak steam.

It took fifty-three hours to reach Antwerp, an average speed of not quite five miles per hour. We could almost have walked it as fast, but we were headed in the right direction all the time, and there was amazingly little complaining.

The camp at Antwerp was bare-bones efficiency, close to the dock where our ship, a Victory, was undergoing final inspections and minor (we hoped) repairs in preparation for sailing. Unlike the train engine that had brought us here, the ship was not laden with bullet holes in the boiler tubes. It was having almost as much difficulty in getting up a head of steam, though. Day after day, welders and steam fitters labored to make the engine reliable enough to get us across the Atlantic to Boston, our destination port.

Our officers received their liquor ration. We did not. At the suggestion of the colonel, I suspected, the officers kept their whiskey and donated the gin to the enlisted men. It was a nice gesture, and appreciated. Eight men shared each bottle. Some did not care for gin, and by the rights invested in me as commander of this group, these men became my partners in sharing the bottle we had. A few in the other groups could not develop an appreciation for gin, and left partly-filled bottles with me. It was a happy time, for I found that with some synthetic lemon juice, such as I once made for riding the ammo truck across France, gin could become quite tolerable. It became my breakfast fruit drink, after which I usually walked to a service club, where I could buy a cup of excellent coffee for five cents, and delicious doughnuts for five cents each. There was also a small but interesting library of books at the club. I read new authors and learned to appreciate the horror stories of H. P. Lovecraft.

At noon, I returned to our Nissen hut in time to join the others for lunch at the mess hall, and sometimes a little more gin at my bunk, just to dilute the after-taste of S on S, or whatever other horror the cooks had found.

Mike Walinski, one of the cooks in our old company, came in one day. We'd been good friends.

"Got something to tell you, Russ," he said.

"Sure, Mike. Tell away. Want some gin?"

He made a face. "No thanks. Remember when we were back on the Seine River, in France? And remember how a lot of us were sick?"

"Yes, Mike," I replied. "I remember it only too well. Bernie Vernal told me we were supposed to get oranges there, one for each man, but they vanished during the night, probably to Paris."

"Definitely to Paris," Mike said. "They came in during Abe Solinger's shift. He took them to Paris and collected the money for them. A lot of money."

"Solinger?" I'd never liked him. Cooks worked twenty-four hours on, twenty-four hours off, with a first cook in charge of each shift. Solinger was a first cook, second in command to the Mess Sergeant. He was a three-stripe sergeant, so held a company grade, as did most of our other sergeants.

He was nasty to the point of being abusive to all who worked under him. He was fat, something he should not have been, and for reasons unknown to most of us, appeared filled with malice toward all. He laughed at every misfortune of others. He was Jewish, something he made into a joke at times, especially when the menu called for non-kosher meat, such as ham. "Best beef I ever ate," he'd say.

"I'm glad you told me, Mike, but what can be done about it now?" I asked.

"You haven't heard the whole of it yet. The oranges were the biggest item, but Solinger was dealing with the black market right along. One week, it would be coffee, the next butter, the next something else. On his shift, we were always running short on something."

"And no one ever did anything about it?"

"It was hard to prove. No black marketeer would come forward to testify. The rest of us had only our own suspicions, with a lot of circumstantial evidence. He was always careful. But the army wasn't quite as stupid as it sometimes looks. They knew what was happening. They put investigators on it, and finally had enough to call for a board of inquiry, maybe a court martial."

"And did they do any of that?" I asked.

"Sure, and Solinger admitted a lot of it, but not all. They decided on a fine and a dishonorable discharge."

"Nothing more?"

"No," said Mike. "He was supposed to come home on the same ship with us, although he's not in our group. You're in charge now, at least with the guys here. Is there anything at all we might be able to do to see a little justice done?"

"Are you suggesting what I think you are?"

"Why don't you get Gregg Scott and Sam Weldon and have a meeting about it. There's more stuff I can tell you, then. None of it is pretty, and maybe you'll all agree on what should be done."

"Okay, Mike," I said. "I'll do just that. How about tonight, just after dark, in a corner of that service club. It's open until nine."

"I'll see you there. Want me to tell the others?"

"Sure."

I had most of a day to think about it, and realized I already knew some of what Mike would probably bring up. I didn't know the extent of Solinger's black market activity, but I did know something about his attitude after we'd learned about the Nazi concentration camp killings. Six million people had died, with the Jews in greater numbers than any of the others.

When Solinger first heard about it, I was standing near him. "Hey," he'd said, "might be a market there for soap and medicines. You suppose any of those prisoners has enough money left to buy some? Maybe there are still relatives, here or in the U.S., who'd spring for a few bucks to help out. I'll check it out. Any of you bleeding hearts want in on what might be a gold mine?"

All of us had turned away in disgust. Even for his own people, hurting badly and needing everything imaginable, all he could think about was a way to make a few bucks for himself from their misfortunes. He cared no more for them than he had for those of us who had been deathly sick and could have been made well by the oranges he'd sold.

We met at the service club and all agreed that once our ship had passed Land's End in England, and was well out into the Atlantic, we'd shove the fat bastard overboard. Troopships were always overloaded by fifty percent, which meant the open deck would be crowded at all hours. In the night, with the sounds of a few hundred guys talking and the ship's engines running, it was unlikely anyone would hear the splash or notice the disappearance of one ugly monster whose only thoughts were for his own illegal profits. We'd do it, any time two of us were in the right place at the right time. The world would be a far better place without this poster boy for the Nazi plans to exterminate all Jews.

After a ten day wait, and just as my gin ran out, it was announced that the ship was ready for boarding. Duffle bag strap slung over my shoulder, and shipping orders in hand, I led my group to our assigned quarters. It was down one deck, and our officers were on the same level, but more nearly amidships, where the ride was normally smoother.

We expected our compartment to be crowded, and it was. Canvas bunks, supported on pipe frames, were stacked five high. The aisles between were just two feet. Two of us, in passing, needed to turn sideways.

Duties were few. I was asked to assign two men each day as a cleanup crew. They would sweep the floor (deck) and clean what the sailors called the companionway, a steel ladder by which we could go up to the next level and back down to our "home."

This was not an onerous duty, and each man assigned to it needed to do it only once on the voyage home. A sailor came every morning with a bucket of soapy water and some rags.

Still, some, especially from companies other than mine, found ways to ignore or avoid doing anything at all that might contribute to our group welfare. Even this, I could deal with, because less than half the group would ever be asked to do anything.

We managed well enough until one of the officers decided a daily inspection of quarters should be conducted. He was a major, and reminded me altogether too much of the "mad major of Southampton." There was no mud here, but a surprising amount of dust and common dirt. The cleanup crew finished with a bucket of dirty gray water each day, which they tossed overboard. Where the dirt originated was a small mystery, but it was there, fresh and in need of disposal. Maybe dust from outer space, falling minute by minute on each of us?

The major, unknown to us until we had arrived in Antwerp, showed up every morning wearing white cotton inspection gloves.

"These stairs," he announced one time, "are to be cleaned every day, Sergeant. You were ordered to see to that. Why hasn't it been done?"

"Sir," I replied, "it has been done, just fifteen minutes before you arrived. It's been done every day on this trip."

He wiped his white-gloved hand across a tread of the companionway. It came away gray. "Look at that, sergeant! And you're telling me these stairs were cleaned? A falsehood of this magnitude constitutes insubordination. Are you aware you can be court-martialed for this?"

I was in no mood for this. I was on a ship taking me where I didn't want to go, doing a job I cared little about. Kay's last letter had been discouraging to the point of being downright gloomy.

Abe Solinger had never showed up, and we had passed Land's End yesterday.

I stood at attention, stared at the major, and said in a clear voice, "It was not a falsehood, sir. Those stairs were cleaned, with soapy water, just fifteen minutes ago. Probably a hundred men have gone up and down them since then."

He held up his gloved hand again. "This says to me that you do not even have a passing acquaintance with the truth. Since you apparently insist on denying the evidence, and are unable to show proper respect to your superior, you leave me no choice. I will file charges immediately, Sergeant. You may expect a court-martial before we reach port, and I have no doubt you will be sentenced to at least five years in Leavenworth." He spun around on his heel and walked away.

The two men who had cleaned the companionway came over to me. "We'll testify for you, Sarge, if that asshole goes ahead with this stupidity. Where do his kind come from?"

"I'm not sure," I replied. "I think he must have a wife at home who will mop the floor with him when he gets there, so he's got to exercise his authority while he still has it. We'll just have to wait it out and see if anything comes of this. Thanks for the offer. I will call on you if necessary."

Mike stopped by the next day. "Far as I could learn, Abe Solinger bribed some clerk at the port facility in Antwerp to assign him to a different ship. He must have got wind of our plans. We meant well, at least, and people like him eventually get what's coming to them."

"Let's leave it at that, Mike." I said. "We've got no reason to lose any sleep over it."

Nor did we. The Abe Solingers of the world and the insane majors might do their worst, but somehow the world would right itself, given a little time. I never knew what stopped the major, but suspected that the colonel squelched his court-martial plans with a little common sense. In spite of everything, there were those persistent signs of rationality, such as a colonel who had the rank and authority to insist on treating others with at least a minimum of dignity and respect, thereby earning the same for himself.

We reached Boston on schedule, disembarked and went to Camp Myles Standish, where we were sorted out into groups headed for different separation centers. Each of us was given five minutes for a telephone call to home. Fifty or sixty switchboard operators kept busy placing our calls and telling us when our time was up. We paid for these calls. In the land of the free, everything had its price. We'd get used to it.

At the separation center (Fort Devens), we were allowed another phone call, for which we also paid out of pocket. This was to inform our families of the exact time and place where we'd be once more free men.

The discharge process included a talk intended to make membership in the reserves an attractive option. Ninety percent of the officers joined, and two percent of the enlisted men.

We left by the front gate, where my parents waited for me with the family car. Waiting for Jake Goldman, of the Trier wine incident, was a limousine and chauffeur, sent by his father, who was too busy to come himself. We watched Goldman try to make the most of this, but felt only pity for him.

It was over.

# 38

## *The End and The Emptiness*

Not all of it was over, though. For a month after returning home, there was no letter from Kay. Finally, an envelope arrived by registered mail. Inside, I found the ring we'd bought together in Leeds, a touching poem, and a letter. Kay explained that her family was still adamant in their refusal to accept her marriage plans. She could not go ahead without their approval, and therefore felt it best to end our relationship at this time. This was the last I heard from her.

A month later, Mrs. Taylor wrote a final letter. Kay, she said, had taken her discharge from the military in England. She had not gone home to Eire. Instead, she was now living with a family in Lancashire.

This hurt, because I was aware of the implications. England was, in some ways, still emerging from the feudal age. Well-to-do families liked to have a "domestic" living with them, to do any number of chores involved in keeping a household running smoothly. Irish girls were prized for this duty. They were usually honest, worked hard, and accepted almost any working conditions. A bed, possibly a small room, and regular meals were most of what they expected, with a small monthly stipend that was likely little more than an American could earn in an hour or two.

There was no way I could be certain of all this, but Kay had never mentioned to me any friends in Lancashire. If my guess were true, she had chosen this life in preference to a home in which her abandoned feelings for an American soldier would likely be criticized as long as she lived. I could do nothing about it. Between us stood the rock-solid barrier of the church, with the equally formidable disapproval of her family, and quite possibly my own.

My mother had corresponded with Kay. There may have been negative comments after I'd notified my family that I considered joining Kay's church. My father had written directly to me, expressing his opposition to such a choice. I never questioned either of them about this. The damage had been done, as much by Kay's family as my own. We could not fight the world and expect to achieve any sort of victory, or the kind of peace and contentment we both desired.

There was some bitterness on my part, some disappointment on Kay's, I was sure. For years, it colored my perceptions of all religions and all churches. I saw them as the root causes of everything that was disagreeable in humanity, fostering divisiveness, promoting bigotry, and encouraging wars while their leaders spoke of peace. The history of religion was a record of brutality and bloodshed, a sad and sickening comment on our human need for something honestly spiritual.

First love, it's been said, is the only true love. That may be so, if our definition of love is narrow or constricted. Most of us have the capacity to broaden that definition, almost infinitely. After a few years, I found ways to do that. I hoped Kay did the same.

September, 1943.
The author at eighteen, on a visit to his aunt in Washington, D.C.
This was close enough to Aberdeen to make a twenty-four hour pass
practical every other weekend.

At nineteen, in Belgium

# *Epilogue*

The inability to bring vigilante justice to our former first cook was at first a disappointment, but soon faded to insignificance. Everything of which he'd been a part was now in the past, unable to affect us any longer.

What did affect us, and I found this was nearly universal among returning veterans, was the vast gulf that had developed in the value systems between the folks at home and us. Their entire lives were wrapped tightly around things and events that, to us, were of no consequence. If they could not understand where we stood on major issues, or why, we understood even less of their reasons for what seemed a pointless existence. I was far from alone in expressing the wish to see, and hear, an artillery shell drop and explode in the center of town, or a bomb. Maybe that would wake them up.

Family arguments ensued, and veterans frequently found refuge in a barroom with others of our kind. Veterans' organizations tried to smooth things out, but with only limited success. They, too, were part of "the establishment," organized by and for the survivors of that older war. Only time could be effective in blending the best interests of the different generations.

Even in the company of sympathetic veterans, I often felt alone. None of them had the same experiences I'd had. None of them, except the occasional surviving infantry platoon sergeant or squad leader, could ever understand.

In all the years that have followed, my company has never had a reunion. Three of us made a feeble attempt to stay in touch, but that didn't last, either. Beyond a sharing of our shortcomings, there was little we could offer each other concerning our role in that war. We now lived in a limbo of denial. What we'd done, it seemed, counted for less than nothing. That same army that had desperately needed us, and could not have won the war without us, now refused to recognize our existence, either in the present or in the history of that great conflict. If mentioned at

335

all, our role was denigrated, made to seem inconsequential, a thing to be either forgotten or despised.

Many authors have written about World War II, and some, notably Stephen Ambrose and Paul Fussell, have done so creditably. Both characterized the army's replacement system as insensitive, uncaring, and wasteful. They were correct. It was a relic from World War I, and should have been thoroughly overhauled before it became part of a modern army and a different, possibly more enlightened, world. Ambrose went on to lay the blame where it properly belonged, with the commanders, starting with General Eisenhower and including Generals Bradley and Patton. However, neither Ambrose nor Fussell, nor anyone else to my knowledge, ever looked "inside" the system. They never talked to those who made it work, and were then condemned for their efforts.

The Soviet army was the only other one that used the same method for keeping their fighting units up to strength. Russian soldiers who operated that system were probably just as hated for their part in it as we were. Yet, none of us asked for this duty. We were assigned to it, and then left on our own, unaided by those who should have been aware of its deficiencies, but apparently were too busy with other concerns to notice.

The British divisions fought and died until there were only a handful of men left, when they were retired from the front, their place taken by another complete fighting force. Some of the Anzacs marched in their victory parade in Melbourne with only a dozen men present, yet still called themselves a "division." Their marching order was spaced out, to allow a spot for each original member. The line of a dozen men, accompanied only by the spirits of those others, could be a quarter-mile long. Maybe it was better that way.

Recognition was what we most wanted, and never received. In due time, we did have battle stars to pin on our theater ribbon, five of them in the case of my company. We knew, as well as most others, that the only thing a battle star meant was that we'd been there. We were in the "combat zone" at the time of active hostilities, whether or not we participated in them.

The most prized awards, such as the combat infantry badge, and the unit citations, could never be ours. They could belong to the division headquarters staff, two or three miles in the rear of our normal position, but they could not be ours. We were only "attached to," never a part of, any fighting unit. When an infantry or armored division was too exhausted to be efficient any longer, they were usually brought back to the rear for rest and recovery. We stayed in place, and were attached to the division moving up to replace the one sent back. Except for that single twenty-four hour pass granted to Ed and me in Stavelot, we were expected to be on duty every hour of every day. There was never a time for rest or recovery, never a time for even the slightest physical or emotional mending.

Even the points that determined who would go home first were given to us grudgingly, it seemed. We were not wanted in the army, nor were we wanted outside of it. No one wished to be reminded of what we'd done.

Most of us, when we had time for it, developed a "pariah complex." There was no real need for this, but it was a fact of our existence. We'd sent too many young men forward to die, often senselessly, because they were so pitifully unprepared for what they would face. Our training programs were hardly worthy of the name. All we had were numbers, a large population from which to draw the necessary manpower, so that's what we used, and used and used until even that resource was strained, and old (by our standards) men with families showed up for combat duty.

Courts-martial or reassignment as part of the next lot of replacements were the twin clubs held over us to insure that we gave our maximum effort to the job at hand. It sometimes seemed not to matter what we did, or didn't do, we could still be punished for it.

Accurate numbers are not possible, because possession of any sort of written record in a replacement company was a capital offense. Execution could follow. Yet we knew, within reason, how many men we'd sent to the line. From our small company alone, it was nearly twenty thousand. Near the end, many of them were either in their thirties or just eighteen years old. I'd been eighteen when I first arrived in Europe, and back then, the same old lies were being broadcast denying that such a thing happened. "No American boy under the age of nineteen,"

President Roosevelt had told the nation in one of his fireside chats, "will ever be sent to serve on foreign soil." Did he think that England was not "foreign soil?" The politicians did not bother with these lies when it became too obvious that the truth was only a sometime acquaintance of theirs, and their promises little more than wool pulled over the eyes of a gullible public. What did it matter, anyway? By that time, the Germans were so desperate they were drafting fourteen-year-olds for frontline combat duty. All nations that embark upon a great war finish it with the sacrifice of their children.

If pride in our accomplishment has been impossible, I have learned over the years to be satisfied with the knowledge that I did my best, and that this was no small thing. My special training was utilized to the limit and beyond. With but few exceptions, during that time in the Argonne when our supply lines completely failed, every one of those twenty thousand men and boys went to the line with a properly operating weapon and with his combat load of ammunition. That was my responsibility, and I did not fail.

Yet, we left the army with the sense that we had failed, that somehow we'd been responsible for too many deaths, too many mutilated and mangled bodies that, even if alive, could never be whole again.

There was much that could have been done better. As the war progressed, we greeted a steady stream of previously wounded, most of them infantrymen on their way back to their companies. The squad leaders and platoon sergeants among them, if assigned to us for a week or two, and given the incentive to do it, could have taken the new replacements in hand and taught them much about survival on the line. Casualties could have been halved.

That possibility was never considered. The replacements had been trained at a camp in the States, and were looked upon as just so many warm, live bodies, ready to fill the gaps left in a division's ranks by the endless, and generally unavoidable, losses in combat. The squad leaders and platoon sergeants were the experienced leaders who would see them through their "baptism of fire." Those leaders could not, even for a short time, be excused from that. The need for their service was simply too desperate. It was a shortsighted way to look at the situation, but division and army commanders were incapable of reacting to anything that was not colored by some degree of desperation and immediacy.

The replacement companies, chronically short of manpower, always depended on those same infantry leaders for a little temporary help. We existed on the ragged edge of exhaustion and the imminent collapse of the system. Yet, we were told repeatedly how "lucky" we were that we were not sent forward to the line. It was a strange sort of luck. It undoubtedly saved our lives at times, yet exacted a heavy psychological toll for the privilege of working ourselves close to a full mental and physical breakdown.

At the end, we had nothing to show for any of it. People at home asked what I did in the war. I told them I was a small arms specialist. "Where? In what division?" usually followed. My answer was that I was "attached" to several divisions at various times. All of that was true, but it wasn't the whole truth. Not once was I able to say what I really did, which was being a key part of a unit that sent thousands to their deaths.

That weighed heavily at times. It was more than the fact that in the army itself, we had become pariahs—a group that did one of the dirtier jobs for the military, a job no one else would ever want to do. It was also that we had to share the blame for those thousands of deaths. Each of us, to some extent, bore the stigma of "survivor's guilt." We had lived. They had not.

For reasons not too different from ours, those few infantrymen who had managed to survive through the whole war while replacements filled and refilled their company's ranks felt the same. The rifle companies bore the heavy brunt of all the fighting. Many had an almost unbelievable casualty rate, far above a hundred percent.

It was difficult to make others, especially civilians, understand how that was possible, but we knew. If a company of two hundred and forty men went on the offensive and suffered a hundred casualties, we sent them a hundred replacements. If the next offensive cost a hundred and fifty casualties, we sent that many replacements. It did not take long for the total number of replacements to become greater than the original strength of the company. A two hundred percent casualty rate was common. Four hundred percent was not unknown in the rifle companies. Bill Mauldin called those few remaining original members "fugitives from the law of averages." They ended the war with the same "survivor's guilt" that we had.

Questioning the justice or injustice of the system was an exercise in futility. Beyond the obvious benefits from what was learned and practiced on the battlefield, there was no good answer to why some survived and some did not. None of us had a choice in the matter. We did what we'd been assigned to do. We followed orders, just as others did, but that never shielded members of a replacement company from the psychological abuse of those who resented the fact that we lived. Strangely, or not so strangely, such abuse did not come from the seasoned infantry veterans. From those, we received only understanding, and as much help as they could give us in the short time they spent with our company. They were our friends.

There was an odd delayed reaction to all this in our civilian life. In some instances, we might behave with an irrational recklessness. In other circumstances, we might display an equally irrational withdrawal from the realities of daily living, almost cowardice in the face of all the ordinary demands society placed on us. It cost some of us jobs, others a marriage, still others the relegation to a role of "displaced person." (Those were the people from Europe who no longer had a native land, and therefore were made homeless by nothing more (or less) than the juggling of boundaries and the politics of the immediate post-war period.)

We were not, in fact, physically "displaced." We had a nation and we had a home, but they were not the same as those we'd left behind two or three or four years earlier. We'd been "displaced" not by a shift in national borders but by our own inability to recognize any niche in the world where we might be comfortable with others and with ourselves. We no longer "belonged." We'd come from a milieu in which only life and death had normally mattered. All else was small, petty, or insignificant. Here, in the world we no longer knew, life and death played only bit parts in a drama composed almost entirely of the trivial.

You might think it would change, that the guilt would end some day and everything would become as it had once been. That doesn't happen. There is an ongoing, often painful acceptance of the way society (or our perceptions of it) had changed, with adjustments that let us inhabit our small part of the world without becoming a danger to others or ourselves. On the surface, we've lived normal lives. In due time, we learned to act normally, although that word may have had different definitions for most others. We fit in, sort of. We became upstanding citizens, mostly. We lived every day without hope of escape from the guilt. Why did we survive? Why had I lived while twenty thousand others had not?

Yet, there is a sort of justice in the world. Given time, things balance out. All we ever need to do is be prepared for the unexpected. A case in point was our ex-first cook—the one we planned to dump overboard in the North Atlantic. He made Newsweek magazine about a year after we came home. He'd apparently used his black market profits to buy a meat market in New York. Such establishments are subject to federal regulation, something Abe should have known, but didn't seem to take seriously. After all, he'd always been able to buy his way out of any trouble in the past. This time, it didn't happen. Examiners found that he'd tampered with the meat scales, and cheated every one of his customers by charging them for a pound of meat when he handed them less than fifteen ounces. It was a little ploy to squeeze a bit more juice from the poor fools who patronized his store.

The federal examiners could not be bought, so Abe went to trial. Newsweek gave him almost a half page, with a picture. I never knew how it all turned out, and didn't care, but at least there were others who had become aware of the sort of lowlife that he always was. We could be grateful for small blessings!

Wars usually achieve a climax of some sort, but not always a satisfactory conclusion. In Europe, the climax came with the crushing of Germany from both west and east. On the other side of the world, it was with the atomic bombs. Loose ends remain, though, and any search for the sort of "closure" sought by many victims of violence, or their surviving kin, is inevitably doomed to failure. A world war is simply too huge. At least in part, closure is obliterated by the changing "climate" of international relations. Former enemies become friends and allies. In the passage of time, old friends can become new enemies.

This raises questions, not the least of which is "Was it worth it?" Was it worth the lives of 405,000 young Americans to stop the Axis powers in their quest for world domination? For a twenty-first century pacifist, the answer must be a reluctant and conditional "Yes."

Was it also worth those lives to assure a better position in the post-war economies for our multi-national corporations, such as Ford and Woolworth, and probably many others? How many of those 405,000 lives were spent for no high moral purpose, but simply to gain more present and future wealth for the already rich? At this late date, it's doubtful anyone can accurately answer that, but it did happen. It happened, we saw it happening, and it must be viewed as the dark underside of modern warfare. In serving the cause of freedom for our countrymen, we also served the unmitigated greed of our impersonal corporate empires. Most of the dead never knew that, but we who live with our "survivors' guilt" know it. We also know that was the part of it all that was not worth the loss of even one young American boy with honor in his heart and patriotic fervor in his mind. Nor should it ever be.

Now, if the ghosts of those twenty thousand dead would just leave us alone!

The kids with whom we became friends were terrific. It never seemed to matter how much harm our army had done to them. All of that, they accepted as necessary to eliminate the presence of German soldiers in their nation. At the end of the war, France had 50,000 orphans living mainly in culverts beneath the streets. We'd bombed their homes, killed their families, and frequently passed regulations that prohibited us from offering any aid. They survived by begging, stealing, and hoping for something better.

Special to me were two brothers in France, Claude and René Totel. They found us in the Argonne Forest, and visited almost daily. It was a time when supplies failed to reach us, and as often as not, we were the recipients of help, and they were the givers. They both wrote letters to me, at first while I was still in the army, later when I'd returned to civilian life.

Three kids in Stavelot, Belgium, were also very special. Yvan (we spelled his name "Ivan"), Léone, and Hèléne were bright points in our daily existence. They were all twelve or thirteen years old, and all studied English to make conversation easier with us. Their native language was Walloon, a French dialect. They also spoke Flemish, the other national language of Belgium. Yvan had passable skills in German, which we used when neither of us could find the right word in the other languages.

Following are letters, one from each of the kids.

Claude was twelve, a serious young man who took responsibility for his younger brother whenever they were outside their home in the nearby village of St. Gobain. It was our understanding that their father had died, but we never knew under what circumstances. They had their mother, they had each other, and for a time, they had a select few American friends, of which I was one.

343

René was Claude's younger brother. Ten years old, he was the youngest of my five European friends. He stuck with me like another body part, happily doing anything whatever that would make life a little easier for us. We did what we could to reciprocate.

Yvan (Ivan in English) lived close to the school we occupied on Stavelot. The best linguist in our little group, it was Yvan we'd call on when a translation was needed.

Léone lived across the street from the school. She had the finest sense of humor. She was also bright and filled with the joy of life and high expectations. It was Léone who continued to write the longest. Her last letter was dated in April, 1950. She became a teacher, and later a nun.

Hèléne was beautiful, at twelve destined to become the subject of intense admiration by any males she favored with her company. She was also a good student, and learned English quickly. Her letters were fewer than those of the others, but always written in English.

The small photographs of Claude and René have survived the passage of years. Unfortunately, pictures of the other kids have been lost in a lifetime of moving and other disruptions.

English text of letters from Claude and René follows reproductions of their letters.

Claude

St Gobain le 10 Février 46.

Monsieur Russell spooner

Je viens vous faire ces quelques lignes
pour vous donnez de mes nouvelles
qui sont bonnes pour le moment.
Je viens vous dire mon cher cammarade
Russell que j'ai eu des nouvelles
de votre père et de votre sœur.
Depuis que vous être parti mon
cher Russell je pense toujours

à vous. Je crois que le camarade
Vivier est avec vous. Nous

Nous vous avons jamais oublié
mon cher Russell. René pense
toujours à vous et il est content
d'avoir eu des nouvelles de vos
parents.

Je ne vois rien à vous dire ce soir
en espérant d'avoir des nouvelles
assez souvent Ceux qui pense à vous
Claude et René Je vais vous quittez
en vous ~~embrassant~~ serrant une
poignet de main affectueuse

Claude
Cotet Rue Pelouze
st Gobain (Aisne)

René

Jeudi 27 Décembre 45

Mon chere grandfrère

Je viens te faire ses quelques
lignes pour te donner de mes
nouvelles qui sont assez bonne
pour le moment et j'espere qu'il
en est de même pour toi Mon
chere grand frere et à soeure
Virginia Nous a envoyer tes
fauteaux je disait ou qu'il est
bien Mon frère Russell tu
faisait un beaux petit sourir
tes parent aussi sont bien

surtout t'a reçure ta mère
et ton père vait Mon petit
Russelle il ne fait pas beau
a St gobain il plent toujour
enfin nous n'avons pas amore
a se plaindre nous auont
encore de la nage je suis
content comme ça je peut
n'amuser dans la cave
tu nous a envoyait une plante
ou s'était le devant de ta
maison il y a deja de la
neige Mon frère Russelle
je t'ernine ma letre en
t'embrassant de loin

Un qui pense a vous jour et
nuit René Votre fille de
vervie gobain

## Translations:

From Claude—

### St. Gobain 2-25-45

Mr. Russell Spooner,

I am just writing these few words to give my news, which, for the moment, is good. I would like to tell you, my dear friend, that I have received news of your brother and sister. (This was an error in translation on the part of Claude's schoolteacher. I have no brother. He may have been referring to my father.)

Since you've been gone, my dear Russell, I think of you always. I believe that our friend Vivier (Called "Bernie" in the book.) is also with you. (He was, off and on.) We have never forgotten you, my dear Russell. René thinks of you often and he is happy to have received news from your parents.

I have nothing more to say to you this evening. I'm hoping to have news of you often. Two who think of you are Claude and René. I am going to leave you with an affectionate handshake.

Claude

From René—

### Thursday, Dec. 27, 1945

My dear big brother Russell,

I am writing you these few lines for the moment to give you news that is good enough here and I hope it's the same for you. My dear big brother, your sister Virginia sent us your photos. They were good. My dear brother Russell, you had a big smile on your face. Also, your sister, mother, and father smiled as well.

Russell, the weather is awful here. It always rains but we have not yet started to complain.

We already have a lot of snow. I am fine because I can still have fun in the courtyard. You sent us a photo that showed the front of your house with snow. My dear friend Russell, I conclude my letter with a hug from afar.

Someone who thinks of you night and day—René.

(drawing of a heart.) Mark so you'll come back to St. Gobain.

A letter from Yvan—

Yvan Legros
Rue de Silo n° 18
Stavelot. Belgium

Stavelot Belgium.
29th August 1965

Dear Russell

I have received your nice letter this morning just when I go outside my bed. I was very glad when I received it. I will write you now and I hope this suits you be all right. Do you think me forgive you maybe? How could do I that? I don't forget. (I beg your pardon... I correct WE don't forget) an american friend but you and we are hoping you be right. Now the peace and quiet are coming back again on the country, you know. I'm so glad which you have received my photo and that you think it. I should be glad too if you could got me a picture of yourself soon, because I have a big admiration for you and my parents also. We like you very much and we hope see you again soon on our next holiday. I understand which you could forget the murders of cris in Marmady ▉▉▉▉▉ ........... I hope you are not me. Certainly my dear friend we can wait you everytime and my brother, mother and father I went to you typists and exhibition. I was very sorrowful when my father said me the ~~~~ president Roosevelt's death. What do you think of your new.... I'm hoping shall be as good as predecessor, you know. Who I'll go to America with you now and I shall be glad of that. Really, you are a very good friend for me and you shall be welcome in my home on your next visit. I hope too which you haven't rain now and a best time there. we have a sun strong and hot and you could easy tan in tents. I will close now and I too wait to answer from you soon. Thanks. hand from all your friend Tracy

A letter from Léone. This one was written in English for the first three pages, in French for the last page.

Liège, le 19.12.46.

Dear Spooner,

Are you dead, sick, married or d'ont you like any more to write. I'am very sad to get news from you so long long time ago. So I write to you to see if you d'ont forget me. I'm in Liège to the Normal school three years ago. I'll be teacher for little babies. You have no told me if you had any brothers and sisters tell me yes or no and send me some pictures.

from your family and you
specially. I go back home in
Stavelot to morrow for Christmas.
and because it's my birthday.
also I get sixteen years.
I d'ont speak any more to
Héline. Do you remember about
my big dog he has been killd,
he was was very sick and ......
I'm very sad.
Here it's very cold. Wen do you
think to come in Belgium. I
hope so quick it's longing to
me. Wat are you doing in
the curlion life tell me about
your life in America.
Well I hope to get some news.

from you very soon. Because you
are not very generous.
Well I finish here my letter
because I have to go work.
with my sister Madeleine.
I once again. I'm wainting
some news from you so quicker
than you can.
I love thruly.
Your little girl from Belgium
Icone

Well I send you all my
wishes for Christmas and a very
happy new year.

Etudiez vous le Français? j'étudie.

un peu l'anglais, c'est amusant.
cela me rappelle quand vous étiez
à Stavelot. Maintenant il n'y
a plus d'Américains, c'est très
triste. J'attends impatiemment une
photo de vous, il y a longtemps
que je ne vous vois plus, mais je
pense souvent à vous. Tous les
jours matin je demande au
facteur s'il n'a pas une longue
lettre de vous, et il dit non
jamais alors je suis fort triste.
Maintenant je termine ma
lettre car la place me manque.
et j'espère que vous pourrez la
traduire facilement.

S. Demolin
1, rue de Spa.
Stavelot

A letter from Hèléne:

The 13. 12. 45

Dear Spooner

I hope you had a good journay,
and you are now close to your
dear parents, who must have
waited your back with great
impatience. I write you again,
for my first letter had gone
away with military address,
and I suppose, you did not
receive it
In this letter I wish you a
Merry Christmas and a happy
New Year
Here in S.tavelot. a year ago,
the 16th, you left us, and the

19th germans began shelling
our little town, Whoch is
nearly quite destroyed
At school, competitions are
going to begin at the 15th
December to 4th februar
I hope you are going to send
me a picture from you, Which
I shall put into my album
With pleasure
I close my little note, hoping
to hear soon from you

Yours faithfully,

# Glossary of Military Terms Used During World War II

AA = anti-aircraft weaponry

Ammo = ammunition.

ATS = Army Territorial Service. The British equivalent of our WACs.

AWOL = Absent without leave.

Bazooka = A rocket launcher, fired from the shoulder. It was used against German armor.

Bouncing Betty = Type of German S-mine, used as an anti-personnel weapon.

Brit = Anyone, military or civilian, who was a native of Britain.

Casual = A soldier without an assignment, or in between assignments.

Charge of Quarters = A soldier, usually an enlisted man, in charge of a company headquarters during the hours when others would be sleeping or otherwise not available.

D-Day = Debarkation Day. The day troops went ashore from their ships.

Dog Tags = The metal identification tags worn on a cord or chain around the neck by every soldier.

H-hour = The time when an attack was initiated.

HQ = Headquarters of any unit.

Jimmy = The standard truck of two and a half ton capacity. Most were built by General Motors, and the name derived from the GM logo on the radiator of each. Later, during the Korea conflict, they were called a deuce-and-a-half.

KP = Kitchen Police, the enlisted men assigned to help the cooks, usually in cleaning and dishwashing.

Kraut = German. It was not a word harsh with criticism, more an acknowledgment of basic differences between them and us. The French called them "Bosch." To the English, they were "Jerries" or "Huns."

MG (or mg) = machinegun

Million Dollar Wound = The loss of a hand, foot, or eye, or any other permanently disabling loss.

Mortar = An infantry weapon, basically a metal tube on a base with elevation and direction adjustments. The mortar "round" was similar to a small bomb, fired by dropping it tail-first down the tube, where an explosion propelled it up and out.

MOS = Military Occupational Specification. The number that describes a soldier's duties, usually with alternate duties that might be assigned.

Musette Bag = Normally, a container for an officer's personal luggage. It might also serve as a carrier for special items, such as grenades.

Noncom = Non-commissioned officer, such as a sergeant.

Piece = a weapon, usually one carried by a foot soldier, but this could also refer to artillery.

Section 8 = The psychiatric ward in a military hospital.

Section 8 Case = One who is psychologically unfit, in need of counseling or medication.

Shelter half = A canvas cover that was half of a standard two-man "pup tent."

SOP = Standard Operating Procedure

T of O = Table of Organization. A paper spelling out the details of a unit's manpower and equipment.

Top Kick = A company's First Sergeant.

Tracer = In ammunition, a bullet that glowed as it traveled through the air.

UXB = Unexploded bomb.

978-0-595-35615-7
0-595-35615-X